America's Jews in Transition

America's Jews in Transition

Chaim I. Waxman

Temple University Press   PHILADELPHIA

Temple University Press, Philadelphia 19122
© 1983 by Temple University. All rights reserved
Published 1983
Printed in the United States of America

Library of Congress Cataloging in Publication Data

Waxman, Chaim Isaac.
America's Jews in transition.

Bibliography: p.
Includes index.
1. Jews—United States—History.   2. Jews—United
States—Social conditions.   3. Judaism—United States—
History.   4. United States—Ethnic relations.   I. Title.
E184.J5W285 1983   973'.04924   83-9157
ISBN 0-87722-321-1
ISBN 0-87722-329-7 (pbk.)

In Memory of
Professors
Werner J. Cahnman
Nathan Goldberg
Hyman B. Grinstein

Contents

Tables and Maps

Preface

Although the subject of this book, American Jewry, has long been an interest of mine, it was not until the fall of 1972, when I began teaching a course entitled "The Sociology of the American Jewish Community" at Brooklyn College, CUNY, that I even considered writing a book on the subject. Subsequently, having taught similar courses at the University of Pittsburgh, at Yeshiva University's Wurzweiler School of Social Work and Ferkauf School of Education, and at Rutgers University, having lectured widely for Jewish organizations and institutions in many cities, and having been actively involved with the Association for the Sociological Study of Jewry, I have had the opportunity to deepen my understanding of American Jewry and to sense the need for a comprehensive work on it.

I was introduced to the historical and sociological analysis of American Jews by the three prominent scholars to whose memory this book is dedicated. Nathan Goldberg was a teacher par excellence and a pioneer in the sociological study of American Jews. He was clearly the undergraduate teacher who had the most influence upon my future career. Both at Yeshiva College and Yeshiva University's Bernard Revel Graduate School, Professor Goldberg served as an unusually dedicated teacher and scholar. Hyman B. Grinstein, also of Yeshiva University, generated a warmth and enthusiasm which made American Jewish history come alive. Werner J. Cahnman, who was a teacher of mine at both Yeshiva University and The New School for Social Research, was a prominent historical sociologist with a rare capacity to drive people to realize their potential more fully. May their memories be blessed.

To list all my colleagues from whom I have learned and who have shared in this book would be impossible, but I should like to acknowledge my deep appreciation to Marshall Sklare for his careful and critical reading of this manuscript. Most of his valuable suggestions have been incorporated into the text. I have exchanged ideas for several decades, with Charles S. Liebman and Egon Mayer, and they have had great influence upon my thinking. Irving Louis Horowitz has been a source of great inspiration and invaluable assistance in more ways than I can enumerate. Jeffrey S. Gurock was kind enough to read several chapters; his time, comments, and encouragement are greatly appreciated. I shall also keep a promise and thank my many students who have seriously considered and challenged many of the ideas I discussed with them in the course of writing this book. Barbara S. Nadel, in particular, was extremely helpful in clarifying some arguments in the last chapter.

Portions of several chapters have appeared elsewhere, in such publications as the *American Behavioral Scientist*, *The Annals* of the American Academy of Political and Social Science, *American Jewish History*, the *Journal of Jewish Communal Service*, and *Tradition*. I am grateful for the opportunity to place them in a broader perspective.

I also thank the Memorial Foundation for Jewish Culture for a grant that enabled me to complete this book and to Rutgers University for providing so many support services without which I could not have written it.

I was fortunate to have had the encouragement of David M. Bartlett, Director of Temple University Press, from the inception of the writing of this book, and to have had the superb editorial skills of Jane M. Dieckmann. I thank them both.

To my dearest friend and wife, Chaya, and to our children, Ari, Shani, and Dani, I offer my deepest appreciation for their love, understanding, patience, and encouragement.

Finally, for our many friends who asked when they called during weekday hours and found me at home: "What's the matter, Chaim, you're not working today?"—I hope this book will convince them that professors don't work only while they are in the classroom.

Introduction

One of the most serious weaknesses of many writings in American Jewish history and sociology is that they often study what was and is happening to American Jewry in a vacuum, that is, as if American Jews were "a people apart," completely isolated from and unaffected by what was and is happening to and within American society as a whole. On the other hand, there is an opposite weakness in which Heine's famous proverb, "Wie es sich christelt, so judelt es sich" ("As Christianity goes, so goes Judaism")* is accepted so unqualifiedly that one is blinded to the unique history, patterns, and trends in American Jewry.

Within the field of the sociology of American Jewry these two tendencies are correspondingly related to at least two of the three dominant perspectives from which most analyses proceed—survivalism and assimilation (Sklare, 1974). The survivalist, being ideologically committed to Jewish survival, is prone to be overly insular, to judge contemporary developments in terms of some preconceived notions of the American Jewish community. These are, in turn, frequently based upon misconceptions about Jewish communities in the past, and/or upon the tendency to focus on some developments within the contemporary community, however unrepresentative they

*The proverb is frequently attributed to Heine, though I have been unsuccessful in locating it in his work. It actually precedes him by many centuries; a similar proverb is found in the twelfth-century book, *Sefer Hachasidim*, by Rabbi Judah ben Samuel, the Pious (c. 1150–1217): "It is known that as is the Gentile custom in most places so is the Jewish custom."

may be, as if they were the wave of the future and a confirmation of a faith in survivalism. The assimilationist, on the other hand, is convinced that Jews will inevitably assimilate, and tends to view all manifestations of Jewish group self-consciousness as "false consciousness," as superficial, and/or as nonauthentic manifestations of ethnicity.

While I am convinced of the necessity of a comparative perspective for the understanding of contemporary American Jewry, I reject simplistic notions of so-called value-free sociology. On the contrary, the perspective of this work is unambiguously survivalist. Where a critical stance manifests itself in this book, particularly in the final chapters, it is within the age-old Jewish tradition of the "*Al Cheyt* complex,"* or constructive self-criticism, rather than that of an outside objective (or subjective) observer.

Approximately ten years ago, Charles S. Liebman wrote a very perceptive sociological analysis of American Jewry in which he characterized the American Jews as "ambivalent" (Liebman, 1973). Through his analysis of American Jewish religion, politics, and family life, Liebman argued that American Jews live with two opposing sets of values—those of integration into American society versus those of Jewish group survival. These two values to him are mutually exclusive, and his book concludes with his pessimistic perception that the stronger value of integration will ultimately be victorious over the weaker one of survival. Liebman's perspective, however, should not be confused with the assimilationist one mentioned earlier. On the contrary, in this book he is unequivocally survivalist, and his very pessimism places him within the old and persistent Jewish survivalist tradition which sees Jewry as "the ever-dying people" (Rawidowicz, 1974, pp. 210–24; Sklare, 1976), which sees each generation of Jews as the last, and which makes monumental efforts to insure that it will not be so. Liebman identified the American

*The term derives from the traditional Jewish prayer recited nine times on the Day of Atonement, in which one confesses to a long list of sins, which hardly any (if any) individual could have committed in toto; as each sin is enumerated, one beats one's breast lightly, symbolically.

Jewish condition as ambivalent because he implicitly identified integration with assimilation, and he foresaw that value as winning out over the more weakly held value of survival.

A somewhat similar analysis, though from a different perspective, was presented in an essay by Seymour Leventman (1969), in large measure a sequel to his book with Judith R. Kramer, *Children of the Gilded Ghetto* (1961). Leventman defined "the problem of the Jewish Community" as the "preoccupation with position in two social worlds, Jewish and non-Jewish" (p. 33). He delineates three generations of Eastern European Jews in the United States; the first, the immigrant generation, was concerned primarily with ingroup survival and the establishment of a rich Jewish community and culture analogous to, though not exactly replicating, the Eastern European *shtetl* community and culture. The second generation, having achieved a measure of economic security, sought commensurate social status in the larger society, found that it could not attain it, and set about to transform and build the institutions of the Jewish community along patterns of the larger society, thereby "having their cake and eating it." The third generation embellished that which the second generation had created. Ingenious as the second and third generations were in creating and gilding an entirely new community, Leventman saw no future for the gilded ghetto in the fourth and fifth generations, primarily because as occupational opportunities opened up in the larger society, or, to use Milton Gordon's conceptual framework (1964), as "structural assimilation" proceeded, an increasing number of American Jews would not find satisfaction by remaining within the ghetto confines and would leave the community to "make it" in the larger society.

Appropriate as these analyses may have been for the American Jewish community of the 1960s, significant developments in both American Jewry and American society during the 1970s render them inappropriate for American Jewry in the 1980s. These developments have dramatically restructured both the nature of American Jewish self-consciousness and the relationship between American Jewry and

American society, with the result that several divergent trends are manifesting themselves among today's American Jews. For one, a polarization is occurring along the identification-assimilation continuum, that is, those who do identify with the Jewish community do so more intensely than did the preceding generation, whereas those who do not are considerably more assimilated than was the previous generation. Moreover, growing evidence suggests that the assimilation process is much more complex, multidimensional, and multidirectional than had been previously perceived. One manifestation is that an increasing number of American Jews are unaffiliated with the American Jewish communal structure, but have not undergone "identificational assimilation" (Gordon, 1964, pp. 70–71), the loss of identification with the ethnic group.

One of the first major theoretical analyses which pointed to the multidimensional character of assimilation was Milton Gordon's *Assimilation in American Life* (1964), wherein he distinguished between "cultural assimilation" and "structural assimilation." Cultural assimilation, or as it was called previously, acculturation, is the process in which immigrants take on the culture of the host society. In the United States, this means Americanization, or the adoption of American norms and values. Structural assimilation, on the other hand, refers to the immigrant group's entrance into the important institutional structures of the society, particularly on the primary group level. While these two types are the major variables in the assimilation process, Gordon indicates that there are five others: (1) "marital assimilation," or intermarriage; (2) "identificational assimilation," the development of an identification with the larger society and the loss of identification with the ethnic group; (3) "attitude receptional assimilation," or the ceasing to experience prejudice; (4) "behavior receptional assimilation," the ceasing to experience discrimination; and (5) "civic assimilation," the absence of value and power conflict between the minority and dominant groups. These are steps, or subprocesses, of the assimilation process. Not only are there varying degrees of the overall process; each of the subprocesses may, likewise, take place in varying degrees (pp. 68–71). Having developed this model of variables, Gordon then proposed that cultural assimilation takes place first, that it may take place without any other types of assimilation and continue so indefinitely, but that once structural assimilation takes place as well, all other types of assimilation are inevitable.

If we apply this theoretical model of variables and propositions to American Jews, it would appear that, if even relatively complete assimilation has not occurred, it must be due to structural assimilation being rather low for American Jews, for surely their cultural assimilation is high. In a very critical review of Gordon's book, Marshall Sklare finds Gordon to be an ideological assimilationist and interprets him as placing the responsibility for the low rate of structural assimilation among American Jews at least as much on their own ethnocentrism as on the resistance of the dominant group, especially in the immigrant generation, to welcome an ethnic minority group. Moreover, the ethnocentrism itself is simply a reaction formation to the persistence of prejudice and discrimination. To this Sklare replied, "Those like myself who believe they belong to a long and profound tradition rather than merely to an ethnocentric ideology will find Gordon's social eschatology singularly unattractive" (Sklare, 1965). Above and beyond the question of Gordon's personal ideological proclivities, his theoretical model, even with its more recent reformulations (Gordon, 1978, pp. 65–93), though valuable, is not satisfactory when applied to the contemporary American Jewish situation: in terms of sociologically objective criteria American Jews today have a relatively high rate of structural assimilation, but not anywhere nearly as high a rate of identificational assimilation. Even with the significant increase in intermarriage, our analysis will indicate that the issue is far more complex than Gordon's discussion of marital assimilation would show. As far as cultural assimilation is concerned, the evidence presented will show that, here too, not only different degrees but different types of cultural as-similation exist, and that while there has been a very high rate of one kind, there has been a significant reversal, especially in the last decade and a half, in the trend of the other. These developments, to be explored in the following chapters, were unpredictable even as recently as the late 1960s and remain unexplained and uncategorized by Gordon's theoretical scheme, or any other existing sociological theory of ethnicity, for that matter.

Something or some things must have occurred within both American society at large and the American Jewish community to have produced a contemporary American Jewish situation so different from that envisioned by sociologists of ethnicity and religion in general and sociologists of American Jewry in particular. Until now we have been dealing with American Jewry as an ethnic group, and the sociology of ethnicity has been unable to explain the prevalent trends within contemporary American Jewry. But American Jews are not only an ethnic group; in fact, they have only relatively recently come to be perceived as such.* They are also a religious group and have been so perceived for a much longer period of time. We should, therefore, look to the sociology of religion for an explanation of those trends and patterns.

The religious patterns in American society during the past six years or so make it hard for us to believe that in the mid-1960s Harvey Cox's ideas in *The Secular City* (1965) were so widely discussed, a group of "radical" theologians were proclaiming the "death of God" (Altizer and Hamilton, 1966), and one of the most prominent sociologists of religion, Peter Berger, made this prediction: "By the 21st century, religious believers are likely to be found only in small sects, huddled together to resist a worldwide secular culture "(*New York Times*, 1968)." Hardly anyone observing American society at that time could have foreseen the rise of new religious movements that have their greatest appeal among young adults, a trend toward greater traditionalism in the established religions in the United States, the election of a president in 1976

---

*The first full-length sociological treatment of American Jews as an ethnic group was *The Jew within American Society* (1965) by C. Bezalel Sherman.

whose campaign had clear religious overtones, and the rise of the Moral Majority to a major position in 1980. While Peter Berger wrote *A Rumor of Angels* (1969), in which he clarified his earlier work, *The Sacred Canopy* (1967), to those readers who may have misinterpreted him to be asserting the obsolescence of religion and suggested that religion provides "signals of transcendence" which allow for a sense of order and hope, he too must have been surprised by the sudden appearance of religion in the public sphere. Berger, along with Thomas Luckmann (1967), saw religion as playing a role within the private sphere only. It was supposed to be increasingly "invisible." And in the private sphere as well even so staunch a critic of secularization theory as Andrew Greeley (1972b) was forced to admit: "It would appear that a bit of the numinous" has worn off, at least in the area of sexuality (p. 193). If hard pressed, he would have probably conceded that it had worn off in other areas within the private sphere as well.

Their inadequacies as prophets notwithstanding, Berger and Greeley had in their theoretical arguments the basic ingredients for understanding the very reassertiveness of religion in both the private and public spheres of modern society. Though in his sociology of religion Berger concentrates upon theological belief and behavior, he and Greeley both have emphasized the strong interrelationship between religion and ethnicity. Greeley has explicitly written of "religion as an ethnic phenomenon" (1972a, pp. 108–126), and Berger has identified religious and ethnic groups as among the most important "mediating structures" in society (1977a, pp. 130–41; see also Berger and Neuhaus, 1977). It is thus not mere coincidence that reassertion of religious consciousness in the private and public spheres and reassertion of ethnicity, the so-called rise of ethnicity, occurred at more or less the same time. Both occurred as manifestations of the search for meaning and order, "nomos," in an American society characterized by a relatively great disenchantment with modernity, chaos, and anomie during the 1960s.

The contemporary American Jewish situation thus is very different from our assumption when viewed from the perspective of the 1960s. For American Jews, moreover, there were several additional factors. First, the inextricable inter-relationship between religion and ethnicity in the Jewish group self-definition has always been much more strongly perceived than it was and is among Catholics and Protestants in American society, despite the shifts of the differential emphasis on one or the other component of group identity during American Jewish history. This interrelationship is expressed in traditional Jewish literature by Rav Saadia Gaon (circa 882–942), for example, who asserted in his classic work, *Haemunot Vedeot (The Book of Beliefs and Opinions)*: "Our nation is a nation only by virtue of its Torah [religious beliefs and laws]," and Rabbi Judah Loew of Prague, the renowned Kabalist of the sixteenth century (circa 1513–1609), who in *Tifereth Yisrael* maintained that the Torah is realized only through the nation of Israel. Empirically, this interrelationship is clearly mani-fested in the responses of some American Jewish college students to questions designed to analyze the ways in which they define and relate to Israel, Zionism, and the Jewish people (Waxman and Helmreich). Among the masses of American Jews, in contrast to some of their theologians and religious leaders, there has been little room for distinctions between Jews as a religious group and Jews as an ethnic-national group, although there were shifts and variations during different periods in which one was emphasized more than the other. The differential emphasis was much more ideological than behavioral.

The contemporary American Jewish condition is very different from the 1960s because of internal forces as well. There was a particular Jewish dimension to the student movement of the 1960s, which began with the Free Speech movement and saw its first eruption at the University of California at Berkeley in December of 1964; in the "long hot summers" of the mid-1960s, beginning with the Harlem riots in the summer of 1964; in the Black Power movement, which initially in CORE and SNCC and then in other organizations removed whites, among whom Jews were disproportionally represented, from the leadership and which was the first significant public renunciation of the ideology of the melting pot and the adoption of an ideology of cultural pluralism; and in the establishment of ethnic studies programs on college campuses across the country. The Six-Day War of June 1967 had an entirely unprecedented and unpredictable impact upon America's Jews. There was a distinct Jewish dimension to the antiwar (Vietnam) movement, the New Left, the New York City teachers' strike in the fall of 1968. And there have been important consequences for contemporary American Jewry from the Yom Kippur War, repeated denunciations of Zionism as racism, the interpretation of affirmative action as quotas, and the emergence of a new Orthodox Jewish element, composed of highly educated and affluent professionals.

A firm belief in the intrinsic value of knowledge and understanding and a reformist spirit inherited from traditional Jewish thought and from the traditions of early American sociology are both elements in this book. Especially where knowledge and understanding have implications for the future, one is obliged to make them explicit. With Rabbi Tarphon in *Pirkei Avot*, I affirm: "Yours is not to complete the work, but *neither are you free to abstain from it*" (*Sayings of the Fathers,* 2:21). The implications of the contemporary situation for the future of American Jewry will be specified when appropriate.

Chapter 1 provides a social historical overview of the formative years of the American Jewish community, 1654–1880. It will analyze the historical forces that helped mold the patterns of the earliest American Jewish settlements and their organizational structures and will then consider the growth and development of American Jewry in the nineteenth century, which, Michael Harrington (1965) notwithstanding, might appropriately be labeled "the accidental century."

The following three chapters will analyze the character and development of the first three generations of Eastern European-American Jewry, covering the years 1881–1964. Without minimizing the impact of the previous Sephardic and German-Jewish contributions to the development of the American Jewish community, one should remember that in 1880, there were approximately 250,000 Jews in the United

States, whereas by the mid-1920s there were approximately four million Jews in the country, the overwhelming majority of whom came from Eastern Europe, and that there were very important differences in the cultural experiences and self-conceptions of the two groups. Understanding those differences is a prerequisite for understanding American Jewry in the twentieth century.

Chapter 5 will systematically explore the internal and external developments in the formative years of the fourth generation, 1964–1975. As suggested earlier, the basic changes in American Jewry and American society during this period of rapid social and cultural change will be explored. The effect on the shape and character of American Jewry will be detailed within a dialectical perspective. At the same time the reciprocal impacts of American Jewry and world Jewry, and especially Israel, upon one another will be analyzed.

Chapters 6 through 9 are an exercise in sociological stock taking. They will present data and analyses of the contemporary American Jewish patterns of size and geographic distribution, occupation, education, and income, political attitudes and behavior, anti-Semitism, American Jewry, and the State of Israel, American Jewish family patterns, including intermarriage, religious affiliation and Jewish education, recent Jewish immigration, and trends in leadership and decision making, including social movements which challenge traditional patterns of organization, such as the *Havurah* movement and the Jewish feminist movement.

The concluding chapter will present the case of American Jewry as a challenge to the dominant perspectives in the sociology of ethnicity and the sociology of religion and will suggest that the group's uniqueness lies in its particular religioethnic character.

While American Jewry is less ambivalent today than it was fifteen years ago, a clearer picture of American Jewry at present and of the prospects for its future tends to lead one, especially a survivalist, to wavering between optimism and pessimism. Definite signs encourage each view, and this ambivalence can make the participant observer's psychological frame of mind quite difficult. But if knowledge and understanding do not make for bliss, they free us to recognize that we are not mere passive pawns in a predetermined historical destiny; rather we are active participants in the future we create.

America's Jews in Transition

1. The Formative Period, 1654–1880

The American Jewish community may be said to have originated with the arrival in New Amsterdam on September 7, 1654, of twenty-three Jewish refugees from Brazil. Although individual Jews had arrived earlier, this was the first group to come. How their forebears got to Brazil and why they were now fleeing from the country are interesting and pertinent questions. To answer them, we have to go further back into history. Already by the early medieval period, two major centers of Jewish life had developed in Europe, one in Germany and Western Europe and the other in Spain. Each of these centers developed its own subcultural traditions. Germany, in Hebrew, is known as Ashkenaz, and those Jews who followed the traditions of the center became known as Ashkenazim; Spain, in Hebrew, is known as Sepharad, and those who followed in the traditions of the Spanish center became known as Sephardim. When in 1492 the Spanish Inquisition threatened Jewish survival in the empire, many Jews who survived the massacres and tortures converted to Christianity. Many did so only publicly while secretly maintaining Jewish traditions; they became known as Marranos. Many other Jews fled to countries in which there were no inquisitions. During the years immediately following 1492, Brazil got an increasing number of Marranos, some of whom had fled there on their own while others after 1548 were deported there by the mother country as convicted but "penitent" heretics. Although Brazil was a Portuguese colony at this time, the Inquisition had not been formally introduced there, and the Marranos were able to gain substantial positions in the economy of the country—in medicine, commerce, and industry. In the second decade of the seventeenth century, the Dutch embarked on the conquest of Brazil, and they captured the city of Recife in 1631. Under the Dutch, many Marranos returned publicly to Judaism and a congregation was established. When in 1654 Portugal recaptured Brazil from the Dutch, the Inquisition was officially and brutally extended to Brazil, and again many Jews fled. The twenty-three Jews who arrived in New Amsterdam came there because it was then a Dutch colony, and they anticipated that they would be able to rebuild their community in relative freedom (Roth, 1941, pp. 271–95).

Peter Stuyvesant, then governor of New Amsterdam, was of a different mind, however. He was not keen on having this alien group within his midst, and he urged the directors of the Dutch West India Company, which owned the colony, to allow him to deport the Jews. These Jews, on the other hand, wrote to their fellow Jews in Amsterdam and asked them to bring pressure upon the company to allow them to remain. The directors carefully deliberated all aspects of the issue and on April 26, 1655, they rendered their decision and wrote to Stuyvesant accordingly:

> We would have liked to effectuate and fulfill your wishes and request that the new territories should no more be allowed to be infected by people of the Jewish nation, for we foresee therefrom the same difficulties which you fear, but after having further weighed and considered the matter, we observe that this would be somewhat unreasonable and unfair, especially because of the considerable loss sustained by this nation, with others, in the taking of Brazil, as also because of the large amount of capital which they still have invested in the shares of this company. Therefore after many deliberations we have finally decided and resolved to apostille upon a certain petition presented by said Portuguese Jews that these people may travel and trade to and in New Netherland and live and remain there, provided the poor among them shall not become a burden to the company or to the community, but be supported by their own nation. You will govern yourself accordingly [Schappes, 1971, pp. 4–5].

Stuyvesant was not happy with the order, and he continued to make life difficult for this small group of Jews. He seriously restricted their rights to trade, and he refused to grant them permission to own real estate. Again the Jews wrote to Amsterdam, and on June 14, 1656, Stuyvesant was ordered to allow the Jews to engage in trade and to own real estate. But other restrictions prevailed. Jews were barred from holding civic office and from holding public religious services.

In 1664 the British captured New Amsterdam and renamed it New York. In 1674 the duke of York granted freedom of religion in the colony, and by the 1690s, the twenty Jewish families had an official synagogue, on Beaver Street. By 1706 they had an official constitution and called themselves Congregation Shearith Israel (the Remnant of Israel), and in 1729 they built their synagogue building, on Mill Street, which they continued to use for almost a century.

This synagogue, as generally was the case within traditional Judaism at the time and especially among the Sephardim, was not simply a house of prayer; it was the overarching institution of the community from which virtually all communal services, such as kosher food, education, and social welfare, flowed. It was a synagogue community in the very real sense that the entire institutional structure of the community was centered in the synagogue. It was, according to the literal translation of the term *"Kehilat Kodesh"*—which they called "Congregation"—a sacred community. It provided a range of services for its members and correspondingly exerted very broad and strong social control over them. Conformity with communal norms, including financial support, was maintained by the subjective allegiance of the members and by the threat of sanction, the ultimate one being the denial of burial rights.

By the middle of the eighteenth century, the Jewish population in North America was concentrated in five major areas: New York, Newport, Philadelphia, Charleston, and Savannah. The common denominator of these cities was that they were all port cities, indicating the Jewish involvement in commerce and trade. The New York community, the oldest and largest, numbered about sixty families. The Newport community, second both chronologically and demographically, was composed of approximately thirty families. Its synagogue, Yeshuat Israel, was formally dedicated in 1763. It became known as the Touro Synagogue in recognition of Rev. Isaac de Abraham Touro, who was the first *Hazan* (Reader) or leader of the services. In 1947, the synagogue was rededicated as a national historical shrine, being the oldest standing synagogue building in the country. The Philadelphia community, Mikveh Israel, and the Charleston community, Beth Elohim, had about twelve families each, while the Savannah community, Mikveh Israel, had less than ten.

Each of these five communities was established by Sephardim, Jews of the Spanish-Portuguese tradition, and their leadership and liturgy remained Sephardic even though, as in New York's Shearith Israel, the majority of the membership already at the time of the Revolution was Ashkenazi. In fact, few Sephardim arrived after 1760. From the very beginning of the eighteenth century, more Ashkenazim— from England, Germany, and Poland—than Sephardim immigrated. The Ashkenazim seem to have integrated quite well into the Sephardic communities, so well in fact that the rate of intermarriage between the two groups grew considerably during the century. Nevertheless, differences remained between them and at times resentments manifested themselves, as in the case of Abigail Franks, who on August 3, 1740, wrote to her son, Naphtali, of opposition to the marriage of Rachel Levy (Ashkenazi) and Issac Mendes Seixas (Sephardi). The couple subsequently parented eight children, the most prominent being Gershom, who served as *Hazan* of Shearith Israel for half a century (Hershkowitz and Meyer, 1968, pp. 75–76; Pool, 1952).

A very important feature of these synagogue communities was the absence of rabbinic leadership. Rabbis did not begin to appear significantly on the American scene until well into the nineteenth century, and the traditional rabbi-scholar elite did not come until the twentieth century. As recently as 1900, Rabbi Jacob David Wilowsky, the rabbi of Slutsk, Lithuania, publicly proclaimed "that anyone who emigrated to America was a sinner, since, in America, the Oral Law is trodden under foot. It was not only home that the Jews left behind in Europe, he said, it was their Torah, their Talmud (Oral Law), their *yeshivot* (schools of Jewish learning)—in a word, their *Yiddishkeit*, their entire Jewish way of life" (Davis, 1963, p. 318). The synagogue Reader was not ordained; he invariably was the male who was most Jewishly educated in the community. Since the contracting of marriages does not, strictly speaking, require the personal involvement of an ordained rabbi, according to traditional Jewish law, the absence of rabbis did not present insurmountable problems for the community. Matters relating to divorce and other issues, which did require ordained rabbis, were referred to the rabbinate in Amsterdam and London.

While the absence of ordained rabbis did not severely impair the day-to-day routine of the Shearith Israel community in New York or the other communities, it did have great impact upon the cultural life of American Jewry. Specifically, it meant the perpetuation of a rather low level of Jewish education which, in turn, affected the degree to which the community could maintain its members within the fold. Instruction of children was the responsibility of Minister in each community, and usually consisted of three to five years of learning to read Hebrew, to understand basic passages from the Bible and Prayer Book, and to become acquainted with the fundamentals of the synagogue service and the Jewish ceremonial calendar.

One of the earliest synagogue-community schools was begun by Shearith Israel in 1755. This school was an all-day school; in addition to Hebrew, general education, including such subjects as Spanish, English writing, and arithmetic, was also provided. The school lasted until the American Revolution, when most of the city's Jews left New York (Grinstein, 1945, pp. 228–29). Subsequently, several other attempts were made to establish Jewish day schools in New York during the nineteenth century, but they were short-lived. The Jewish day school movement did not really begin in the United States until the twentieth century.

At the outbreak of the Revolutionary War, the Jewish population in the country numbered between 1,000 (Rischin, 1954, p. 29) and 2,500 (Marcus, 1970, III, 1329) individuals, out of a total population of between two and two and one-half million. Because they were concentrated in five cities, however, they took on greater significance than the one-tenth of one percent of the total colonial population which they actually were. Both numerically and in the level and character of their service, Jews figured prominently in the military aspects of the Revolutionary War, as well as in its financial and economic aspects (Rezneck, 1975). Most Jews supported the revolution because of political and economic grievances against England and because of the growing sense of Americanism which was inclusive of Jews. Those who remained loyalists did so primarily out of a sense of obligation to England and/or because they had economic contacts with British firms.

The outcome of the Revolutionary War was uniquely revolutionary for Jews in that the United States was the first country in modern times to grant complete equality of rights to its Jews. The Constitution, which was ratified in 1789, proclaimed in Article VI that "no religious Test shall ever be required as a Qualification to any Office or public Trust under the United States." In 1791, the first ten amendments to the Constitution, the Bill of Rights, were adopted. The first amendment guaranteed that "Congress shall make no law respecting an establishment of religion, or prohibiting the free exercise thereof; or abridging the freedom of speech, or of the press; or of the right of the people peaceably to assemble, and to petition the Government for a redress of grievances."

The constitutions of individual states, however, did not proceed uniformly with respect to equality of religious rights. Whereas New York State's constitution abolished religious discrimination in 1777, Virginia passed its Statute of Religious Freedom in 1786, Pennsylvania's constitution was adopted in

1790, and Maryland did not grant political rights to Jews until 1824. Nevertheless, even where they did exist, most religious discrimination statutes were not strictly enforced and, for the most part, were not directed against Jews in particular. And in those states in which the great majority of the country's Jews lived, complete religious equality was guaranteed by both federal and state constitutions.

When George Washington was inaugurated in 1789, Jewish communities wrote congratulatory letters to him, and his responses were warmly received. To the Hebrew Congregation of the city of Savannah, he wrote:

> I rejoice that a spirit of liberality and philanthropy is much more prevalent than it formerly was among the enlightened nations of the earth; and that your brethren will benefit thereby in proportion as it shall become still more extensive. Happily the people of the United States of America have, in many instances, exhibited examples worthy of imitation—the salutary influence of which will doubtless extend much farther, if gratefully enjoying those blessings of peace which (under favor of Heaven) have been obtained by fortitude in war, they shall conduct themselves with reverence to the Deity, and charity towards their fellow-creatures [Schappes, p. 78].

Similarly, in his response to the Hebrew Congregation of Newport, Washington rejoiced over the United States as the model of equality, and concluded: "May the children of the Stock of Abraham, who dwell in this land, continue to merit and enjoy the good will of the other inhabitants, while every one shall sit in safety under his own vine and fig-tree, and there shall be none to make him afraid" (ibid., p. 80).

While there were many Americans who did not quite share Washington's views of equality in general, nor his favorable disposition toward Jews in particular, the condition of Jews in the country at the end of the eighteenth century was relatively much better than it had been elsewhere, because of the novel American ideal of equality and the Biblical inspiration that imbued many Founding Fathers. To many, America was the "New Zion," and Jews were viewed as the descendants of the Hebrews of old. Anti-Semitic incidents occurred, but anti-Semitism never became rooted in the political tradition of American society.

The 1790s marked the beginnings of the decline of the homogeneous synagogue communities of the United States. Until then, there was but one synagogue in each city and town which had a community of Jews, and the Sephardi tradition prevailed in each even when the majority of members were Ashkenazim. However, in 1795 a group of Ashkenazim from the Mikveh Israel congregation in Philadelphia broke away from that congregation and formed their own synagogue which, somewhat ironically, they named, Rodeph Shalom ("Pursuer of Peace"). This move marked the beginning of a trend that became the norm in the following century, namely, the founding of synagogues according to traditions of their members, even when there are other synagogues in the community.

The demise of the monolithic structure of the Colonial, Sephardi-ruled synagogue was inevitable, given the dramatic increase in Jewish immigration to the country during the first decades of the nineteenth century. Whereas in 1790 there were approximately 2,500 Jews in the United States, in 1818 there were about 3,000 Jews, in 1826 the number doubled to about 6,000, and by 1840 there were an estimated 15,000 Jews in the country. During this period the country became a haven for the economically uprooted and religiously persecuted. Along with increasing immigration, the country was undergoing a rapid western expansion. As Jews spread throughout the country, they established synagogues as the central institutions in their local communities. During the second decade of the nineteenth century, however, a new pattern began to emerge. In both Philadelphia and New York philanthropic societies which had initially been founded within their respective synagogues for synagogue members became autonomous. These marked the beginning of Jewish organizations independent of the synagogue, a pattern that had profound impact upon the role of the synagogue and the structure of Jewish communal life in years to come.

In New York the break with the homogeneous synagogue community did not occur until the 1820s. Until this time Shearith Israel was *the* synagogue, and its officials set the standards for acceptable behavior. While there had been declines in traditional religious behavior—such as increasingly public violations of the traditional Jewish norms of Sabbath observance, dietary laws, and even intermarriage—there nevertheless was a single New York Jewish community, Shearith Israel. In 1825, however, a group of Ashkenazi members seceded and formed their own synagogue, Bnai Jeshurun (Grinstein, p. 5). The leadership of Shearith Israel initially opposed the founding of Bnai Jeshurun but ultimately gave it their blessing when they realized that it would be founded regardless. By acknowledging the new synagogue, they hoped to be able to retain some influence over it. This hope was short-lived; by 1840 there were four more Ashkenazi synagogues in New York: Anshe Chesed (1828), Ohab Zedek (1835), Shaarey Zedek (1839), and Shaarey Hashamayim (1839). The same trend persisted in the 1840s, when four more synagogues were founded in New York: Rodeph Shalom (1842), Beth Israel (1843), Temple Emanu-El (1845), and Bnai Israel (1847). By 1860 there were about twenty-seven synagogues in New York City, with only one or two that were newly formed by immigrants upon their arrival. The overwhelming majority of the synagogues were formed by a series of secessions from older synagogues (Grinstein, pp. 50–51).

This pattern established itself across the country. There were secessions from older synagogues in cities where they existed and there was a mushrooming of new synagogues as Jews moved to new towns and cities. As was typical with the growth pattern of the country as a whole, no structure or organization could maintain uniformity and overall control. In the spirit of entrepreneurship, new synagogues were formed, Jewish communal service societies were formed independent of the synagogue, and "men performed marriage ceremonies, gave divorces in an unauthorized fashion, set themselves up as ordained or unordained oracles of Jewish law without the sanction of existing synagogues" (Grinstein, p. 5). In contrast to the Colonial era, nineteenth-century American Judaism was clearly a grass-roots movement. Wherever it developed, it did so from the bottom up, rather than being imposed from the top down.

In the twentieth century there are at least three branches of Judaism—Orthodox, Conservative, and Reform—but until the 1820s there was only one form of Judaism in the United States, at least as it manifested itself in the synagogue: traditional Judaism, which is probably closest to what is Orthodox Judaism today. By the turn of the nineteenth century, there was, for all intents and purposes, no Sephardi immigration. Nineteenth-century immigration was almost totally Ashkenazi, and until 1880 primarily from Germany, Poland, Denmark, and Holland. Most of these immigrants came because of economic incentives and were among the least rooted in their native Jewish communities. Traditional Judaism, therefore, did not control their lives significantly.

The first major attempt to deal with the generally perceived decline of the quality of Jewish life by introducing reforms in the synagogue service took place in Charleston, South Carolina, in 1824. Isaac Harby, an educator, journalist, and dramatist, headed a group of forty-seven members of Congregation Beth Elohim who were unhappy with synagogue service. They organized themselves into "The Reformed Society of Israelites," and they attempted to reform Beth Elohim's service by abbreviating it, by having some parts of the service read in both Hebrew and English, by eliminating the practice of auctioning synagogue honors, and by having a weekly discourse, or sermon, in English. While these initial demands are quite compatible with contemporary centrist Orthodoxy in America, they were radical at that time. Moreover, the leadership of Beth Elohim perceived—and this subsequently proved to be rather accurate—that these demands of the Society were only the beginning of much more drastic reforms later.

The Society was unsuccessful in changing Beth Elohim, and its members therefore seceded and established their own congregation, which then went well beyond the more modest reforms they had initially proposed. The new congregation grew rapidly for several years, but by 1828 it began to decline, and in 1833 it closed its doors for the last time. Harby himself had already left for New York in 1828, where he joined Congregation Shearith Israel. He died six months after his arrival there and was buried in Shearith Israel's second cemetery, which is still located on West 11th Street, between Fifth and Sixth Avenue, in Manhattan. Most other members of the Society returned to Beth Elohim.

Neither the demise of the Society nor the return of most members to Beth Elohim, however, can be viewed as indications of the strength and triumph of traditionalism. Other factors were involved in this initial failure of reform. The leadership of the Society was organizationally inexperienced, Jewishly ignorant, and, unlike the movement of Reform Judaism in Germany, not ideologically motivated (Reznikoff and Engelman, 1950, pp. 135–36). The Society was strongly ostracized by Beth Elohim and was unable to develop the resources for all the other communal needs that the parent congregation provided. More than anything else, the demise of the Society was probably due to the general decline of the Charleston community after 1828 and to the increasing apathy toward Jewish concerns in that community (Jick, 1976, p. 13). Subsequent developments suggest that Harby was somewhat premature when in 1825 he delivered a discourse before the Reformed Society of Israelites and declared: "Your principles are rapidly prevading the whole mass of Hebrews throughout the United States" (Blau and Baron, 1963, II, 563). By the early 1840s the parent congregation, Beth Elohim, left the traditional fold for Reform, and by the 1860s Reform synagogues, some new and many formerly traditional, existed in New York City, Baltimore, Albany, Cincinnati, Philadelphia, and Chicago, as well as many newer and smaller communities. Despite its short life, Charleston's Reformed Society of Israelites paved the way for the coming—in little more than a quarter of a century—of a major movement within American Judaism.

In an effort to combat the chaos in American Jewish

religious life, Rev. Isaac Leeser, who became the *Hazan* at Mikveh Israel in Philadelphia in 1829 at the age of twenty-three (Wolf and Whiteman, 1975, pp. 372 ff.), became involved in a series of activities that had profound impact upon American Jewry for many years to come. Between 1830 and his death in 1868 Leeser wrote Hebrew textbooks for children and works on Judaism, translated the Prayer Book and Bible into English, edited and published the first national Anglo-Jewish weekly in the United States, *The Occident*, and established the first American theological seminary, Maimonides College. He was a driving force behind the establishment of the Hebrew Educational Society, the Jewish Publication Society, and the Jewish Hospital, all in Philadelphia, and was the first to devise a program for the national unification of American synagogues (ibid., p. 373; Davis, pp. 347–49).

Leeser's staunchest supporter in his drive to unify American synagogues was Rev. Isaac Mayer Wise, who arrived in New York from Bohemia in 1846 and was to become the institution-builder of Reform Judaism in America. Wise too was dismayed at the chaotic state of Judaism and Jewish congregational life in the United States, and in 1848 his call for an association of Jewish ("Israelitish") congregations in the country was published by Leeser in *The Occident* (VI, 1848–49, 431–33).

The alliance between Wise and Leeser did not last long, however, for despite his traditional Jewish upbringing and education, Wise became a spearhead of reform. His first position was rabbi of Congregation Beth El in Albany, where he served from 1846 until his dismissal in 1850, the result of a growing dissatisfaction with Wise as an individual and with the many reforms he instituted. He was then immediately hired as rabbi of Anshe Emeth, a new congregation which from its very inception was Reform. He remained at Anshe Emeth in Albany for four years, during which time he traveled around the country extensively, severed his relationship with *The Occident* as well as *The Asmonean*, another publication sympathetic to tradition, and published a book, *The Origin of Christianity*, for which he was scorned by traditionalists who viewed the book as heretical and threatening. The book did help create a name for Wise, however, in Jewish and general American public circles, and he emerged as a major spokesman for American Judaism and Jewry. In 1854 at the age of forty-six, Wise accepted an offer from Congregation Bene Yeshurun in Cincinnati, where he remained until his death in 1900. During those years, he devoted himself to organizing American Judaism and, though he did not quite accomplish that task, he did play the pivotal role in institutionalizing Reform Judaism in America. Wise had dreamed of organizing all the congregations in the country, but the traditionalists refused to associate with him. In 1873, however, representatives of thirty-four Reform congregations did convene in Cincinnati and officially organized the Union of American Hebrew Congregations. Though its name identifies it as American, not solely Reform, it became and is today the synagogue and temple organization of American Reform Judaism. Similarly when Wise's dream of establishing a seminary for the training of American rabbis was realized with the founding of Hebrew Union College in Cincinnati in 1875, its name identified it simply as Hebrew, without the Reform designation. Hebrew Union College today has branches in New York, Los Angeles, and Jerusalem, and is the school of higher learning of American Reform Judaism. And when Wise's dream of establishing a synod of American rabbis was finally realized in 1889, it called itself the Central Conference of American Rabbis, without the specific Reform designation, though it was, and remains, the rabbinical body of American Reform Judaism (Heller, 1965; Wise, 1901).

Leeser and other traditionalists were not the only opposition facing Wise. He had his share of opponents within the Reform rabbinate as well. One of his earliest and most vehement Reform antagonists was David Einhorn, who had come to America in 1855 to become rabbi of Temple Har Sinai in Baltimore. Whereas Wise was the organizer and institution builder, Einhorn was an unyielding ideologist of radical Reform. He had no respect nor patience for Wise's relatively less doctrinaire, pragmatic approach. To him Wise was a

liberal reformer and therefore more dangerous than traditionalists. In 1861 Einhorn wrote an article in the German
language monthly, *Sinai*, in which he declared: "The real
culprits are the so-called reformers. . . . Reform is something
quite different from the elimination of [one or another of the
prayers which are listed]" (quoted in Jick, p. 165). Wise
responded to this attack by denouncing Einhorn as "a Deist, a
Unitarian, and a Sadducee and an apostle of deistical rationalism . . . . Einhorn, you should not have so far forgotten that
your father was a Jew. . . . Reclaim publicly your false
representations of Judaism and your slanders of the Jew."
Wise concluded his counterattack by branding Einhorn "an
enemy of the Jews and Judaism" (ibid.). The two remained
bitter antagonists throughout their lives, and each competed
with the other for the leadership of Reform Judaism in
America. While Wise was successful in his role as institution
builder, Einhorn and his followers, especially his disciple and
son-in-law, Kaufman Kohler, succeeded in having the principles of radical Reform adopted in the Pittsburgh Platform of
Reform Rabbis in 1885, four years before the official founding
of the Central Conference of American Rabbis. Some principles adopted asserted:

> To-day we accept as binding only the moral laws and maintain
> only such ceremonies as elevate and sanctify our lives, but reject
> all such as are not adapted to the views and habits of modern
> civilization.
>
> We hold that all such Mosaic and Rabbinical laws as regular
> diet, priestly purity and dress originated in ages and under the
> influence of ideas foreign to our present mental and spiritual
> state. They fail to impress the modern Jew with a spirit of priestly
> holiness; their observance in our days is apt rather to obstruct
> than to further modern spiritual elevation.
>
> We consider ourselves no longer a nation but a religious
> community, and therefore expect neither a return to Palestine,
> nor a sacrificial worship under the administration of the sons of
> Aaron, nor the restoration of any of the laws concerning the
> Jewish State.
>
> We reject as ideas not rooted in Judaism the belief both in bodily
> resurrection and in Gehenna and Eden (hell and paradise), as

abodes for everlasting punishment or reward [Plaut, 1965, pp. 33–34; Davis, 1963, pp. 226–27].

These remained the principles of Reform Judaism for more than fifty years, and it was not until Zionism had became a major movement, Hitler had come to power, and the ethnic composition of Reform Judaism in America had undergone considerable change, that the principles were altered in the Columbus Platform of 1937.

In response to the successes of Reform, and especially what were considered its extreme and intolerable principles Henry Pereira Mendes, rabbi of New York's Congregation Shearith Israel, and Sabato Morais, successor to Isaac Leeser as *Hazan* of Congregation Mikveh Israel in Philadelphia, organized a group of traditionalist rabbis, educators, and laymen, and established The Jewish Theological Seminary of America in New York City. The founding of this seminary on January 31, 1886, marked the institutionalization of the more moderate wing of traditionalists—who referred to themselves as the "historical school"—into Conservative Judaism (Davis, pp. 231 ff.). In that same year on September 15, a group of traditionalists of Eastern European background founded Yeshivat Etz Chaim to meet the Jewish educational needs of the newly arriving Eastern European Jews. Eleven years later in 1897 the Rabbi Isaac Elchanan Theological Seminary was founded as the seminary for the training of Orthodox rabbis. In 1915 the two schools merged and become Yeshiva College and later Yeshiva University (Klaperman, 1969, pp. 17–33). Thus in the nineteenth century came the institutionalization of three branches of American Judaism.

In addition to religious institutionalization, American Jewry moved toward organizing communally, during the nineteenth century. Three events in particular were decisive. The first was in reaction to a blood libel and subsequent pogrom in Damascus, Syria. On March 24, 1840, Jasper Chasseaud, the American consular representative in Syria, wrote a long letter to the U.S. secretary of state, officially informing him of the affair. The gist of that letter follows:

On the 5th of February last the Revd Capouchin Thomas president of the Catholic Church of Damascus—together with his Servant having, all of a sudden desappeared from that City. . . . The Jew Barber was questioned and taken into prison, and after the application of some torments on his person he confessed that the Revd Thomas had been beheaded in the house of David Arari, a rich Jew, by Seven of his coreligioners of Damascus, and that, in order to take his Blood, it being ordered by their religion to make use of Christian Blood in their Unleavened Bread at Easter . . .

The Seven Jews thus accused, as well as all their high Priests; 64 Children, belonging to those families, and all their Butchers were immediately taken to prison, and after severe Tortures and threats several of them confessed . . .

The inquisition against the jews in that City (in which there may be 30000 Souls of that Nation) continues with much vigour and no jew can show his face out in the streets [Blau and Baron, 1963, III, 924–26].

The American Government apparently recognized that the Jews of Damascus were being used as pawns in a conflict involving the viceroy of Egypt, supported by France, and the Turkish sultan, supported by England. It implicitly rejected Chasseaud's interpretation of the Syrian accusations and expressed its humanitarian concern and sympathies with the position of the persecuted Jews. The affair became a cause cèlébre in newspapers around the world. England, for obvious political as well as humanitarian reasons, reacted most sharply. Jews in England, France, and other Western European countries held mass prayer and protest meetings. In the United States, once the Government officially stated its position in favor of intervention on behalf of Damascus Jewry, mass meetings were held in the Jewish communities of New York, Philadelphia, Charleston, and Richmond (ibid., pp. 927–52). In New York the trustees of Shearith Israel voted not to conduct the meeting in their synagogue because "no benefit can arise from such a course" (quoted in Grinstein, p. 420). The meeting was held in Bnai Jeshurun, and a committee representing the synagogues and socieities of the New York Jewish community was appointed to send a letter to President Martin Van Buren to intercede on behalf of the Jewish prisoners in particular, and all of Damascus Jewry in general.

Secretary of State John Forsyth responded, confirmed that he had already written to the counsul in Alexandria, and enclosed a copy of that letter.

While it is difficult to gauge the ultimate impact of these events upon Damascus Jewry, it is clear that they had profound impact upon American Jewry. The Damascus Affair showed American Jews its need for a representative national body to deal with crises. Also Shearith Israel's refusal to host the mass protest meeting in New York marked its demise as the authoritative parent congregation of New York and American Jewry.

The second event that stirred American Jewry to organized activity was the proposal of a treaty between the United States and Switzerland. Since Switzerland had laws and practices that discriminated against Jews and certain cantons that were completely closed to them, American Jews felt that by ratifying the proposed treaty, the United States Government was giving sanction to the discrimination. Moreover, American Jews were particularly upset as the treaty included a provision that allowed only Christian Americans to live in Switzerland. In 1854 a national committee representing American Jews sent a letter of protest to Congress, and across the country Jews protested through meetings and letters to newspapers and politicians. While these activities were not immediately effective, as far as the treaty was concerned—it was not until 1874 that Switzerland wrote a new constitution that guaranteed religious freedom—they did once again highlight the need for a corporate voice for American Jews (Stroock, 1903; Adler and Margalith, 1943, pp. 299–322).

The third and decisive incident was the Mortara case. On June 23, 1858, seven-year-old Edgar Mortara of Bologna in Italy, was abducted from the home of his parents, Girolamo Mortara Levi and Marianna Padovani Levi, by a Catholic nurse and was hidden in a convent. According to evidence the abduction took place with the approval of the archbishop of Bologna, and it was subsequently endorsed by Pope Pius IX. The abduction was widely criticized in the European and American press, and by some Catholics in Europe. In the United States, however, the Catholic press supported the abduction, on the grounds that the nurse had been hired by the parents. The argument was that if she used that opportunity to baptize the child (secretly, several years before the abduction), the parents had only themselves to blame (Schappes, pp. 385–87). For the third time American Jews held mass protest meetings and wrote to Secretary of State Lewis Cass to intercede with the Italian authorities on the child's behalf. The secretary's reply, however, was quite different from that received during the Damascus Affair. He stated that it was the policy of President James Buchanan's administration not to interfere in the internal affairs of foreign governments. American Jewry was appalled by this response, and though it was not able to secure the return of the Mortara child, it moved with greater urgency to organize itself (Korn, 1957).

On November 27–29, 1859, representatives of twenty-four congregations, eleven of which were from New York and thirteen from other parts of the country, assembled at Cooper Institute in New York and established the Board of Delegates of American Israelites. Since this group consisted primarily of representatives of traditional congregations, most of whom were from the East, and therefore was not actually representative of American Jewry as a whole, it did not accept the long list of priorities urged by Isaac Leeser. Rather a much more limited statement of purposes was adopted: "1) To keep a watchful eye on all occurences at home and abroad. 2) To collect statistics. 3) To aid religious education" (Tarshish, 1959, p. 20).

Dissension within the ranks of American Jewry plagued the Board of Delegates from its very inception. Reform rabbis, in particular, were hostile to the Board. They suspected that because it was composed of traditionalists, it would attempt to co-opt and stifle Reform, and they saw it as an infringement on the autonomy of each individual rabbi and congregation. In addition, some were opposed to the very notion of united Jewish social and political activity. For example, Temple Emanu-El, the first Reform congregation in New York City declared: "It would be a mistake for Jews to act together for

social and political purposes for thus they would become an *imperium in imperio* in America, and others would believe that the Jews felt they were in exile" (quoted by Tarshish, p. 21).

During its brief existence, the Board of Delegates did nevertheless manage to achieve a number of significant accomplishments. At its urging, for example, Congress amended its Act of 1861, which provided for Army chaplains solely from among Christian clergy (Tarshish, p. 22; Schappes, pp. 462–64). In 1862 the Board and many others strongly protested General Ulysses S. Grant's General Order No. 11, which expelled all Jews from his military jurisdiction and which was rescinded three months later by President Abraham Lincoln (Schappes, pp. 472–76). The board was also instrumental in the rejection of a proposed new constitution in North Carolina, which would have restricted Jews from holding public office (Tarshish, p. 23). Owing to the deep divisions within American Jewry, the Board was much less successful in its educational and religious agenda. Though it was founded by traditionalists, during the 1870s the Board attracted an increasing number of liberal Reform members, and in 1878 it merged with the Union of American Hebrew Congregations, lost its autonomy, and became a standing committee of the UAHC (Tarshish, pp. 30–2).

The period between 1820 and 1880 was one of dramatic geographic and economic expansion in the country. Cities were growing, and the country was moving westward. These conditions provided many German Jewish immigrants during that period with unique opportunities, given their historical relationship with the city, and their experience as middlemen as financial and commercial agents in Europe (Stern-Taubler, 1955). They arrived in the United States but did not concentrate in New York City as the later Eastern European Jewish immigrants tended to, and for the most part, began peddling (Glanz, 1947/48, p. 92). Some, who did concentrate in New York, became as wealthy as the wealthiest non-Jews in the country through investment banking, such as Joseph Seligman and Solomon Loeb. Others, such as Emanuel and Mayer Lehman, became railroad magnates in addition to being commodity dealers and investment bankers. Lazarus Straus and his three sons, Isador, Oscar, and Nathan, and Julius Rosenwald, who was born in the United States of German Jewish immigrant parents, are just a few of those who went on to excel in retail merchandising (Birmingham, 1967). While these were the exceptions, obviously, German Jewish immigrants apparently were more successful socioeconomically than other immigrant groups and even American-born non-Jews. For example, a study of late-nineteenth-century Boston found that a significantly higher percentage of Jews attained white-collar status than did native-born non-Jewish Bostonians (Thernstrom, 1973, pp. 124–51). And in a study dealing specifically with that city's German Jewish immigrants during the years 1845–1861, Mostov found that whereas "one-third of Boston's entire work force, and one-fifth of the city's employed Germans in 1850 worked in menial, semi-skilled, and service jobs," only 2 percent of employed Jews did so (Mostov, 1978, p. 145). In terms of wealth, using data derived from the city's tax assessment lists and censuses, he found that whereas "the two middle class categories included less than one-third of the city's taxpayers," they did contain between 50 percent to 75 percent of all Jews in the city (ibid., p. 146). Likewise, a recent study of Jews in Atlanta during the nineteenth and early twentieth centuries found that "in their economic performance, the Jews of Atlanta surpassed not only their northern cousins but also their gentile neighbors. . . . In three of the four decades over which the 1870 population was traced, Jews manifested less skidding and Jews in the proprietor-professional group demonstrated greater stability than both native whites and immigrants. Jews in the 1880 cohort did even better" (Hertzberg, 1978, p. 152).

A problem of course arises whenever groups are compared to one another. In comparing the relative socioeconomic success to one group. German Jewish immigrants, to others, we are dealing with the *relative* success of that group to that of the others, and we can easily fall into the trap of overly generalizing and stereotyping. While unique opportunities for socioeconomic success did prevail in the country during this

period and German Jewish immigrants did take advantage of them as a rule, not everyone was a Horatio Alger. Not only did all German Jewish immigrants not become part of the celebrated "our crowd" (Birmingham); some of them remained poor. Although the American Federation of Labor—cofounded by Adolph Strasser and a Jew, Samuel Gompers—was not organized until 1881, strife, strikes, and labor unions existed in the country from as early as the 1790s. In 1866, the National Labor Union was formed (Rayback, 1966, pp. 47–184). While no specific data on Jews in the early labor movement or poor Jews are available, we can assume that some Jews were involved. Moreover, while the Bnai Brith leader Benjamin F. Peixotto could proclaim in 1865 that "our people (as everyone in this great Republic) have thrived beyond measure. On every side, witness of their wealth and prosperity appear" (Moore, 1981b; Swichkow and Gartner, 1963, p. 30), Jewish charities in fact were on the rise in the country since 1822, especially in New York. The Hebrew Benevolent Society, for example, originally formed by the Ashkenazi members of Shearith Israel, later an affiliate of Bnai Jeshurun, and ultimately the largest Jewish philanthropic agency in New York by the 1850s, "had 2,025 applicants, among whom it distributed $3,567" (Grinstein, p. 146). In addition, there were such organizations as the German Hebrew Benevolent Society, the Society for the Education of Poor Children and the Relief of Indigent Persons of the Jewish Persuasion, the New York Hebrew Assistance Society, the Bachelors Hebrew Benevolent Loan Association, the Young Men's Hebrew Benevolent and Fuel Association, the Hebrew Female Benevolent Society of Shearith Israel, the Ladies Association for the General Instruction of Children of the Jewish Persuasion, the Bnai Jeshurun Ladies Benevolent Society, in addition to other philanthropic organizations concerned with visiting the sick and providing burial rites (ibid., pp. 146–55). The activities of all of these organizations, which derive from the very high priority placed upon philanthropy within Jewish tradition, indicate that Jews still had their share of poor. The American Jewish success story during the nineteenth century, early twentieth century, and even in the contemporary period, as will be indicated later must be taken with more than a grain of salt. The relative context cannot be overemphasized, lest the picture be distorted and those who did not fare so well be overlooked. At the same time, even that relative success is something to be marveled at.

Socially too, Jews in the United States during most of the nineteenth century were relatively successful. Certainly there were instances of anti-Semitism. Probably the most noted were those involving Uriah P. Levy, General Grant, and Joseph Seligman. In 1812 Uriah P. Levy, a native American Jew whose family had been in the country for several generations and who had been a merchant marine, enlisted in the United States Navy. He rapidly rose to become a commanding officer and was deeply resented by his fellow officers who were jealous of the success of this "damned Jew." He was court martialed six times; each time he was found guilty, severely punished, dismissed, but then ultimately vindicated. In 1855 he was among 200 officers who were dismissed allegedly "to improve the efficiency of the Navy." Following mass protests, the Navy appointed a Court of Inquiry to review the cases, during which Levy presented a stirring defense. On January 29, 1858, he was reinstated, with about 65 others who had been dismissed, and in 1860 he became commander of the Mediterranean squadron (Schappes, pp. 375–85; Kanof, 1949/ 50). General Grant's Order No. 11 was discussed above. The Seligman-Hilton Affair took place in Saratoga, New York, in 1877. Joseph Seligman, a German Jewish immigrant who had become one of the country's leading bankers, was barred from registering as a guest in the Grand Union Hotel which, along with other non-Jewish establishments in the city, allegedly displayed signs reading, "No Jews or Dogs Admitted Here." Jews reacted strongly and proceeded to boycott the A. T. Stewart Company because its president, Judge Hilton, was an associate of the Grand Union. Although the wholesale company went bankrupt as a result, upper-class and middle-class Jews found themselves increasingly barred from non-Jewish establishments during the rest of that decade and the next.

Whereas the Seligman-Hilton Affair was already part of a growing pattern of anti-Semitism, the Levy and Grant incidents were more the exceptions than the rule. Except for the relatively small increase during the Civil War period, political anti-Semitism was virtually absent in the United States until the very end of the nineteenth century. Only after a number of German Jews made significant entries into the world of banking, and a growing number of Jews from Eastern Europe began to crowd into the urban slums along with the rising number of Catholic immigrants from Eastern and Southern Europe, did ideological anti-Semitism become pronounced among Nativists, Populists, and others (Lipset and Raab, 1970, pp. 92–95; Higham, 1975, pp. 116–51). Even during the 1890s, when the growing instances of anti-Semitism did indicate the potential for political anti-Semitism, "it is important to note that it was only a potential, that none of the major political and social movements of the day used anti-Semitism as a political tactic. Anti-Catholicism was the anti-Semitism of the Protestant nineteenth century" (Lipset and Raab, p. 95).

One indication of the level of Jewish acceptance and integration into American society during the nineteenth century is the rate of exogamy—marriage outside the group. Historically the marriage of a Jew to a non-Jew who has not converted to Judaism was a very severe violation of Jewish norms and was sanctioned accordingly. Among traditionalists, the marriage was not condoned, and the Jewish spouse was considered dead, for all intents and purposes, and his or her family actually observed many rites of mourning. Furthermore, the prevalence of mixed marriage in which the Jewish spouse does not become an apostate, or convert, to the religion of the non-Jewish spouse, is an indication of non-Jewish acceptance of Jews. It is, therefore, revealing of the state of Jewish and non-Jewish intergroup and interpersonal relations that between the years 1776 and 1840, the rate of intermarriage was 28.7 percent. Of the 699 marriages of Jews during that period whose records are available, 201 involved marriage with a non-Jew (Stern, 1967, pp. 142–43). Also, Grinstein indicates the liberalization of the policies of Congregation Shearith Israel in New York between 1790 and the 1830s with respect to intermarriage that allowed the Jewish spouse to remain within the fold and the congregation (Grinstein, 1945, pp. 375–76). Although specific data are not available, the rate of intermarriage apparently continued to rise until the onset of the large Eastern European immigration at the end of the nineteenth century. According to Arthur Ruppin, one of the first sociologists of Jewry: "Before the mass immigration from Eastern Europe began in 1881, the percentage of mixed marriages was fairly high among the American Jews, most of them of German or Dutch extraction; they were particularly frequent in the Southern and Western States where Jews lived in small numbers" (Ruppin, 1973 [1934], p. 321).

Finally, while the nineteenth century was a period of integration, acculturation, and even assimilation for many, for those with strong Jewish identification it was a period also during which they began to view their political behavior from a Jewish perspective. While they certainly did not perceive themselves to be voting solely in terms of Jewish group interests, nor were they, they did begin to perceive that their Jewish heritage and interests influenced their voting perspective. Already in the late eighteenth century, American Jews had supported Thomas Jefferson against the Federalist Party, and the opposition to the Federalists intensified when, in 1814 and 1815, the party proposed a constitutional amendment that would bar naturalized citizens from serving as members of Congress. Jewish support for the Democratic Party grew with President Martin Van Buren's staunch support during the Damascus Affair and continued through the administration of James K. Polk. During the 1850s, however, neither the Democrats nor the Whigs enjoyed strong support from the Jews. "While the Democrats compromised with slavery in domestic affairs, the Whigs, in many states, were allied with the nativist movement. In foreign affairs, both parties had foresaken the Van Buren policy of aiding distressed Jews abroad" (Fuchs, 1956, p. 31).

Jews were so disillusioned with both major parties that

Isaac Mayer Wise perceived that Jews might support the extremist Know-Nothing Party, which, while it was strongly anti-Catholic, did not turn its nativism against Jews. Wise did not trust the Know-Nothing candidates, viewed them as potential anti-Semites, and bemoaned: "The Hebrew vote is almost unanimously in favor of Know-Nothing candidates, and the Know-Nothing leaders entertain strong hopes that they have attracted the Hebrews permanently to their party" (quoted in Heller, 1965, p. 308). There seemed to be no substance to Wise's perception of strong Jewish support for that party. With respect to the slavery issue, while there was no consensus among American Jews, it would be incorrect to suggest that they were neutral on the subject or that they did not see their Judaism and Jewishness as relevant to it—quite the contrary. On January 4, 1861, Rabbi Morris J. Raphall, of Congregation Bnai Jeshurun in New York gave a public speech, "The Bible View of Slavery" (Schappes, pp. 405–18), in which he discussed the Biblical tolerance of slavery. Although Raphall was careful to distinguish between the institution of slavery as it had existed among the Hebrews of old and that of the South in his own times, his discourse was widely viewed as a legitimation of slavery basically. Less than two weeks later, the *New York Daily Tribune*, edited by Horace Greeley, published a strong and informed response to Raphall by a well-known Jewish scholar, Michael Heilprin (ibid., pp. 418–28). Several months later, David Einhorn was forced to leave his position as rabbi of Temple Har Sinai in Baltimore because of his strong support for the abolitionist cause, which he based upon his understanding of Jewish teaching, and which he persisted to declare from the pulpit (ibid., pp. 444–49; Korn, 1961).

When it comes to issues involving Jews directly, moreover, an analysis of the three major American Jewish periodicals during the years 1840–1859—Leeser's *Occident*, Wise's *Israelite*, and *The Asmonean*, published in New York by a layman, Robert Lyon—indicates that they were indeed "pioneers of American Jewish Defense" (Cohen, 1977). Cohen convincingly demonstrates that the "three young editors (all under the age of forty when they commenced publication) undertook herculean assignments in their attempt to protect the far-flung Jewish settlements," and her analysis of *The Asmonean* calls for a corrective in the standard portrait of the politics of American Jews during this period. In reference to the 1860s, for example, Werner Cohn writes: "To a very large extent they were thought of—and thought of themselves—as individually functioning participants in American politics; no one was much concerned over any possible relevance of their Jewishness to their ballotting" (Cohn, 1958, p. 620). In contrast, at least Lyon in *The Asmonean* took a very different position. While he did not call for or favor a distinctly Jewish political party or a permanent coalition with either major party, he did call upon Jews to assert their minority group rights through their voting power (Cohen, p. 136). Although Lyon's assertiveness was not characteristic of the majority of American Jews at the time, he may be seen as the father, or grandfather, of the political stance that was to be adopted by the organized American Jewish community a century later, in second half of the twentieth century.

2. The Eastern European Immigration

The years 1881–1923 constitute one of the most fascinating eras in American history in general, and in the American Jewish experience in particular. It was an era during which approximately twenty-five million immigrants, primarily from Eastern and Southern Europe, arrived in this country. Of the many groups that came, Jews were second only to the Italians in number. In 1880 the Jewish population in the United States was approximately 250,000 individuals, most of whom were immigrants or descendants of immigrants from Central Europe (Glazer, 1972, p. 60). Before 1869, very few Jewish immigrants arrived from Russia, but between 1869 and 1880, when significant numbers of Jews began emigrating from there, an estimated 30,000 of them came to the United States (Wischnitzer, 1948, p. 289, n. 1). The major stimuli for the increased emigration from Russia at this time were the cholera that plagued the northwest part of that country in 1868 and the famine in the same area a year later (ibid. p. 29). In March 1881 Czar Alexander II was assassinated, an event that sparked anti-Jewish riots and massacres in scores of Jewish communities. Following these, laws that restricted the lives of Jews were passed. The combination of economic, political, and physical persecution generated a massive move of Jews out of Eastern Europe; the overwhelming majority of them came to the United States (ibid., pp. 37–130). Table 1 indicates the frantic pace of Jewish immigration into the United States between the years 1881 and 1923, a pace that almost certainly would have persisted had the various forces favoring restriction not succeeded in the passage of Johnson Immigration Act of 1921 and 1924.

This dramatic influx of an estimated 2,787,754 immigrant Jews from Eastern Europe transformed American Jewry and the nature of its communal structure in fundamental ways. From a quarter of a million individuals in 1880, the American Jewish population grew to almost three and one-half million by 1917, and to more than four and one-quarter million by 1927. Whereas in 1877, Jews were 0.52 percent of the total United States population, in 1927 they had grown to become 3.58 percent (Gutman, 1966, p. 354). While in 1880 most American Jews were of Central European background, in 1927, 80 percent or more were estimated to have been of Eastern European origin (Glazer, 1972, p. 83). While the important contributions of the earlier Sephardi and German Jewish immigrations should not be minimized, it was the

Table 1. Jewish Immigration into the United States from 1881 to 1923

1881	8,193	1896	73,255	1910	84,260
1882	31,807	1897	43,434	1911	91,223
1883	6,907	1898	54,630	1912	80,595
1884	15,122	1899	37,415	1913	101,330
1885	36,214	1900	60,764	1914	138,051
1886	46,967	1901	58,098	1915	26,497
1887	56,412	1902	57,688	1916	15,108
1888	62,619	1903	76,203	1917	17,342
1889	55,851	1904	106,236	1918	3,672
1890	67,450	1905	129,910	1919	3,055
1891	111,284	1906	153,748	1920	14,292
1892	136,742	1907	149,182	1921	119,036
1893	68,569	1908	103,387	1922	53,524
1894	58,833	1909	57,551	1923	49,989
1895	65,309				

SOURCE: Mark Wischnitzer, *To Dwell in Safety: The Story of Jewish Migration since 1800* (Philadelphia: Jewish Publication Society of America, 1948), p. 289. © The Jewish Publication Society of America. Reprinted with Permission.

Eastern Europeans, as Leventman says, "whose culture became virtually synonymous with that of American Jewry and that eventually formed the Jewish community in the United States" (Leventman, 1969, p. 35).

Because their cultural and structural backgrounds in Europe were so different from those of German Jews, and because the conditions in the United States had changed by the time of their arrival, the Eastern European Jewish immigrants developed very different patterns of organization from those of their predecessors. In contrast to the German Jewish immigrants of the nineteenth century who disbursed across the country, the Eastern European immigrants, arriving when the United States was becoming urbanized, concentrated in ethnic neighborhoods in the country's largest cities. New York City was their major focal point, and "practically all East European immigrants arriving after 1870 initially found their way to the Lower East Side. Virtually penniless upon their arrival in the city, they were directed to the Jewish districts by representatives of the immigrant aid societies, or came at the behest of friends, relatives, or employers" (Rischin, 1970, p. 79). This resulted in the urbanization of American Jewry, a pattern that persists to this day, although it has been declining somewhat in recent years. To understand the nature of the immigrant community in the United States, we should review their Eastern European backgrounds.

As a result of the partitions of Poland in 1772, 1793, and 1795, large numbers of Jews were incorporated into Czarist Russia, and a smaller but significant number became part of the Austro-Hungarian Empire. Within Russia the Jews were restricted to the "Pale of Settlement," an area of about 386,000 squares miles which spanned the territory from the Baltic to the Black seas and which comprised ten Polish and fifteen Russian provinces (see Map 1). From about 800,000 Jews in 1800, Russian Jewry grew to almost five and one-half million by 1900 (Ruppin, 1973, [1934], p. 43).

The world of Eastern European Jewry was very different from that of German Jews. As Bernard Weinryb aptly puts it, they lived in

Map 1. *The Pale of Settlement at the End of the Nineteenth Century*

SOURCE: *Encyclopedia Judaica* (Jerusalem, Keter Publishing Co., 1971), XIII,
25–26. ©Keter Publishing Co. Reprinted with Permission.

a milieu where the feeling of homogeneity, of *Klal Yisrael* (unity of
Israel), was strongly entrenched, and where a set of Jewish values
and attitudes prevailed, including religious devotion and observance. In Eastern Europe, Jews lived in compact masses. Not
only did they form a majority of the population in many towns and
hamlets, as well as a considerable percentage in the big cities, but
the Jewish sections in these settlements were generally "purely
Jewish." . . .

In contrast with Western Europe, there was a definite sense of
belonging to a "nation" or people. The mode of life was less a
matter of individual choice and more a matter of control by the
group through the medium of public opinion [Weinryb, 1958, p.
15].

During the nineteenth century the world of Eastern European Jewry was the *shtetl*, which is a Yiddish term meaning small town. The nature of the *shtetl* has been grossly distorted and "misapprehended," as Irving Howe indicates (1976, p. 10), in much popular writing about it in recent years. It was not quite the warm, lovely, and joyful community as nostalgically portrayed in *Fiddler on the Roof*. Nor did it have the permanence that is implied in the anthropological study of its culture in *Life Is with People* (Zborowski and Herzog, 1952). It was "a community in the process of disintegration, though the exact degree of disintegration varied from region to region, from community to community, and from group to group" (Weinryb, p. 15). In fact, in the beginning of the twentieth century the majority of Jews in Eastern Europe were urban (Ruppin, pp. 32–36). Most of the Eastern European Jews who immigrated in the United States during the period 1880–1920, and especially those who came before 1910, did nevertheless come from *shtetlach* (plural for *shtetl*), and despite local variations, we can speak of the culture of the *shtetl*. Those who lived there did share a common religion, language, set of values, norms, institutional structure, and sense of belonging.

Judaism in its traditional form was the religion of the *shtetl*; it was its culture also. The person from the *shtetl*, living in a traditional monoreligious culture, would probably not have even understood the Western distinction between religious group and ethnic group. To him or her, there were only *Yidn*, Jews, and *Yiddishkeit*, Jewishness, the Jewish way of life. While there has been some misunderstanding on the matter, within traditional Judaism there is much more emphasis on behavior than on belief. Theology was never a major area of discussion or study, even among scholars. To be a "good Jew" meant to behave in accordance with the norms of traditional Judaism as defined by the rabbi scholars of the community. Belief was probably taken for granted. As poignantly portrayed by Howe:

God was a living force, a Presence, more than a name or a desire. He did not rule from on high; He was not a God of magnificence; nor was He an aesthetic God. The Jews had no beautiful churches, they had wooden synagogues. Beauty was a quality, not a form; a content, not an arrangement. The Jews would have been deeply puzzled by the idea that the aesthetic and the moral are distinct realms. One spoke not of a beautiful thing but a beautiful deed. . . . Yiddish culture was a culture of speech, and its God a God who spoke. He was a plebian God, perhaps immanent but hardly transcendent. Toward Him the Jews could feel a peculiar sense of intimacy: had they not suffered enough in His behalf? In prayer His name could not be spoken, yet in or out of prayer He could always be spoken to [Howe, p. 11].

The language of the *shtetl* was Yiddish, "a medieval German dialect with which Hebrew elements were combined" (Zborowski and Herzog, p. 33). In time, Yiddish developed its own linguistic autonomy, frequently absorbing aspects of the local vernacular. Hebrew was the "holy tongue," reserved primarily for scripture and prayer. Although scholars were relatively well versed in Hebrew, Yiddish was the mother tongue of the masses who used it even for an understanding of scripture and prayer. Whether or not they knew the language of the country in which they lived, Yiddish was the language of *shtetl* Jews, and through it they conveyed their deepest sentiments.

The Eastern European Jewish sense of belonging to a "nation" or people was derived and reinforced from both internal and external sources. Historically within traditional Judaism "the Jewish community as a whole is a unique blend of kinship and consent. This amalgam is apparent as early as the biblical account of the Jewish people's origins: a family of tribes becomes a nation by consenting to the Covenant. It is reflected in subsequent biblical narrative, and postbiblical history gave the blend new meaning" (Elazar, 1976, p. 11). Thus, to the Jew of the *shtetl*, the Jewish community was perceived as the extended family. In addition, Eastern Europe had not developed the distinction between religion and nationality which Germany and the West had. As Glazer points out, Eastern European countries were neither as ethnically homogeneous nor religiously diverse as was Germany. In Eastern Europe there were, and still are, many

different national groups struggling for liberation from oppression. Just as the Poles were and are Catholic, and the
Russians were and are Orthodox, the Jews were and are
perceived by themselves and non-Jews as a separate nation. So
entrenched was this conception of Jews as a people that it
would have been "easier to envisage the Jews abandoning
their religion (upon their arrival in America) and becoming
simply a people than to envisage them abandoning their ethnic
characteristics and becoming a denomination in Reform
Jewish style" (Glazer, 1972, p. 64), as many German Jewish
immigrants had. In the *shtetl*, of course, it would have been
very difficult to envisage them abandoning either their ethnic
or religious character, but their having thought of themselves
as a distinct people is borne out by the responses of Eastern
European Jewish immigrants to the immigration authorities
upon their arrival in the United States. When asked to classify
themselves on a list of "races or peoples," most Eastern
European Jewish immigrants designated themselves as
"Hebrew," rather than "Russian" or "Polish." By contrast,
German Jews had tended to identify themselves as "German."
Among American Jewish leaders, it was primarily German
and/or Reform Jews who objected to the inclusion of the term
"Hebrew" on the list of races, on the grounds that Jews were
neither a race nor a nation (Goldberg, 1945, pp. 90–105).

   The system of social stratification in the *shtetl* was one in
which level and degree of sacred learning, family lineage, and
wealth were the major variables that determined status. The
two major classes of people were *sheyneh yidn*, beautiful or fine
Jews, and *prosteh yidn*, plain or common Jews (Zborowski and
Herzog, pp. 73–80). Status, *yikhus*, was either ascribed (*yikhus
avos*) or achieved (*yikhus atsmo*). Generally, level and degree of
sacred knowledge and learning conferred highest status.
Wealth, provided it was used "properly," in the support of
communal needs, also conferred high status. If, in addition to
one's own achieved status, one also had *yikhus avos*, one was a
descendant of *sheyneh yidn*, scholars or wealthy Jews, then one
was bestowed with even higher status.

   Shtetl Jews fully internalized the biblical dictum that "it is not good for man [person] to be alone," and the biblical injunction to "be fruitful and multiply." Marriage, children, and family life were among the most important values and institutions in the *shtetl*, and it was the sacred responsibility of parents *tzu makhen fun kinder mentshen*, to make people out of children (ibid., pp. 335–38). By *mentshen*, people, was meant obedient, respecting, and refined people who ideally would be *sheyneh yidn* who would bring honor to their parents. Children had responsibilities toward their parents throughout their lives (and after), and the obligation for a child to care for his or her elderly parents prevailed even when, as was often the case, he or she was reluctant to accept that care.

Marriage was not a matter of individual choice. It was carefully arranged by the parents, sometimes through the intermediary service of the *shadkhen*, matchmaker. Although it was assumed that "parents always want the best for their children" (ibid., p. 275) and children usually agreed and went along with the match, the current notion that the children had no say in the match and were forced to enter into marriage over their own objections is not quite correct. Since traditional Jewish religious law does not recognize a marriage as valid unless both the bride and groom agree to it, Zborowski and Herzog are undoubtedly correct when they assert that "those who object . . . succeed in winning their point" (ibid. p. 275).

Sex roles in general and husband/father—wife/mother roles in particular were very clearly delineated in *shtetl* culture. The husband's major role was outside the home. He was busy learning, or engaged in economic pursuit, or both. Many men devoted themselves completely to sacred learning and their wives assumed the economic responsibility for the family, but it was hardly the case with all husbands and wives. Most husbands were earning a living either full or part time. The wife who was the sole economic provider was the exception, though there were many wives who worked alongside their husbands out of economic necessity. Some also worked so that their husbands would be able to spend at least some time each day in sacred learning. The father was the remote authoritarian figure for his son to whom he was a formal teacher, since it was the father's responsibility to make a *mentsh* (good person) out of his son. With his daughter, the father was somewhat more relaxed, easy-going, emotional, and indulgent, since the mother had the more authoritarian role with her.

In the day-to-day activity within the home the mother clearly played a dominant role, though she often held the father up to the children as the court of last resort. In addition many women were engaged in economic activities outside the home so that they had more extensive fields of activity than men. With the children the mother played the role of providing affection. "The stereotype of the "Yiddisheh mammeh," familiar in many lands, has firm roots in the *shtetl*. No matter what you do, no matter what happens, she will love you always. She may have odd and sometimes irritating ways of showing it, but in a hazardous and unstable world the belief about the mother's love is strong and unshakable" (ibid., p. 293). Ironically, it is from this stereotype that the Jewish mother as demanding, overprotective and overbearing, emasculating, and neurosis-producing evolved, in the character of Mrs. Portnoy (Roth, 1969). The stereotyped Mrs. Portnoy is a deliberately gross exaggeration, of course, and Zena Smith Blau has written a much more sympathetic, sober, and empirical analysis of the contemporary "American Jewish mother" (Blau, 1967).

The Jews of the *shtetl* were middlemen engaged in commerce, trade, or skilled work. During the latter part of the nineteenth century, their economic situation increasingly worsened as a result of the abolition of serfdom in the early 1860s, the construction of railroads, and official attempts to promote industrialization (Kuznets, 1975). Thousands of Jews reduced to pauperism and whole communities were virtually destitute. These economic conditions, coupled with the spread of the ideas of the Enlightenment, secular Yiddishism, secular Zionism, and secular Socialism, were too powerful for the *shtetl*—with all of its closedness—to withstand (Dawidowicz, 1967, pp. 5–90). The *shtetl* was disappearing and those Jews who remained in Eastern Europe were moving to the larger cities. In the first half of the twentieth century "East European Jewry stood at the threshold of a new era in which traditional Judaism, at last ready to encounter the modern world, faced two opponents: an aggressive secularism that was aggressively Jewish and a self-destroying assimilationism. The drama in that encounter had resonances of an encounter at the beginning of the modern era, when rabbinic Judaism faced hasidism and haskala [Enlightenment]. But the new drama was not acted out; its dramatis personae were cut down forever" (ibid., p. 89).

For those millions of Jews who did manage to emigrate to the United States at the turn of the century, that occasion, though life saving, was traumatic nevertheless. Not only did they encounter alien cultural and social forces, they were frequently met with hostility, fear, and disdain from their brethren, the earlier German Jewish immigrants who were just beginning to feel comfortable with their integration into American society.

While the Jewish immigrants from Eastern Europe faced many difficulties, most historians agree that, at least until the early twentieth century, ideological anti-Semitism was not one of them. Oscar Handlin points out for example that "after all, in 1899, Tom Watson, later of the Frank case, was still vigorously condemning medieval prejudices against the Jews" (Handlin, 1951, p. 324; on the Leo Franks case, to which Handlin refers, see Dinnerstein, 1968). He argues: "The ten years after 1890 were not only free of anti-Semitism; they were actually marked by distinct philo-Semitism" (ibid., p. 325). Even John Higham, who takes a much less sanguine view toward the depth of anti-Semitism in American society during the nineteenth century and argues that it was not restricted to the Populists who, he maintains, were no more anti-Semitic than others in the society, nevertheless agrees that it was considerably more intense and extensive after 1900 than before (Higham, 1975).

If anti-Semitism was not as serious a problem for the new immigrant Jews as it had been in Eastern Europe and as it was later to become in the United States, the antipathy and animosity of the German Jews was a major problem for them. Even before the large scale immigration from Eastern Europe began, some German Jewish leaders and spokespersons publicly disapproved of the immigration of Jews from Western Russia to the United States. When in late 1869 the Alliance Israelite Universelle held a meeting in Berlin to discuss the plight of Russian Jewry and established a subcommittee charged with providing aid and support for Russian emigrant Jews who wished to settle in Europe and the United States, *The Jewish Messenger*, an Anglo-Jewish newspaper which represented upper-middle-class Reform German Jews, predicted that such aid "would prove disastrous to the immigrants themselves and would create an excessive burden on the American Jewish community" (Mandel, 1950, p. 13). In February 1881 the editor of the newspaper called for more stringent immigration laws because of the number of "utterly helpless" immigrants who were being sent here by the London Board of Guardians (ibid., p. 15), and in 1884 *The American Israelite*, founded and edited by Isaac Mayer Wise, urged the use of the recently passed New York State restrictive immigration laws to turn away about two hundred poor Russian immigrants who were going to arrive shortly (ibid., p. 24).

With the increasing persecution of Jews in Russia and their increasing immigration into the United States, however, no American Jewish leader could publicly urge restrictions on immigration any longer. By 1887 even the editor of *The Jewish Messenger* staunchly defended the Russian immigrants against defamation and immigration restriction (ibid., p. 28).

Not all German Jewish leaders agreed with the early restrictive stance. On April 27, 1870, the Board of Delegates of American Israelites and the Hebrew Benevolent Society cofounded the first known Jewish immigrant aid society in the country, the Hebrew Emigrant Aid Society of the United States, whose function was to provide "temporary relief to those here and soon to arrive" (Wischnitzer, 1956, p. 28). In the view of the society's leaders, the immigrants would best be served by dispersing them in the West and helping them to find employment there. This organization was short-lived, and on November 27, 1881, Jacob H. Schiff—one of the wealthiest, most philanthropic, and highly revered German Jews, who immigrated to New York in 1868 and who went on to become the head of the investment banking firm, Kuhn, Loeb and Company—and a number of other prominent German Jews founded a second Hebrew Emigrant Aid Society, which provided food, transportation, and employment counseling and guidance services (ibid., pp. 29–30), and then attempted to disperse them away from New York City. In 1882, the first full year of its existence, the Society dispersed 2,617 of the Jewish immigrants who arrived in the port of New York that year, to 165 cities in 32 states across the country (Szajkowski, 1951, pp. 272–73).

In 1890 the Baron de Hirsch Fund was established by the French Jewish philanthropist, Baron Maurice de Hirsch, for the purpose of ameliorating the condition of Russian Jews in the United States. It was administered by Samuel Isaacs, Jacob H. Schiff, George Seligman, and Julius Goldman among others, all of whom had been active in relief organizations. Bankers, lawyers, judges, and businessmen that they were, they invested a substantial portion of the Fund in a venture designed to encourage and assist the Russian Jews to become farmers, according to the wishes of Hirsch (Joseph, 1934). Many Russian Jewish immigrants, however, were less than overjoyed with the Fund, because some trustees were opposed to the liberalization of restrictions on immigration and because the establishment of the Jewish Colonization Association, set up by Hirsch and his Fund, was perceived as an effort to strip them of their culture and to inhibit their mobility in the cities.

In 1903 and 1905 there were serious pogroms in Kishinev, Bessarabia, in Russia. Sparked by a blood libel, the first pogrom resulted in the death of almost fifty Jews, the wounding of about five hundred more, and the looting and destruction of more than a thousand Jewish homes and businesses. Mass meetings were held in Jewish communities around the world, protesting the pogrom and the conspiracy of the czarist regime in encouraging it. American Jews were outraged and petitioned President Theodore Roosevelt to officially protest to the czar, which he did; but the czarist government refused to accept the petition. After the second pogrom in August 1905 a group of prominent New York Jews, including Louis Marshall, Jacob Schiff, Oscar Straus, and Cyrus Adler among others, met to consider the formation of a permanent central organization to protect Jews and Jewish interests. Marshall invited fifty-nine Jewish civic and religious leaders from around the country to a meeting in February 1906. At that meeting and at the subsequent one in May, the questions of the desirability and constitution of the proposed committee were discussed in depth. Although the representatives of Bnai Brith and the Union of American Hebrew Congregation's Board of Delegates felt that a new organization was unnecessary, they accepted the majority opinion in favor of it. The question of the committee's constitution was the subject of heated debate between those who favored a democratically elected and representative committee and those who feared that such a committee would be unwieldy and insisted instead upon an exclusive, elitist committee. On November 11, 1906, the American Jewish Committee held its first meeting in New York City and established its membership as no more than sixty American citizens. These sixty members, however, did not have the power to initiate action. The ultimate power of the Committee rested in the hands of a small executive committee which held tight reign over the larger body, its policies, procedures, and directions. Active in many areas beyond those addressed in its founding constitution—"to prevent infringement of the civil and religious rights of Jews, and to alleviate the consequences of persecution"—the American Jewish Committee was nevertheless viewed with ambivalence by the Eastern European Jews, the radicals and socialists, the religiously traditional, and the Zionists, because it was controlled by a self-appointed group of religiously liberal and secular, non-Zionist, exclusivist patricians who, by and large, were American Jews of German and Central European rather than Eastern European background.

It is important to contemplate and understand the motivations behind the establishment of these and other social service and welfare agencies that the wealthy German "Uptown" Jews, the *Yahudim*, as they were disparagingly referred to, developed for their "Downtown" brethren, the *Ostjuden*, the Eastern European Jews. Many of the German Jews unquestionably viewed the Eastern European immigrants as uncouth, destitute, uncivilized, and therefore threatening to their own position in American society. When newly arrived Eastern European Jewish intellectuals started espousing the cause of socialism, moreover, and when so many Eastern European Jews became involved and even leaders in the newly emerging labor movement in the United States, many German Jews, who were middle class essentially, were appalled. There was nothing novel in their fears; middle-class members of minority groups who are themselves of precarious status quite characteristically hold the lower-class members of their group in contempt.

There was something rather novel, on the other hand, in the manner in which the German Jews attempted to deal with their fears and hostilities. They did not, as other middle class members of minority groups have, completely reject and disassociate themselves from their lower-class brethren. They did not respond as did middle-class blacks, for example, the "black bourgeoisie" who were critically analyzed by E. Franklin Frazier. As Frazier portrayed them:

> The emphasis upon "social" life or "society" is one of the main props of the world of make believe into which the black bourgeoisie has sought to escape from its inferiority and frustrations in American society. This world of make believe, to be sure, is a reflection of the values of American society, but it lacks the economic basis that would give it roots in the world of reality. In escaping into a world of make believe, middle class Negroes have rejected both identification with the Negro and his traditional culture. Through delusions of wealth and power they have sought identification with white America, which continues to reject them. But these delusions leave them frustrated because they are unable to escape from the emptiness and futility of their existence [Frazier, 1957, p. 237].

Clearly there are basic differences between the position of middle-class blacks in the middle of the twentieth century and that of German Jews at the turn of the century. The point, nevertheless, is that precisely because German Jews were white and in a somewhat more secure socioeconomic position, they would have had even more reason to reject the Eastern European Jewish immigrants and identify with the larger non-Jewish society. It certainly would have been much easier for them to do so than it was for middle-class blacks to identify with the larger white society.

Rather than totally withdrawing from the Eastern European Jewish immigrants, however, the German Jews undertook to "Americanize" them as rapidly as possible. They did this by establishing such philanthropic organizations as the Hebrew Emigrant Aid Society, which had local committees in more than two dozen cities throughout the country and Toronto (Osofsky, 1960, p. 184), and by establishing educational and training courses and schools for both children and adults. They zealously set out to transform the immigrants, the "wretched refuse" to which Emma Lazarus referred in her famous poem, "The New Colossus" (Jacob, 1949, p. 178), by transforming them into "respectable" Americans as quickly as possible. This objective was explicitly stated in the founding charter of the Hebrew Educational Alliance (the designation "Hebrew" was subsequently dropped from the name), a social and educational agency founded by German Jews in 1893 on the corner of Jefferson Street and East Broadway, in New York's Lower East Side, to provide programs "of an Americanizing, educational, social and humanizing character—for the moral and intellectual improvement of the inhabitants of the East Side" (quoted in Stein, 1956, p. 36).

The Eastern European Jewish immigrants strongly resented what they perceived as the snobbishness of the German Jews and, especially, the Germans' efforts to Americanize them, which the Eastern Europeans viewed as forced assimilation. To some, the German Jews were a greater threat to the cultural survival of Eastern European immigrants than American society and culture itself. In 1903, for example, Isaac

Max Rubinow, a noted physician, economist, and statistician, immigrated to New York City from Poland and, shortly thereafter, wrote a series of articles on the Jewish condition in this country for the Russian Jewish monthly *Voskhod*. He begins by describing the economic, social, and political conditions of the Russian Jews in New York in a very positive and optimistic manner. But then he continues with a very different picture. "If everything is in such perfect condition then the reader may justly ask: 'Why all the fuss?' But the fact is that not everything is as perfect as the reader might imagine" (Rubinow, 1959, p. 108). The problem, Rubinow argued, was the German Jews. The non-Jewish American sympathized with the Eastern European Jewish immigrant for two reasons: because the Jew was a victim of persecution and because he was industrious. "The German Jew, the old timer, however, was ashamed of his Russian cousin, and this shame created an iron barrier between the two groups. This brought about a great deal of misunderstanding. The German Jew forgot that when he first appeared on American soil, the Portuguese Jew who preceded him, regarded him with contempt. The characteristic indication of the state of affairs may be seen in the respectful attitude of the American [non-Jew] towards the members of the [Russian Jewish] intelligensia and in the hostility of the wealthy American Jew towards the intelligentsia" (ibid., p. 110).

Rubinow reserved his strongest indictment for the directors of the Educational Alliance. But, he said, even they cannot be considered fully culpable. Having been Americanized, they simply adopted and internalized the larger American attitudes and techniques of Americanization. "Of course, we should not blame the German Jew either. He blindly adopted the American pedagogic method—a method which calls for the intensive instruction of immigrants in poetry of a patriotic nature. The German Jew accepted axiomatically the fact that the Russian Jew was incapable of transporting his cultural treasures with him to his new environment. He held this "Russian savage" in contempt—a contempt which was very strong in Germany twenty-five years ago, but which has gradually been disappearing, because in Germany, they have become more familiar with Russian culture" (ibid., p. 111).

Though he tries to be understanding Rubinow does not attempt to hide his anger. In the final analysis he is as bitter of the German Jews as Frazier was of the "black bourgeoisie," and his explanation of the social psychology of the German Jews is strikingly similar to Frazier's analysis of the "black bourgeoisie": "The wealthy Jew who suffers a great deal from social ostracism tries his best to erase his individuality and to compel the public to forget that he is a Jew. And when he imagines that he has succeeded, his Russian cousins shatter this idyll by the outward appearance of the latter. This prompts him to exclaim in despair 'Let us Americanize him as quickly as possible'" (ibid., p. 121).

Most contemporary social historians of that period are quite critical of the activities of the German Jews at the time and view them in much the same way that the Eastern European intellectuals did. Most religious traditionalists view the German Jews as assimilationists and their activities as aimed at stripping the Eastern European Jews of the vestiges of their religious heritage. Marxists, on the other hand, define the activities of the German Jews within the framework of exploitation and social control. Gorelick, for example, distinguishes between their activities and the traditional Jewish religious notion of *zedakah*, charity and philanthropy, and finds them antithetical to one another:

> Under traditional Jewish law and practice, charity, or *zedakah*, was part of the religiously mandated social obligation of every observant Jew. Optimally, the donor should not know the identity of the recipient and the recipient should not know the identity of the donor. Such a conception of charity, however, precludes using philanthropy to control or influence the behavior of the poor. Consequently the German Jewish bourgeoisie generally adapted *zedakah* into philanthropy based on Andrew Carnegie's concept of the "stewardship of wealth."
>
> Unlike *zedakah*, the stewardship of wealth presumes that all recipients must prove their worthiness to receive; in fact they

must modify their behavior in ways deemed suitable by the donor. The stewardship of wealth insists that the control of wealth must remain in the ultimate hands of the wealthy; philanthropy must serve the purposes set by the wealthy. Thus, unlike *zedakah*, the stewardship of wealth was an instrument of social control [Gorelick, 1981, p. 28].

On the other hand one historian, having been quite critical himself of the attitudes and activities of the German Jews vis-a-vis the Eastern European Jewish immigrants, has reappraised the negative image of the *yahudi*, the German Jew, on the basis of recent evidence which indicates that many German Jews actually had very positive attitudes toward their Eastern European brethren and staunchly undertook very extensive and meaningful activity on their behalf (Szajkowski, 1973).

In any event, many Eastern European immigrants at the time were, without question, resentful of the German Jews and, rather than participating in the organizations and agencies founded by the German Jews, they embarked on massive efforts to establish their own network of religious, educational, and social service institutions, organizations, and agencies. In 1882 they founded their own Hebrew Emigrant Auxiliary Society which in 1902 merged with the Hebrew Sheltering House, founded by Eastern European Jews in 1889, and became the Hebrew Immigrant Aid Society, HIAS, which today is one of the major international Jewish migration agencies (Wischnitzer, 1956). In 1888 Eastern European Jewish labor leaders in New York organized a federation of Jewish labor unions, the United Hebrew Trades (Weinstein, 1929; Epstein, 1953; Tcherikower, 1961). In 1887, the major Eastern European synagogues in New York City organized in an effort to create a united Orthodox community and appoint a chief rabbi. After extensive deliberations and a search, they elected the popular and respected communal rabbi of Vilna in Lithuania, Rabbi Jacob Joseph, who arrived in New York in 1888. The whole effort failed, however, due to the opposition of Conservative and Reform rabbis, the vehement opposition of Jewish radicals, socialists, and anarchists, the resistance of ritual slaughterers to abide by the regulations which Rabbi Joseph prescribed for the community, and the failure of the Orthodox synagogues to abide by their commitments to him. He died a poor, broken man at the age of 59, on July 28, 1902 (Karp, 1955). The effort, nevertheless, was a significant one in the attempts by Eastern European Jewish immigrants to establish their own mode of Judaism in America.

One of the most unique efforts at organization was in the founding of extensive systems of organization, based upon community of origin in Eastern Europe, which catered to a host of economic, cultural, and personal needs, known as *landsmanschaften*. Mutual aid and interpersonal comfort for those undergoing a crisis were among the major functions of all *landsmanschaften*, and some catered to the religious needs of their constituents as well. Founded in the late nineteenth century, many of these lasted well into the twentieth century. As late as 1938, a survey by the Federal Writers Project found 1,841 of them in New York City with a total membership of 257,067, of whom 38,414 were American born (Shapiro, 1970, pp. 22–23). In the early part of the twentieth century a number of unions of *landsmanschaften* were founded also, known as *verbands*, which consisted of groups of *landsmanschaften* from the same region in Eastern Europe. These *verbands*, or federations of *landsmanschaften*, were a reaction to the prejudices that Jews from each region in Eastern Europe held against others from other regions, and each *verband* set out to found institutions catering to the likes and dislikes of those from its region. Thus when the Galician and Bukhovinian *verband* founded Har Moriah Hospital, the Russian and Polish *verband* countered with the founding of Beth David Hospital. When the Roumanian *verband* founded the Jewish Home for Convalescents, another *verband* founded its own convalescent home and, in addition, an orphan home (Grinstein, 1959, p. 86).

Between 1885 and 1923, twenty Yiddish daily newspapers were established in New York City. By 1924 seven of these were still in publication, and each represented a unique constituency. The *Yiddishes Tageblatt*, or Jewish Daily News, established in 1885, served a religiously traditional and Zionist readership. The *Vorwaerts*, or Jewish Daily Forward, was established in 1887 by the Jewish Socialist Press Federation, under the editorship of the well-known journalist Abraham Cahan, and served as the newspaper of secular Jewish labor. The *Yiddisher Morgen Journal*, established in 1901, was the only morning Yiddish newspaper and contained extensive want-ad listings to which the unemployed seeking work eagerly turned. *Die Warheit*, established in 1905, and *Der Tog*, established in 1914, merged into *Der Tog-Warheit* in 1919, strove to raise the level of Yiddish literary standards and to provide an outlet for a variety of expression from the constructive forces of American Jewry. The *Freiheit*, established in 1922 by the Workers' Party of America, espoused the cause of Soviet Communism (Soltes, 1969 [1925]). In the 1950s *Der Tog* and the *Yiddisher Morgen Journal* merged and continued publishing for several more years, alongside the remaining *Vorwaerts* and *Freiheit*. By the end of the 1970s, because of declining readership, only the *Vorwaerts* remained, and it is published only as a weekly at the present time. Likewise, its ideology has undergone considerable change from what it was at its inception; today, it espouses the liberal-democratic position, is strongly supportive of Israel, and is much more sympathetic to religious traditionalism.

In addition to the New York Yiddish press, which reached Jews throughout the country, there were Yiddish newspapers in other cities that had substantial populations of Eastern European Jews, such as Chicago, Cleveland, and Philadelphia. None of these, however, even remotely approached the prominence of the New York Yiddish newspapers, nor did any of them survive as long.

Despite the vehement objection of the Eastern European Jewish immigrants to the German Jewish attempts to Americanize them, the very creation of the Yiddish press, as with the other institutions, organizations, and agencies that the Eastern European Jews established, did serve the function of Americanizing them—helping them to overcome the cultural shock which they experienced upon their arrival in the United States and to learn the American social and cultural systems and encouraging them to progress in those systems. As Soltes found in his study of the Yiddish press, it was "an Americanizing agency" which, nevertheless, was cherished because it was determined by the Eastern Europeans themselves, rather than being foisted upon them and controlled by others.

The Yiddish theater made its debut in New York on August 12, 1882. During its history it provided for the performance of both indigenous Yiddish plays as well as translations into Yiddish of well-known non-Jewish plays. It frequently served as the starting point in the careers of many actors and actresses who went on to varying degrees of prominence in Broadway and cinema (Lifson, 1965). By the late 1960s, there no longer were any regular Yiddish theaters in New York, although the Central Synagogue in Manhattan does house the Folksbiene Theater, which intermittently offers Yiddish performances in limited engagements.

One interesting institution which, invariably, was established in the Eastern European Jewish immigrant neighborhoods of virtually every city in the country was the Turkish Bath. Though not intrinsically Jewish, this establishment probably had its origin in both the religiocultural values of cleanliness in the Jewish tradition and in the conditions of the immigrants, namely, that there were very few apartments in which the poor immigrants lived which were equipped with private baths, let alone hot water. On the East Side of New York City, for example, the typical immigrant houses consisted of walk-up "railroad" flats equipped only with cold water, and a community toilet shared by all the families on each floor. The bath was usually located in the kitchen and came with a collapsible tabletop, which enabled it to be used as a table when not being used as a bath. Obviously this was not conducive to frequent bathing by the tenement dwellers. In addition, the crowded conditions of those apartments made regular bathing at home even more impractical. Jacob Riis provides a vivid contemporary view of the housing conditions in the Eastern European Jewish neighborhood on New York's Lower East Side, which he termed "Jewtown":

> It is said that nowhere in the world are so many people crowded together on a square mile as here. The average five-story tenement adds a story or two to its stature in Ludlow Street and an extra building on the rear lot, and yet the sign "To Let" is the rarest of all there . . . In Essex Street two small rooms in a six-story tenement were made to hold a "family of father and mother, twelve children, and six boarders . . . These are samples of the packing of the population that has run up the record here to the rate of three hundred and thirty thousand per square mile. The densest crowding of Old London . . . never got beyond a hundred and seventy-five thousand [Riis, 1970 (1890), pp. 70–71].

Nor was there a time during the day when one was afforded sufficient privacy to bathe at home, because the home frequently doubled as the workplace.

> The homes of the Hebrew quarter are its workshops also. . . . You are made fully aware of it before you have travelled the length of a single block in any of these East Side streets, by the whir of a thousand sewing machines, worked at high pressure from earliest dawn till mind and muscle give out together. Every member of the family, from the youngest to the oldest, bears a hand, shut in the qualmy rooms, where meals are cooked and clothing washed and dried besides, the livelong day. It is not unusual to find a dozen persons—men, women, and children—at work in a single small room [ibid., p. 72].

Since baths were not convenient at home and "only some 8 percent of Russian Jewish families [in New York's Lower East Side] had baths, according to a study of 1902, and these often without hot water," the bathhouse developed as a characteristic of the immigrant Jewish neighborhood. As Rischin points out: "In 1880, one or two of New York's twenty-two bathhouses were Jewish; by 1897, over half of the city's sixty-two bathhouses (including Russian, Turkish, swimming, vapor, and medicated bathhouses) were Jewish" (Rischin, 1970, p. 87). Not only did these bathhouses contribute to the relatively lower disease and death rates of the Eastern

European immigrant Jews, as compared to others (Lindenthal, 1981), they became part of the cultural traditions of their children as well. The popularity of saunas among American Jews in contemporary Jewish community centers and even of health spas, such as those of Elaine Powers and Jack Lalane, probably has its roots in the bathhouses of the immigrant neighborhoods.

Following the precedent already established by their Jewish predecessors in America from the beginning of the nineteenth century, the Eastern European immigrants founded an array of new synagogues as their numbers multiplied. According to Glazer, there were 270 synagogues in the country in 1880; "by 1890 there were 533; by 1906, 1,769; and in 1916, 1,901 . . . and there were perhaps scores or hundreds more that no census reached" (Glazer, 1972, p. 62). In contrast to the German Jews who established Reform synagogues, virtually all the synagogues established by the Eastern Europeans at this time were Orthodox. Wirth's description of the typical synagogue in Chicago's immigrant Jewish neighborhood underscores the point made by Howe (p. 11) that the *shtetl* notion of beauty was not as a form:

> The synagogues of the Polish and Russian Jews were from the beginning of their settlement in Chicago separate from those of the Germans. In January, 1926, there were forty-three orthodox synagogues on the near West Side. Most of these are small, only a few having over one hundred members. They are made up largely of immigrants who originate from the same community in Europe. . . . For the most part these synagogues are either converted Christian churches, or buildings that were once used by congregations that have moved to other parts of the city. . . . [F]ew of those now there have been kept in repair. . . . They are equipped with a basement, which is used for the daily services and meetings, while the main floor is occupied only on the Sabbath and on holidays [Wirth, 1928, pp. 205–6].

The mushrooming of Orthodox synagogues during this period led in part to the prevalent but incorrect notion that all Eastern European Jewish immigrants were Orthodox when they arrived in this country, and only later did many of them and their children leave Orthodoxy for the Conservative and Reform synagogues or for no synagogue affiliation at all. This characterization is incorrect on several grounds. As I mentioned before, throughout the nineteenth century Eastern European Jewry, including the *shtetl*, was in major upheaval and change, including religious change. Many Jews in Eastern Europe had, in varying degrees, rejected the prevalent religious traditionalism. And many who did not maintained traditional Jewish religious patterns not so much out of ideological commitment to Orthodox ideological principles, but as the cultural patterns they had internalized. When they immigrated to the United States, they founded synagogues because the synagogue was a central institution in their native communities, and they founded Orthodox synagogues as the only kind of synagogue with which they were familiar. It would be more accurate to describe them as Orthoprax, as conforming with Orthodox habit or custom, rather than as ideologically committed Orthodox. Moreover, there were even among them varying degrees of Orthopraxy in what might seem to be a paradox but is not, namely, the "non-observant Orthodox," whom Sklare defines as "heterodox in personal behavior but who, when occasionally joining in public worship, do so in accordance with traditional patterns" (Sklare, 1972, p. 46). Thus, while the Orthodox synagogue was the one chosen by the typical Eastern European immigrant who was so inclined, without question wide variations in intensity of religious commitment and a complete religious-secular spectrum already were present in the first, the immigrant generation (Liebman, 1965, pp. 27–30; Singer, 1967).

Another indication that most Eastern European Jewish immigrants were not committed to Orthodoxy is the paucity of Jewish education during this period. While the Jewish population in the United States in 1900 was estimated to be 1,085,135, with approximately 200,000 being children, "only 36,000 received any kind of organized Jewish instruction at any one time" (Winter, 1966, p. 11). Of these, about 25,000 were enrolled in religious schools attached to synagogues, and the remaining 11,000 were enrolled in communal supplementary schools (ibid.). Although many presumably received their Jewish education from private teachers, it is apparent nevertheless that the majority of Jewish children did not receive any Jewish education.

Those concerned about this state of affairs set about to correct it through one of two principal avenues. One segment with Samson Benderly, one of the most highly regarded Jewish educators in the country, at its helm, organized the Bureau of Jewish Education in New York City. As director of the Bureau, which was to be a model for Jewish communities around the country, Benderly addressed himself to the Jewish educational needs of all segments of the community he represented, and he went on to organize elementary Jewish education, to establish the first communal Hebrew high school in New York, to found Jewish nursery schools, to organize adult Jewish study classes, to design a Jewish summer camp, and to found the first School for Jewish Communal Service in the country in New York City (Winter, 1966). The Bureau of Jewish Education was part of an umbrella organization—the New York City Kehillah—which nobly attempted, but perhaps too much in the tradition of noblesse oblige, to unite New York Jewry, to ease the plight of immigrants, and to enhance Jewish life in the city by creating a model community (Goren, 1970). The Kehillah, which lasted from 1908 to 1922, was organized in response to the allegation by Theodore A. Bingham, New York City's police commissioner, that 50 percent of all criminal classes in the city were Jews. Headed by a young dynamic, American-born Reform rabbi, Dr. Judah L. Magnes, the Kehillah sought to recreate in American fashion the organic Jewish communal structure that had existed in Europe by integrating all the various components and organizations of New York Jewry. But America in the twentieth century was not Europe in the previous centuries. The Kehillah advocates failed to recognize an essential characteristic of American society observed by the French political and social analyst Alexis de Tocqueville during his brief visit to the country in the 1830s, namely, the important role voluntary groups play in maintaining and strengthening America's unique type of democracy (Tocqueville, 1969 [1850], pp. 513-17). In the final analysis, the Kehillah "experiment" failed because of inability to reconcile the deep differences among the many constituent factions, such as the elitism of the "Uptown" German establishment and the participatory democracy of the "Downtown" Eastern European masses, the Zionists and non-Zionists, the religious and secular, the politically radical and the politically conservative (Goren, 1970, pp. 214-52). After the demise of the Kehillah, the Bureau of Jewish Education survived, but in a considerably weakened form.

Others sought to improve Jewish education by establishing autonomous all-day schools, *yeshivas*, or Jewish parochial schools, which would provide intensive Jewish education in addition to the prescribed secular curriculum. By 1917 New York City had four such schools, in addition to the previously mentioned Yeshiva Etz Chaim. They were the Rabbi Jacob Joseph School, founded in 1900 on the Lower East Side's Henry Street; Yeshiva Rabbi Chaim Berlin, founded in 1906 in the Brownsville section of Brooklyn (Landesman, 1971, pp. 234-36); the Talmudical Institute of Harlem, founded in 1908 (Gurock, 1979, p. 112); and Yeshiva Torah Vedaath, founded in 1917 in the Williamsburg section of Brooklyn. On February 19, 1917, the first yeshiva outside of New York—the Yeshiva Torah Ve-Emuna Hebrew Parochial School, now known as Yeshiva Chofetz Chaim—Talmudical Academy, was founded in Baltimore, Maryland, by Rabbi Abraham Nachman Schwartz, the "Chief Rabbi" of Baltimore's Russian Jews (Fein, 1971, p. 192). Within the following ten years seventeen day schools had been founded in the country with a combined enrollment of 4,290 pupils (Schiff, 1966, p. 37). Although these schools encountered considerable opposition within American Jewry on practical, economic, and ideological grounds and the overwhelming majority of Jews sent their children to public schools, the day schools did persevere and became the pioneers for the development in the following generations of a range of yeshivas which were to provide intensive Jewish education on the elementary, high school, college, and postgraduate levels.

Virtually every student of this period has been greatly impressed with the rapid rate of economic and social mobility of the Eastern European Jewish immigrants as compared to other immigrant groups. As two of the pioneers in comparative ethnic relations observe: "Most of the Irish had taken three generations to work themselves out of poverty, the Italians two, the Jews had moved somewhat faster" (Glazer and Moynihan, 1970, p. lv). Moreover, as recent critical sociologists have pointed out, a vast mythology has been created according to which the rapid mobility of these immigrants is attributed to the high value traditional Judaism places upon education, as witness the high status accorded the scholar in the *shtetl*. According to the proponents of this myth, the immigrant Jews adapted the value of sacred learning to American realities, transformed it into the value of secular learning, zealously sent their children to elementary school, high school, and college and thus were able within a single generation to rise from the lower class to the middle class. This is a gross distortion, and the realities of the mobility of the Eastern European Jewish immigrants were quite different.

As a number of recent studies demonstrate, although Jews and Italians immigrated during the same period, their cultural and structural conditions in Europe, their reasons and purposes for emigrating, and their situations upon immigrating were quite different. The Italians were to a large extent a rural peasant group who immigrated because of the severe economic hardship suffered in the wine-growing regions of southern Italy; many men were induced to come to the United States temporarily, make some money, and then return to the home country. The situation of the Eastern European Jews was vastly different. While they were not quite urban in the contemporary sense of the term, the occupational backgrounds of the Jews and the skills which they brought with them differed greatly from those of the Italians. From early medieval times, Jews in Europe were barred from owning land and were encouraged to deal in financial matters.

For centuries they were the classic middlemen of Europe (Ruppin, pp. 130 ff.; Kessner, 1977, pp. 24–43; Kuznets, 1975). Even in the highly agricultural economy of Russia in the nineteenth century, only a very small percentage of Jews had farm-related occupations; they worked more in urban jobs, handicrafts, needle trades, and other consumer-goods trades (ibid.).

The Eastern European Jews not only came for economic reasons, but also because of harsh religious persecution. The pograms and anti-Jewish legislation in fact were part of a long history of persecution in Europe. These Jews did not, therefore, consider Eastern Europe their home as the Italians did Italy. When the Jews left Eastern Europe, they harbored no hopes of returning; their departure was final. They came to the United States to stay. They also had a reference group to whom they could look in their hopes for making a better life for themselves—their German-Jewish predecessors who were rather successful. They brought their wives and children with them or sent for them rather soon after their arrival, and they were determined to stay and gain a security for themselves or at least for their children which was not possible in Eastern Europe (cf. Sarna, 1981, for a penetrating analysis of exaggerated claims of few Jews returning to Eastern Europe.)

The streets in the neighborhoods where they settled were not quite paved with gold, however; nor was their road to economic mobility as smooth as it is frequently portrayed. The initial antipathy of the German Jews has already been discussed, as well as the crowded conditions (described by Jacob Riis) in which they lived. The following is a more vivid and detailed description of the immigrant Jewish neighborhood on New York City's Lower East Side:

> Their five- and six-storey tenements, their fronts lined with balconies and fire-escapes, looked down on the mass of pushcarts, peddlers and customers, through which a few wagons might try to force their way, or children, hauling loads of old wood they had picked up for fuel. Everyone was bartering in loud Yiddish for old clothes and hats, legs of chicken, over-ripe tomatoes, single eggs and ounces of tea. A stranger, picking his way across a sidewalk crammed with boxes of goods from the shops, entered a dark hall, so dark that he might fall over a child, so dark that a little girl who

had lost a toy could expect to find it when the gas was turned on in the evening. On each floor above the shop and street level was a landing with two toilets, large sink, and cold-water tap, and at either end two apartments of four rooms. To describe these as parlour, kitchen, and bedrooms would be misleading, for at night all rooms might be needed for family and lodgers to sleep in, chairs being pushed together to form beds for smaller children. The best room looked on to the street. The others—the kitchen with its highly ornamented iron stove, its work-table, the dining-table and chairs where the family could just find room to eat—and the smaller rooms had windows only on the airshaft which separated tenements. Some indeed lacked windows altogether, and district nurses needed to light candles before visiting patients. During the day, one room might be needed for some industrial task, like making trimmings for dresses, at which mother and quite small children would be busy. Intense summer heat, smells from the rubbish which piled up at the foot of the airshaft, noises from street and neighbours, bugs in the walls—all these were normal incidents of tenement life [Taylor, 1971, pp. 168–69].

Despite these hardships, the Eastern European Jews remained convinced that with hard work and a bit of luck their conditions would improve. Perhaps luck was on their side, for they did arrive at a most propitious moment—the birth of the burgeoning clothing industry. Given the backgrounds and skills with which they came and with so many of the industry's employers being German Jews, the immigrant Jews were presented with a unique opportunity and very many of them took advantage of it. They entered the garment industry in large numbers, and this in turn presented them with another opportunity, to organize and play a pivotal role in the developing labor movement. Abraham Cahan, along with other radicals and socialists, appealed to them in their language, Yiddish, and fostered a strong labor ideology among them; Morris Hillquit organized them into an ethnic labor federation, the United Hebrew Trades, in 1888; and Abraham Cahan founded and edited the newspaper of the Jewish labor movement, *Der Vorwaerts*, the Jewish Daily Forward, which became the most widely read newspaper among immigrant Jews [Epstein, 1965].

During the first ten years of the twentieth century, it has been estimated that approximately one-third of all arriving

Jewish workers in New York City earned their livings in the garment industry and an additional one-third worked in trades as butchers, carpenters, shoemakers, and the like (Kessner, pp. 37–38). In the country as a whole, the occupational patterns of Russian Jewish immigrants were similar. More than one-third, 35.3 percent, of those employed were in the garment industry, 25 percent were in the building trades, and 20 percent were in such occupations as proprietors of retail stores and peddlers (Goldberg, 1947, p. 16).

But it was not luck alone which enabled the immigrant Jews to gain a modicum of economic security. It also took many years of relentless sweat and toil, often with unsanitary and unsafe working conditions, frugality, and at times organized conflict with employers. Jacob Riis was perhaps taking some liberty with his literary license in his description of "Jewtown," but he makes the point nevertheless:

> Thrift is the watchword of Jewtown, as of its people the world over. It is at once its strength and its fatal weakness, its cardinal virtue and its foul disgrace. Become an overmastering passion with these people who come here in droves from Eastern Europe to escape persecution, from which freedom could be bought only with gold, it has enslaved them in bondage worse than that from which they fled. Money is their God. Life itself is of little value compared with even the leanest bank account. In no other spot does life wear so intensely bald and materialistic an aspect as in Ludlow Street. Over and over again I have met with instances of these Polish or Russian Jews deliberately starving themselves to the point of physical exhaustion, while working night and day at a tremendous pressure to save a little money. An avenging nemesis pursues this headlong hunt for wealth; there is no worse paid class anywhere [Riis, 1970 [1890], pp. 71–72].

Perceptive as he was, Riis misunderstood the object of their drive. It was not wealth, nor even money per se, which they sought. Rather, after centuries of persecution and insecurity, they yearned for a degree of security, if not for themselves then for the children, which had been inconceivable in Europe. In a sense, it was another form of the same drive that impelled the pioneers of Zionism to create a Jewish homeland in what was then Palestine so that they could finally taste freedom.

For many Eastern European Jewish immigrants, gaining freedom and economic security in America meant a national liberation. They foresaw the possibility of freedom and they were determined to take advantage of it. Moreover, they were not going to give up their religious and cultural heritage in order to enjoy the benefits of that freedom and security. They were willing to make certain adjustments, but they were convinced that they could have their cake and eat it, that they could gain economic security and maintain their own group identity.

World War I imperiled two-thirds of the world's Jews, ten million of them in Eastern and Southeastern Europe and in the Middle East; both Eastern European and German American Jews responded in not quite a united effort, but in ways that did lead to their first major "joint" effort. A group of Orthodox Jews, the majority of whom were of Eastern European background, formed the Central Committee for the Relief of Jews Suffering Through the War on October 4, 1914. Later that same month, the American Jewish Committee called together representatives of forty organizations who established the American Jewish Relief Committee. The Central Committee for the Relief of Jews refused to join the new Relief Committee and on November 27, 1914, the Joint Distribution Committee was established as the agency to distribute the funds raised by both the Central Committee and the Relief Committee. When in 1915 the socialist and labor groups established their own People's Relief Committee, its funds too were distributed by the Joint Distribution Committee. The three autonomous relief committees were indicative of the deep divisions among the three factions of American Jewry, and it took years for the chasms to be bridged. The Joint Distribution Committee was a significant but small step toward bridging those chasms. Today, despite the disappearance long since of the divisions, that organization, which is American Jewry's major agency for overseas aid, retains its traditional designation as the American Jewish Joint Distribution Committee (Handlin, 1964; Bauer, 1974, 1981).

While the war promoted some unity among the factions

in the area of relief, it exacerbated the hostilities between the Eastern European and German Jews with respect to an issue which was growing dramatically in significance, namely, Zionism. The different Jewish group self-definitions with which the German and Eastern European Jewish immigrants arrived in the United States were discussed previously; namely, German Jews defined themselves as a religious group, whereas the Eastern European Jews defined themselves much more in national terms as an ethnic group. Their increasing activity on behalf of Jews in war-torn Europe and the growing importance of the Jewish settlements in what was then called Palestine served to enhance the spirit of Jewish nationalism among the Eastern European Jews in the United States. In 1914 the Federation of American Zionists, a weak organization founded in 1898, adopted a plan for reorganization which was to culminate in the founding of the Zionist Organization of America in 1918, under the leadership of an outstanding lawyer from Boston, who was later to become a justice of the Supreme Court of the United States, Louis D. Brandeis. Brandeis was a dynamic personality, and he was able to attract a group of highly respected American Jews, such as Judge Julian W. Mack and Professor (later United States Supreme Court Justice) Felix Frankfurter, to work with him on the Provisional Committee (Urofsky, 1975, pp. 81–163; Shapiro, 1971, pp. 24–76). With them a major segment of Eastern European American Jewry had leadership that rivaled the stature of the American Jewish Committee leadership, and rivals they were. Whereas the German Jewish elite was composed of bankers and wealthy businessmen who were rather conservative politically, Brandeis and his colleagues were judges, lawyers, and others who espoused political reform and supported many progressive causes. They also opposed the aristocratic exclusivism of the German Jewish elite and advocated a democratically organized "congress" of American Jews. At the end of 1916, 140 delegates representing virtually all factions within American Jewry met to determine the procedures for electing the congress; with America's entry in the war in 1917, however, the congress was postponed and the first American Jewish Congress was convened in Philadelphia in December of 1918. According to the original plans, with which the representatives of the American Jewish Committee finally agreed, the congress was to be a one-time event. However, because conditions were unsettled after the war, a second congress was convened in Philadelphia in 1920, at which time Rabbi Stephen S. Wise urged the Zionists and other delegates representing Eastern European Jews to make the congress an ongoing entity. Although the new organization was no more democratically representative than the American Jewish Committee and although its stated objectives—"to further and promote Jewish rights" and "to deal with all matters relating to and affecting specific Jewish interests"—were virtually identical to those of the committee, the American Jewish Congress, as it was named, did represent broader segments of American Jewry, had a specifically Zionist ideology, and adopted more militant tactics than the Committee's in promoting what it perceived to be Jewish interests.

As the period of the first generation—the Eastern European immigrant generation—came to a close, American Jewry had laid the foundation for the organizational structure that was to encompass the American Jewish community of the following generations. The immigrants had by and large overcome the challenges of economic survival; their children set out to take full advantage of what they saw as the openness and opportunities of American society.

3. The Acculturation
of the Second Generation

Having achieved some economic security during the course of the first—the immigrant—generation, the second generation set out to take full advantage of the opportunities that American society presented to them. If their parents had not already done so, they moved out of the immigrant neighborhoods to the more modern, middle-class neighborhoods of the large cities in which they lived. In New York City, for example, there was a mass movement of Jews from Manhattan to these neighborhoods in Brooklyn and the Bronx during the 1920s and 1930s (Moore, 1981a). They went to particular areas, such as Eastern Parkway and Flatbush in Brooklyn and Pelham Parkway and the Grand Concourse in the Bronx, to some extent in response to appeals to prospective Jewish tenants from Jews who had established a foothold in the construction and real-estate industries and who specifically catered to the middle-class and ethnic desires of their fellow mobile Jews (ibid., pp. 19–58). A similar pattern developed during the 1940s when, in the rush to suburbia, Jewish builders of suburban communities encouraged fellow Jews to move to these new communities (Gans, 1958, p. 210).

In his study of the residential patterns of Jews in Chicago during the 1920s, Louis Wirth analyzed the migration from the immigrant neighborhood, the "ghetto," to the area of second settlement and its effects upon the Jewish community. As he saw it, the first to leave the ghetto were those who were most successful economically and usually least tied to Jewish tradition, The *"all-rightnick,"* the Jew who "in his opportunism, has thrown overboard most of the cultural baggage of his group" and who "represents the type of business man to whom success is everything" (Wirth, 1928, pp. 248–49) is the major figure in the initial development of the second area. The social organization of the second area comes to reflect the secularization and assimilation of the new generation of economically mobile Jews. Distinctive 'social types' emerge in the new area, such as "the *Lodgenik*, or joiner; the *Radikalke*, or the emancipated woman; the society lady or the philanthropic woman who goes back to the ghetto 'to do something for these poor people,' of whom she was recently one; and the *Ototot*, or the almost emancipated person who clings to a little beard" (ibid., p. 250).

The plain, small synagogue of the immigrant neighborhood was replaced by the beautiful, magnificent, and "pretentious" synagogue structures of the new neighborhood. In place of the Orthodoxy of the ghetto synagogue, Conservative Judaism became increasingly important in the second area.* Initially founded by moderate traditionalists as a bulwark against Reform, this uniquely "American religious movement" (Sklare, 1972), responded to the changing needs and values of American Jewry and reshaped Judaism accordingly. Second-generation Jews, who found Orthodoxy to be too confining and inhibiting in their drive for economic and social mobility, but who strongly wished nevertheless to retain their Jewish ethnic and religious identity, embraced Conservative Judaism as being the ideal alternative between the "too religious" Orthodox and the "non religious" Reform. The Conservative synagogue became the central institution of the new Jewish community, and the religious and secular ethnic activities of the community both were centered within it. The conception of the synagogue as such a center was most clearly articulated in the work of Mordecai M. Kaplan, one of the most influential thinkers of Conservative Judaism and the

---

*Wirth exaggerated the significance of Conservative Judaism in Lawndale, Chicago. Marshall Sklare provides data showing that Orthodox Judaism remained prominent in this second-generation area of settlement (Sklare, 1972, p. 292, n. 11).

founder of a later fourth branch of American Judaism, Reconstructionism (Liebman, 1970). As Kaplan argued, "to fulfill the comprehensive purpose called for by present-day conditions, a synagogue must not be monopolized by a particular congregation. It must belong to the entire Jewish community. It should be a neighborhood center to which all Jews to whom it is accessible should resort for all religious, cultural, social and recreational purposes" (Kaplan, 1934, p. 425).

While the Conservative synagogue never quite became the neighborhood center that Kaplan hoped it would become, in the second-generation community it came to encompass both religious and secular functions for its members. If one looks at the listing of synagogues in the telephone directories of the large cities, especially in the eastern part of the country, one finds many with "Jewish Center" as part of their names. Most are Conservative synagogues founded during the periods of the second- and third-generation communities. Most Orthodox synagogues retained the designation "Congregation," whereas the Reform synagogue usually called itself "Temple."

Though he was not all that happy about it personally, Wirth pointed out the interesting pattern of development of successive Jewish settlements. The first Jewish residents move to the new neighborhood to escape the ghetto and to ease their assimilation into the larger society, only to find themselves followed by more Jews; these later ones are the least assimilated and they in turn establish many features of the older ghetto in the new community. The new neighborhood then becomes a new Jewish neighborhood, and those who wanted to escape from it now find themselves once again "trapped" within it. They are trapped within the Jewish community to a large extent because they are not accepted socially by their non-Jewish neighbors despite their wealth. "The realization that wealth alone does not bring a superior social position has come as a sudden and sad realization to many" (Wirth, 1928, p. 260).

In these new "gilded ghettos" (Kramer and Leventman, 1961) the gap between cultural assimilation and structural assimilation (Gordon, 1964) began to manifest itself most conspicuously, and it was the Jewish community's flexibility of communal structure which enabled it to adjust so rapidly to the new conditions, thereby preventing its disintegration. The pace of cultural assimilation, or "acculturation" as most sociologists refer to it, was quite rapid. It was most evident perhaps in the rate of secularization, or the increasing defection from the traditional religious system. As Warner and Srole found in their study of "Yankee City," for which the research was conducted between 1930 and 1935, "the progressive defection of successive generations of Jews from their religious system in a process apparently nearly completed among the children of the immigrants themselves" was much more obvious than the defections among other groups. As they said: "The religious subsystem of [the Yankee City Jewish] community is apparently in a state of disintegration" (Warner and Srole, 1945, pp. 199, 200), primarily because of the economic factor. If Jews were to successfully compete in the economic sphere, they had to break with the traditional religious patterns that restricted them. The Sabbath is a case in point:

> The Jewish Sabbath falls on Saturday. In Russia the Jews, comprising an important part of the merchant class, maintained their own work rhythm in the week, and non-Jews had to adapt themselves to it. On Saturday their shops were closed, whereas on Sunday they were "open for business."
> The work rhythm of the American week, however, is Christian. Sunday is the Sabbath, and Saturday is a work day, the most important day in the week. This rhythm the Jews are powerless to resist. They must accept it or lose out in the competitive race [ibid.].

Though they readily dropped those religious traditions that inhibited their successful participation in the competitive race, Yankee City Jews did not opt for mass identificational assimilation. Nor did their actions result in the disintegration of the Jewish community. Rather, the very nature of the community underwent basic change. As Warner and Srole defined it:

In all other aspects of the Jewish community, the process of change is one of a replacement of traditionally Jewish elements by American elements. In the religious system of the Jews there is no such replacement. The Jews are not dropping their religious behaviors, relations, and representations under the influence of the American religious system. There are no indications that they are becoming Christian. Even the F[1] generation [the native-born generation] can only be said to be irreligious [p. 202].

In other words the Jewish community was culturally assimilating without, however, disappearing. While the class system in Yankee City was open and "the Russian Jews climb its strata faster than any other ethnic group in the city" (Warner and Srole, p. 203), there were certain requirements, nevertheless. Definite norms of behavior were expected of those rising in the class system which were at odds with the norms of traditional Judaism, and all but those who immigrated as adults adopted the American norms.

But even as they shed their traditional Jewish norms, they did not eliminate the religious element from the group self-definition. They did not cease to define themselves as a religioethnic group and proceed to become solely an ethnic group. Rather, they embraced what they perceived as a progressive form of Judaism which, at the same time, was rooted in tradition. Conservative Judaism was Americanized Judaism to them, in much the same way that American Reform Judaism was for their predecessors in the mid-nineteenth century. Conservative Judaism was uniquely suited to the children of the Eastern European immigrants in that it provided them a framework within which they could behave as Americans while espousing an ideological commitment to tradition; this framework also maintained an explicit emphasis on the ethnic character of Judaism.

Though much of this situation is implicit in the analysis of the Yankee City Jewish community, Warner and Srole were not fully aware of the process. They explained what they saw as the disintegration of Judaism in Yankee City as related to the collapse, in the face of an open-class system, of the Judaistic religious system "which, for centuries, served an

isolating function and was continuously preserved intact"
(ibid., p. 202). What they failed to perceive was the ability of
Jews and the Jewish communal structure, including the
religious structure, to adapt to changing conditions. From a
sociological, rather than theological or religious ideological,
perspective, Conservative Judaism can be defined as precisely
such an adaptation. The second generation did not cease to be
religious, in their perception; rather, they redefined the
religion. Whether such redefinition, especially without a
consistent ideology, is viable in the long run is another matter;
it will be discussed later, when we look at some challenges
facing the Conservative movement today. For the majority of
the second generation Eastern European Jewry in the United
States, Conservative Judaism was functional in that it enabled
them to resolve what might have otherwise been an impossible dilemma: how to retain the restricting traditional
Jewish norms even though they were not ideologically com-
mited to them, without ceasing to define themselves within a
religious group self-definition, which would have been hardly
acceptable to either themselves or to the larger American
society. Even if there had been strong Orthodox leadership, it
probably could not have prevented massive defection. In fact,
there was not a strong Orthodox leadership yet because the
bulk of the rabbi-scholar elite remained in Europe and those in
the United States did not have the time or the resources to
develop structures that would allow for economic mobility
within the Orthodox fold. Subsequent developments, as will
be discussed, changed this situation considerably, but not until
after World War II.

In the meantime, the second generation experienced
economic mobility with a vengeance and, in the course of its
cultural assimilation, swelled the ranks of Conservative
Judaism. Data comparing the occupational distribution of
foreign-born and native-born Jews in London and Stamford,
Connecticut, and Staten Island, New York City, indicate that
whereas 18 percent of the foreign born were in industry, less
than 11 percent of the native born were; whereas more than
62 percent of the foreign born were in trade, 53 percent of the

native born were; and while less than 7 percent of the foreign born were in the professions, more than 19 percent of the native born were (Goldberg, 1947, p. 52). In Cleveland, an analysis comparing the occupational distribution of Jews from 1923 and 1930, indicates a "drop in the sample of needle trades employees . . . from 83 to 65, among peddlers-hucksters from 46 to 27, and among laborers from 44 to 33. On the other hand, lawyers increased from 15 to 20, and salesmen from 39 to 60" (Gartner, 1978, p. 272). And in a study of the occupational status of Jews in Detroit during the depression, in 1935, 12 percent of the Jewish youth were found to be in the class of professionals, proprietors, managers, and officials; almost 46 percent were in the class of clerical, sales, and kindred workers; almost 9 percent were in the skilled class of craftsmen, foremen, and kindred workers; and 33.5 percent were in the semiskilled and unskilled class. Among non-Jewish youth, 4 percent were in the professional and proprietory class; 21 percent were in the clerical class; 15 percent were in the skilled; and 59 percent were in the semiskilled and unskilled classes (Fauman, 1958, p. 123).

Related to economic mobility, though probably more as an effect rather than a cause (Slater, 1969; Greer, 1972; Steinberg, 1974; Gorelick, 1981), is the educational mobility of the second generation. So significant were the increases in Jewish enrollments in colleges and universities that, beginning in the 1920s, even colleges and universities in the Eastern part of the United States which had always been open to Jews adopted quotas which were designed to limit and reduce Jewish enrollments (Broun and Britt, 1931), because of the significant increases in Jewish applications and the fear of the administrations that the Jewish influence was becoming too great.

The most frequent explanation of the drive toward higher education among the children of the Eastern European Jewish immigrants is that it was rooted in the traditional Jewish value of learning. Milton Gordon, for example, asserts: "The traditional stress and high evaluation placed upon Talmudic learning was easily transferred under new conditions to a desire for secular education, if not for the parent generation, at least for the children" (Gordon, 1964, p. 186). Similarly, Talcott Parsons argues, the "high prestige of the Law itself, on the one hand, and that of the men who were its trustees, on the other, effected among the people an attitude of high respect for 'learning' in general. Such an attitude could readily be extended to cover other fields of study outside of that of Jewish Law, or the Talmud. The strong propensity of Jews to enter the learned professions can certainly, at least in part, be looked upon as a result of the traditional high regard for learning" (Parsons, 1942, p. 106; see also Wirth, 1964, p. 103; Fuchs, 1956, pp. 178–80).

Others are skeptical of the cultural roots of American Jewish educational mobility, however. Miriam Slater, for example, argues there is not continuity, but discontinuity between the goals of Eastern European Jewish learning and American academic success. She asserts that "insofar as such goals were internalized we should expect them to be a deterrent to desiring higher education" (Slater, 1969, p. 372), because the method and objective of traditional Jewish learning were completely at variance with and in opposition to those of secular education. Liebman too argues that "there has always been a strong antiphilosophical, antispeculative tradition in Judaism (though not the only tradition), and most of the Eastern European religious leadership, particularly in the nineteenth and twentieth centuries, opposed secular education and the pursuit of any nontraditional Jewish study that was not value neutral" (Liebman, 1973, pp. 140–41).

While Slater and Liebman are correct in that Jewish traditional learning and secular education were, in many respects, antithetical to each other, this does not mean that those who zealously pursued secular education were consciously rejecting Judaism. Many of them did in fact perceive their secular educations as the fulfillment, or operationalizing, of the Jewish emphasis on study and knowledge. Their educational mobility was a manifestation of the Americanization and secularization of Jewish values, not the rejection of them. The Eastern European immigrants and their children perceived that traditional Jewish sacred learning would not promote economic and social mobility, which they viewed to be good for Jews as Jews, but would actually hinder it. They therefore adapted the Jewish value to the social requirements of the secular American society. Louis Wirth was sensitive to the social psychology involved in his analysis of the intellectual as one of the "Jewish types of personality": "The ideal of intellectuality which, in the ghetto of the Old World, produced the type of student known as the *Yeshiba Bochar*, or talmudical student, and the *Melammed*, or rabbinical teacher, persists, though it may be in secular form. In the olden days when religious learning was the highest virtue, a prosperous merchant would prefer a poor but learned student as the future husband for his daughter; in the modern ghetto a lawyer, a doctor, an artist, or a writer are the prizes that the rich businessman will seek as his sons-in-law" (Wirth, 1964, p. 103).

To the Eastern European Jewish immigrants and their children, pursuing secular education was not the rejection of Jewish values; rather, it was the realization of them, albeit in a somewhat different form. While a minority looked to higher education as a vehicle that would enable them to realize their complete assimilation into American society, the majority had no such agenda. They sought to assimilate culturally, to acculturate and enjoy the good American life, but they maintained their Jewish group identity through structural isolation.

One further manifestation of the cultural assimilation of the second generation, the children of the Eastern European Jewish immigrants, is the low birthrate pattern which emerged during the 1930s. While the evidence is only suggestive, based upon a small number of limited community studies rather than a solid data base, it does indicate that the American Jewish birthrate declined significantly during the 1930s, even more so than did the general American birthrate as a result of the depression. Also, the available data indicate that the increase was less in the American Jewish birthrate after World War II while the general American population was experiencing a sharp increase, a "baby boom" (Goldscheider, 1967; Goldberg and Sharp, 1958, pp. 108–10). In the one study which indicates that Jews were in fact part of the postwar "baby boom," namely, an extensive study of three generations of the Jewish community of Providence, Rhode Island (Goldstein and Goldscheider, 1968), they nevertheless seem to have had a lower increase in birth rate than did the larger American society. In any event, the decline in the Jewish birthrate is clear when we compare pre-1910, when the average number of children born was 3.5, with the 1925–29 marriage cohort, when that average dipped to 1.9 children (ibid., p. 122).

Culturally assimilated as they were, second-generation Jews did not manifest commensurate patterns of structural assimilation. On the contrary, they remained structurally isolated due to internal and external forces. They wanted to maintain their Jewish communal affiliations and associations and were forced to by the barriers imposed by the larger, "host" society. They moved to neighborhoods which, "gilded" as they were, became largely populated by Jews. Despite the "openness" of American society, the interpersonal relations of these Jews were carried on largely with other Jews. Nathaniel Zalowitz, writing in the *Jewish Daily Forward* in 1926, observed about New York City:

> Once there was only one kind of Jewish neighborhood, of which the old East Side was the "shining" example. But today you have a Ghetto for the Jew who owns a Rolls Royce and half a dozen other cars besides. The rich Jew no less than the poor one prefers to live among "unsere leute" (our own kind) and the Gentile thinks so too. . . . What else (if not voluntary "ghettos") would you call the districts in the various large American cities in which two-thirds or more of the Jews live and have their being? . . . The majority of the Jews . . . inhabit certain sections only. That, I urge, is the true earmark of Ghetto life [quoted in Moore, 1981a, p. 22].

Their desire to maintain a Jewish group existence manifested itself in the plethora of Jewish communal organizations and agencies, especially philanthropic and social-welfare ones, which were created and developed. Jewish federations and communal welfare funds became central fund-raising and disbursing agencies in increasing numbers of cities with significant Jewish populations. The concept of a Jewish federation in the United States, or a Jewish community chest, dates back to 1895, when the Federated Jewish Charities of Boston was organized (Elazar, 1976, p. 160). The original idea of federation was to make fund raising more efficient. With the masses of new immigrants, a variety of social and educational agencies had emerged. These developments paralleled those of the larger society when, in the second half of the nineteenth century, many private social welfare agencies had sprung up across the country and attempts to organize them led to the formation of the Charity Organization Society (COS). Though not directly related, the American COS was modeled after the London COS, which was organized in 1870 for the expressed goal of coordinating the efforts of and designing guidelines for London's numerous charitable organizations (Waxman, 1977a, pp. 81–86). During that same period, in Philadelphia in 1870 and in New York in 1874, local Jewish welfare agencies joined forces and formed the United Hebrew Charities, in the belief that "private charity must be purged of its sentimentality and organized into an effective force" (Bremner, 1960, p. 98). These societies, and the increasing number of nonsectarian ones, led the movement toward "scientific philanthropy" during the rest of that century and played a central role in the emergence of professional social work in the beginning of the twentieth century.

At the turn of the century, it became increasingly apparent that the traditional patterns of fund raising within the Jewish community, namely, with each agency raising its own funds independently, was wasteful and self-defeating. The joint fund-raising campaign of the Boston Federation proved to be so successful that other Jewish communities soon followed suit. In 1900 a National Conference on Organized Jewish Charities was held, and representatives from thirty-six cities attended. By 1917, there were forty-seven federations in the larger American cities. Also, the federation concept was adopted by many general, non-Jewish social welfare agencies, and federation became the model for community chests and councils of social agencies in cities and towns across the country (Leiby, 1978, p. 118).

The initial task of federations, joint fund raising, promoted community organization by encouraging the diverse local Jewish agencies to engage in collective communal activity. By the time of the community of the second generation, federations took on the roles of coordinating the programs and activities of the various member communal agencies, determining unmet communal needs, and establishing new agencies to meet them. As such, federations became the centers of local Jewish communal power. As Maurice Karpf observed, "especially since the War, and more especially during the third decade of the present century, federations became communal agencies whose function it is not only to provide financial support for their constituent societies but to plan for the community needs along constructive lines. Today, with few exceptions, the federations aim to support, coordinate, and control the needed social service agencies and activities in their respective communities" (Karpf, 1971 [1938], p. 103).

The many advantages of federations notwithstanding, their emergence as centers of control and power in local communities and nationally with the establishment of the National Council of Jewish Federations and Welfare Funds in 1932 (Lurie, 1961, p. 116), led to several rifts within the organized American Jewish community during the following decades. While the antagonisms between the German and East European Jews had subsided during the period of the second generation, two other schisms began to grow. One struggle was between two competing conceptions of Jewish communal centrality—the federation and the synagogue—and the other involved the legitimacy and representativeness of the federation leadership. This second issue will be discussed in a later chapter; while its seeds were sown with the federation's assumption of strong communal control, the actual struggle did not break out until later. The conflict of the federation and the synagogue, however, appeared virtually at the beginning, when with the secularization of the Jewish community philanthropy became a major avenue of expressing one's Jewishness.

The conflict between the synagogue—especially the rabbi—and the federation essentially is a conflict between the two components of the corporate nature of the Jewish community—religious and ethnic. The rabbi, as the religious leader, defines his role as the authority on all matters related to Judaism, including the welfare of Jews and the Jewish community. As he sees it, Jews are first and foremost a religious group and the synagogue must always be the central institution of the Jewish community. He is particularly mortified when executives of secular Jewish social service agencies, and especially Jewish federation executives—who are fairly ignorant of Jewish learning, as the overwhelming majority of them in the second and third generations were—claim to be the most important leaders of the Jewish community and are in the position to control Jewish communal power. The Jewish social service executive, on the other hand, defines his role as even more basic to the Jewish community. He sees himself as providing for the survival and well-being of the community, without which there will be no synagogue nor rabbi. Moreover he often sees the rabbi as the "scholar-saint," who aspires to be the "religious specialist" (Carlin and Mendlovitz, 1958), but who has neither the professional training nor the ability to play a significant role in the service of the Jewish community outside of his very limited spheres. Although this conflict has abated somewhat in recent years, in the fourth-generation community, due to the declining rate of synagogue affiliation and the growing sensitivity to religious tradition and increased Jewish knowledge among federation executives, the issue is still a topical one and attracts a large audience whenever it is on the agenda of the annual convention of the Council of Jewish Federations (Raphael, 1979, pp. 199–254).

The structural isolation of the second generation was maintained not only internally, but also by the barriers imposed by the larger society. Overt and covert anti-Semitism were rampant in the United States during the 1920s and

1930s. In the early 1920s, it was in response to the large Jewish immigration and, in the 1930s, to the depression and the increasing involvement of the government in the European war against Hitler's Germany. Henry Ford's publication of the libelous *Protocols of the Elders of Zion* and *The International Jew* in his newspaper *The Dearborn Independent*, the tirades of such Fundamentalist preachers as Gerald Winrod and Gerald L. K. Smith, the agitations of the radio preacher, Rev. Charles E. Coughlin, and the poet, Ezra Pound, and the baitings of the Ku Klux Klan, were among the overt manifestations of anti-Semitism (Selzer, 1972, pp. 114–200). Quotas restricting the number of Jews in colleges and universities and the barring of Jews from core positions in the American economy were others. In an effort to belie the allegation in the 1930s that Jews controlled the American economy and were responsible for its ills, *Fortune* magazine undertook a study that showed that Jews played virtually no role in the major commerical banking houses nor in heavy industry, such as steel, automobiles, coal, rubber, shipping, and transportation (*Fortune*, 1936, pp. 39–46). Rather, "to find Jewish participation in industry it is necessary to turn to the light industries. And even there it is necessary to turn from the manufacturing to the distributing end" (ibid., p. 48). While the editors of *Fortune* did not claim that these patterns were the result of discrimination against Jews, subsequent public opinion polls during that decade by *Fortune* and others (Stember et al., 1966, pp. 32–34) and reports indicating that Jews were absent in various occupations and other social settings (McWilliams, 1948, pp. 113–41) demonstrated rather conclusively that systematic anti-Semitic exclusion was at work.

The barriers to structural assimilation imposed by the larger society produced two interrelated effects upon the well-to-do businessmen and professionals of the second generation. One was an increase of what Kurt Lewin refers to as "leaders from the periphery":

> In any group, those sections are apt to gain leadership which are more generally successful. In a minority group, individual members who are economically successful, or who have distinguished themselves in their professions, usually gain a higher degree of

acceptance by the majority group. This places them culturally on the periphery of the underpriviledged group and makes them more likely to be "marginal" persons. They frequently have a negative balance and are particularly eager to have their "good connections" not endangered by too close a contact with those sections of the underpriviledged group which are not acceptable to the majority. Nevertheless, they are frequently called for leadership by the underpriviledged group because of their status and power. They themselves are usually eager to accept the leading role in the minority, partly as a substitute for gaining status in the majority, partly because such leadership makes it possible for them to have and maintain additional contacts with the majority [Lewin, 1948, pp. 195–96].

Lewin saw leaders from the periphery as damaging for the organization and activity of a minority group, and he suggested that the percentage of them among the leadership of American Jewry had increased since the end of World War I. While he did not explain the reason for the increase, the analysis presented here makes it predictable. Given the increased cultural assimilation, especially the greater educational and economic mobility on the one hand, and the increased imposed barriers to structural assimilation, anti-Semitism on the other, there would be a greater number of those who would experience the social-psychological stresses that according to Lewin, characterize the leader from the periphery.

Another and somewhat related response to the imposed structural isolation of the second generation had important consequences upon that generation's communal organization and development. The rising educational and economic mobility on the one hand and the structural barriers on the other produced a relatively high number of second generation Jews who experienced "status inconsistency." Status inconsistency, as analyzed by Lenski, is a phenomenon which tends to emerge in societies whose systems of social stratification are multidimensional. In American society, for example, education, occupation, and income are variables and dimensions of stratification. So too is ethnicity. As societies become increasingly complex, certain individuals probably will occupy a higher status in one part of the stratification system than in another. This is especially the case with racial and cultured minorities. The black or female doctor, for example, is of high professional status but of low racial or sexual status. Since all individuals think of themselves in terms of their highest status and expect others to treat them accordingly, but often find they are treated by others in terms of their lowest status, these individuals of inconsistent statuses frequently experience great stress. Lenski discusses different possible reactions to the status inconsistency experience (Lenski, 1966, pp. 86–88), but one in particular is of relevance at this point, namely that people of inconsistent statuses "are likely to find social interaction outside the bounds of the primary group (where others tend to be like themselves) somewhat less rewarding than does the average person" (ibid., p. 87). For the economically successful members of the second generation in particular, their status inconsistency, deriving from their being socially excluded by and from the larger society, forced them to seek the status to which their economic position entitled them within the primary group, the Jewish community. Jewish communal workers and fund raisers, according to Kramer and Leventman, played a pivotal role in helping to ease the plight of those experiencing status inconsistency and in responding to the needs and demands of the masses of the second generation who sought not status, but Jewish institutions.

Excluded from the general community, businessmen and professionals, supported by Jewish patronage, were susceptible to the attractions of an ethnic community. Their communal sentiments were readily converted into social reality by the professional community organizers among Jewish social workers and fund-raisers. Traditional welfare activities became the basis of formalized secular organizations, reaffirming sentiments of mutual identity and strengthening communal bonds. The now overorganized structure of the second-generation community has continued to impose communal ties and sentiments on its members, which in turn support the structure. It is no longer possible to determine whether the structure is a consequence of the sentiment or the sentiment a consequence of the structure [Kramer and Leventman, 1961, pp. 12–13].

Because of the high value placed upon charity and philanthropy in Jewish tradition, fund raising became "an important principle of organization in the Jewish community" (ibid., p. 100). The wealthier members of the community contributed more, proportionately, to Jewish philanthropies than the less wealthy, but not because they were any more committed as Jews. Kramer and Leventman maintain that "philanthropic contributions are more than indices of traditional Jewish values; they reflect particular life styles as well. For most North City Jews, conspicuous charity is less a matter of religious or ideological commitment than a conventional social obligation serving as a source of status" (ibid., p. 101).

An implicit but pronounced social criticism exists in this portrayal of the patterns of giving in the North City Jewish community and by implication in the whole American Jewish community, a criticism that this giving is inconsistent with Jewish culture and the role of philanthropy within it; the authors themselves are aware of it. As they point out, "Philanthropy has always been a legitimate way to consume wealth conspicuously" (ibid., p. 99). In the social stratification of the highly traditional Eastern European *shtetl*, wealth, provided it was used in the support of communal needs, was one of the major variables determining status. It should not be surprising therefore, that the more wealthy members of the second-generation community adopted this traditional Jewish pattern to alleviate their status inconsistency. That their philanthropy entailed elements of self-interest and was not altruistic is correct, of course. Judaism has always acknowledged the reality of self-interest in human action. As Lenski points out, altruism is not a factor in human motivation, and invariably an element of self-interest is involved, even if it is enlightened self-interest (Lenski, pp. 27–30). From a moral standpoint therefore, the issue is not whether there was any self-interest involved but rather how the individuals directed and put their self-interest to work. While Kramer and Leventman are correct in that many wealthy members of the second-generation community who gave to Jewish philanthropic causes were not necessarily motivated by Jewish traditional values alone, they did in fact manifest traditional Jewish patterns in the manner in which they attempted to resolve their dilemma of status inconsistency.

Finally, on a broader national level, the structural unity of the second generation was reinforced by the serious rise of threats and actions against Jews in foreign lands, especially in Europe with the rise of Nazism and in Palestine with the rise of Arab nationalism and anti-Jewish massacres. The two major American Jewish overseas aid organizations, the Joint Distribution Committee (JDC) and the United Palestine Appeal (UPA), founded by the Zionists in October 1925 (Urofsky, 1975, pp. 325–26), recognized that competing for contributors was inefficient, but the ideological differences between them—especially about whether helping Jews in their countries was preferable to encouraging them to go to Palestine—precluded any united fund-raising campaign. The Council of Jewish Federations and Welfare Funds had a special reason for wishing that the two overseas aid agencies should come to some agreement, since it ran the fund-raising campaigns in the local communities. After several years of negotiations, the Council of Jewish Federations worked out a formula with the JDC and UPA, and the two overseas aid agencies became the major partners of a new body, founded in 1939, the United Jewish Appeal (UJA) (Lurie, 1961, pp. 136–43). For several years the United Jewish Appeal itself remained rather unstable and its relationship with the Council of Jewish Federations was precarious at best. This initial effort at cooperation established a pattern that spread during the period of the third generation, namely, the increasing coordination of fund-raising activities between the Council of Jewish Federations and the United Jewish Appeal in Jewish communities throughout the country. As a result of these efforts, not only were fund raising streamlined and more dollars raised; the joint campaigns have resulted in the Council of Jewish Federation's rise to a position of dominance in domestic Jewish communal affairs. Concurrently the United Jewish Appeal became the major fund-raising agency involved in overseas aid, and the United Palestine Appeal, subsequently renamed the United Israel Appeal, became the major power block within the UJA.

These developments were part of the process through which American Jewry, in its cultural assimilation, has created a "community and polity," a corporate sense of community, "embracing within it both the strictly religious and not so clearly religious dimensions of Jewish existence, the ethnic ties of individual Jews," and the voluntaristic "political dimension if they are to survive" as a community (Elazar, 1976, pp. 4, 6). It was not until the third-generation community that serious questions began to arise as to that corporate will to survive.

4. Religion without Religiosity: The Third-Generation Community

If the second generation was the era during which American Jews were largely acculturated but remained structurally isolated, the third generation was one of increasing acculturation and decreasing structural isolation imposed from outside; yet they remained a people apart. At the same time, the self-definition of the group underwent acculturation; American Jews in the third-generation community increasingly defined themselves as a religious group, rather than an ethnic one.

In an intensive study of Protestants, Catholics, and Jews in the city of Detroit, Lenski found the religious associations of Jews became greatly weakened while their communal bonds remained stronger than for the other groups. In terms of religious associations, 12 percent of the sample of Jews reported that they attended no synagogue or temple services at all; 56 percent reported attendance only on the High Holy Days, or a few times a year; 20 percent reported attending at least once a month; and only 12 percent reported weekly attendance (Lenski, 1963, p. 36). In terms of communal bonds, however, the evidence indicated that those of the Jews were stronger than for any other groups surveyed. Of the Jews reporting 96 percent said that all or nearly all of their relatives were Jewish, and 77 percent reported that all or nearly all of their close friends were. Also, all the married Jewish respondents reported that they were "lifelong Jews married to a lifelong Jewish spouse" (ibid., p. 37). These findings led

Lenski to conclude that "the vigor of Jewish communalism more than compensates for the weakness of the religious associations" (ibid., p. 319). Ironically it was precisely in terms of the weakest element in their group bonds, the religious, that Jews defined themselves as a group in the third generation. Suggestions about why and how this developed are found in Gans's study on the origin and growth of the suburban Jewish community of Park Forest (Gans, 1958).

The years following World War II witnessed a great housing boom, and during the late 1940s and 1950s America's middle class became suburbanized. Park Forest, a suburban community thirty miles from downtown Chicago, started in 1948 and was incorporated as a village in 1949. The community numbered about 1,800 families, of whom about 150, or close to 9 percent, were Jewish. Of these, twenty families, three-quarters of whom involved mixed marriages (between Jews and non-Jews), had no connections with the formal Jewish community, and another 30 families were too new to the community to have developed strong ties. Gans studied a sample consisting of 44 of the remaining 100 families and found them to be young—the median age for the husbands, the male heads of households, was 35, and of their wives, 30; highly educated—only 9 percent of the male heads and 25 percent of the wives had no college education; and of middle to upper-middle income status. Of the sample 36 percent were professionals and 48 percent were in business and industry, though only 14 percent of these were owners (Gans, pp. 206–8). When those who were active in the formation and leadership of the Jewish community were compared with the inactive members, the actives tended to have slightly more and older children, to have slightly higher mean incomes, and to be of somewhat higher educational and occupational status. Culturally, the Jews of Park Forest were virtually indistinguishable from the non-Jews. Moreover, in contrast to the residential patterns of the second-generation community, not only did they live like others in Park Forest, they also lived with them. Park Forest had no distinctively Jewish section. "The Jewish families were scattered at ran-

dom, and only rarely were two Jewish families to be found in adjacent houses" (Gans, p. 209).

The informal Jewish community developed in four stages: "contact, recognition, acquaintance, and friendship" (Gans, p. 210). The formal organizations were set up largely through the efforts of the several men among the early residents in the community who worked for American Jewish organizations and agencies. Their professional involvement in Jewish organizational activity provided them with a special incentive to form Jewish organizations in Park Forest. They invited a group of their friends and acquaintances to a meeting and, because most of those there had no special interest in any particular organization, they decided to form a B'nai B'rith lodge. Two women who were new to the community and wanted to develop contacts with other Jewish women in the community organized a meeting about a month later in which it was decided to set up an affiliate of the National Council of Jewish Women.

Shortly after these two organizations were founded, an interesting and revealing split developed between the men and the women about the orientation of the Jewish communal organization of Park Forest. The men wanted an adult-oriented community in which the religious and/or cultural activities would center around the adult population, and in which the children would learn to be adults by assuming adult functions. Thus the men wanted a synagogue that would have a Sunday school through which the children would be socialized into the adult community. The women, on the other hand, wanted a child-oriented community in which the activities would be centered around the children and their needs as children as perceived by the parents "while at the same time most of the adults abstain from religious-cultural activities and involvement in the community" (Gans, p. 215). Thus the women wanted a Sunday school for the children, but without the involvement of adults. In the end the child-oriented Sunday school, in which the children were taught about Jewish customs primarily as historical and cultural phenomena but not as religious normative imperatives, was adopted. The parents "conceived the institution to be a school in Jewish identity, in '*Jewishness*,' not in *Judaism*" (Gans, p. 219).

Not long after, the adult activities of the formal Jewish organizations also became child oriented. The Jewish holidays, especially the "happy holidays" of Passover, Purim, and Chanukah, became instruments for creating and reinforcing Jewish identification and as such were primarily oriented toward the children. Chanukah, in particular, loomed large as the Jewish counterpart of Christmas, and parents spent lavish sums on Chanukah decorations, religious objects, and presents.

Most of the families were religiously nonobservant and unaffiliated with synagogues or temples. The only observances that were maintained were the child-oriented and parent-oriented ones, such as keeping a kosher home for parents, keeping the traditional numbers of days for holidays for parents, observance of circumcision and of memorial services. Even the founding of the synagogue was not based upon intrinsic religiosity, but on the need to demonstrate Jewish group solidarity to Park Forest's non-Jews.

Despite their solid middle-class status, acculturation, and secularization, Park Forest's Jews carried on their more informal and intimate social interaction almost exclusively with other Jews. They professed strong ingroup feelings and were quite open about feeling more comfortable with other Jews. Even those who were more highly educated and denied "chauvinistic" ingroup feelings, tended to have more Jewish friends and associates than non-Jews, not because they were Jewish but because they shared a common subculture. As Gans characterizes the community: "Their adjustment to American society and their present position in it can be described . . . as behavioral acculturation, but with continued social cohesion and isolation" (p. 231).

Six years later, in 1955, Gans returned to Park Forest to determine what changes, if any, took place during the intervening years. The Jewish population had grown to 600 families, approximately 10 percent of the total suburban community. The socioeconomic composition of the Jewish

population was similar to what it had been earlier. Several new Jewish organizations existed, and in 1951 Temple Beth Sholom, an Eastern European Reform congregation, was founded. The acculturated and secularized character of the community manifested itself in the Temple, where attendance at religious services was low but attendance at a lecture series on secular Jewish topics was high. Although no pork was served, the Temple's kitchen was not kosher. The most popular functions in the Temple were dinners, dances, and bazaars. Participation in these social activities of the Temple would probably have been even greater, had they not been fund-raising activities that were quite expensive to attend and participation was prohibitive for those of modest means. The Temple also had a congregational Sunday school, which was much more adult-oriented than the other Sunday school in the community, the child-oriented community school founded in 1949.

Despite many indications of considerable formal Jewish communal growth during these intervening years, Gans was skeptical of the suggestion that a real Jewish revival was taking place in Park Forest. Rather he interpreted the trends as the transformation of the informal community patterns that had previously existed in the urban setting into more formal ones (p. 243). The child-oriented functions of the formal organizations still persisted and, though there were many new Jewish organizations and activities, active voluntary community participation was still the exception rather than the norm. When there is participation, "it is more likely to express itself in passive response than active support" (Gans, p. 244). The Temple is the center of most of the community's activity, but mainly because it is ideologically and institutionally diffuse and is able to adapt itself to its members' wishes. As Gans interpreted it, what was taking place in Park Forest and, by implication, in American Jewish communities across the country, was not a real Jewish revival; rather, the organizational structures were manifestations of what he was to later term "symbolic ethnicity" (Gans, 1979), that is, manifestations "of the need and desire of Jewish parents to provide clearly visible institutions and symbols with which to maintain and reinforce the ethnic identification of the next generation" (Gans, 1958, p. 247). When, in the years 1958–1962, Gans lived in and studied the new suburban community of what was then called Levittown, New Jersey, he interpreted the formal Jewish communal developments in the same perspective (Gans, 1967, pp. 73–82). Accurate as this interpretation may have been in the third-generation community, its applicability to the fourth-generation community is questionable, as will be discussed later. Gans may have overlooked the possibility of the formal organizations functioning in ways other than those intended by those who established them, especially when conditions and events within American Jewry and within American society changed so dramatically from the period of the third-generation community.

While Gans's studies, despite his interpretations, emphasized the persistence of structural isolation in the third-generation community, other studies of other communities found somewhat different patterns. In their study of the Jews of "North City," Kramer and Leventman found that there were changes in the occupational patterns between the second generation and third generation members of the community. Specifically, they found an increase in salaried employment among the third-generation members of the community and in the number of those who enter traditionally non-Jewish occupations (Kramer and Leventman, pp. 134–36). Also, there were indications that the life-style of the third generation was more influenced by occupation and less by ethnicity (ibid., p. 200).

The friendship patterns in North City were similar to those found by Gans in Park Forest. Most of the third-generation Jews had their closest friendships with other Jews, and many of them publicly eschewed the "chauvinistic" basis of their social relationships (ibid., pp. 175–78). But Kramer and Leventman were more forceful in their prediction of the trend than was Gans. They asserted that "being Jewish is no longer necessary or sufficient grounds for association" (p. 178), and

they implied that the stated willingness of the third generation to develop friendships with non-Jews would become an increasingly prevalent trend as occupational assimilation continued, as witnessed in their increasing tendency to belong to non-Jewish organizations as well as Jewish ones (ibid., pp. 178–83).

Occupational assimilation also affected marriage patterns, Kramer and Leventman suggest. Although most of the third generation Jews preferred endogamy for themselves and their children, they were not quite confident about their children's preferences. They also assumed that if faced with the exogamy, intermarriage, of their children, they would inevitably come to accept it (ibid., pp. 180–81). Since opposition to exogamy had, in the past, been rare and very strongly opposed and sanctioned, this attitude of almost fatalistic apathy indeed indicated a radical departure from traditional Jewish norms.

A relatively high degree of uncertainty about the spouses their children might choose was also evident in a study of "Riverton," an industrial town of about 130,000 people, of whom about 7 percent, or approximately 8,500, were Jews. Conducted in the early 1950s by Sklare and Vosk, this study sought to determine the nature of the Jewish community's sense, definition, and perception of itself and its relationship with its non-Jewish neighbors. While both parents and children strongly expressed that they wanted Judaism and the Jewish people to survive, that they felt more comfortable with other Jews than with non-Jews, and that intermarriage was not a good idea, they seemed much less adamant about intermarriage than did previous generations. As Sklare and Vosk summarize the attitudes of the parents: "Most thought it unlikely that the children would marry non-Jews, but were not prepared to affirm this with absolute certainty. "I hope I am right," was the common response. Almost all would be unhappy, were intermarriage to occur and would do all in their power to prevent it. Still, faced with an accomplished fact, the large majority would make their peace with their children" (Sklare and Vosk, 1957, p. 34). While the attitudes of the children were fairly similar to those of their parents in a dislike for intermarriage, when faced with a forced-choice question between love and Jewishness, 75 percent of the children, including some who came from strictly Orthodox homes, opted for love. This compares with 40 percent of the parents who, on the forced-choice question, opted for love rather than Jewishness for their children (ibid., p. 36).

The Jewish group self-definition of Riverton's Jews shows the impact of Americanization in that it is different from the self-definition of the first, the Eastern European immigrant generation. Whereas the immigrant generation defined itself as either a religioethnic or an ethnic group, with the primary emphasis upon the ethnic element in the group self-definition, the third generation defined itself primarily as a religious group. As Sklare and Vosk conclude, "Riverton Jews—and American Jews in general—see themselves primarily as Jews by religion." Belonging to a synagogue, "for the Americanized Jew of Riverton," therefore, "has become a mark of identification and a ticket to the larger community" (ibid., pp. 25, 26). The revival of synagogue affiliation which they found in Riverton was not a real religious revival. Rather, it was "congregationalism" that was being revived. "What has happened is that more Jews are affiliated with the synagogue, not that more are religious" (ibid. p. 26). This interpretation is virtually identical with that of Gans, in his follow-up study of Park Forest, and with that of Herberg in his analysis of the religious affiliation patterns of Protestants, Catholics, and Jews in American society during this period (Gans, 1958; Herberg, 1960). For the third generation, religion was significant for its social identification value, but did not imply religiosity (cf. Marty, 1976). In this secularization process most traditional religious rituals were dropped. Only those that could be integrated within the framework of American cultural values were retained. As Sklare and Vosk put it:

> The rituals which have survived best . . . are not those designed to remind the Jew every day, and indeed every moment, that he is a Jew and that God expects a certain course of behavior from him,

but rather those that are occasional and joyous, that involve the young, and mark the transition from one stage of life to another. It is also revealing that those which have survived do not demand rigorous devotion and daily attention, do not involve an unsupportable isolation from non-Jews, and are acceptable to the larger community as appropriate symbols of the sacred order [ibid., p. 11].

Although Sklare and Vosk were fairly sanguine about "the problem of intermarriage" among Riverton's Jews because, "the deep urge to preserve Jewish identity compels them to keep their sons and daughters from the kind of association with Gentile children which might lead to marriage" (p. 36), evidence from other studies suggested that the parents were not as successful in this as they thought they would be. In a review of studies of Jewish intermarriage, Erich Rosenthal reported that data from a study of the Jewish community of Greater Washington, D.C., by Stanley K. Bigman in 1956 indicated an overall Jewish intermarriage rate of 13.1 percent, with that rate rising to about 18 percent for third-generation American Jews. Moreover, "the Washington data revealed that children in at least 70 percent of mixed families are lost to the Jewish group" (Rosenthal, 1963, p. 32). Subsequent data demonstrated rather conclusively that in fact the intermarriage rate has risen rapidly since the 1950s. A review of those studies and an analysis of their implications will be presented in a later chapter.

Two of the most extensive and intensive studies of Jewish communities during the period of the third generation were those of Goldstein and Goldscheider, of Providence, Rhode Island, and Sklare and Greenblum, of "Lakeville," a suburb of Chicago. The Providence study was conducted during the early 1960s as part of a larger study of the Greater Providence Jewish community, and was an analysis of the demographic, social class, family, fertility, marriage and intermarriage, and religiocultural patterns of a sample of foreign-born Jews, native-born children of immigrants, and native-born children of native-born Jews in the community at that time. By the time of the study, only 17 percent of the Jews of Providence were foreign born; approximately 40 percent were third-generation Americans (Goldstein and Goldscheider, 1968, p. 40).

In general, the social patterns of the three generations of Providence Jews follow the patterns found in other communities. In only one respect were they different from other studies, namely, there was a lower proportion of third-generation Jews in the professions among Providence Jews than was the case in the other communities studied. Goldstein and Goldscheider suggest that this lower proportion of professionals may be due to the limited employment opportunities for many professionals within Greater Providence and, thus, those who do have professional education and training move elsewhere. Also "since the 25–44 year group of the third generation is heavily weighted toward the younger end of this age category, a number of persons may still have been receiving their training and therefore would have returned to the community to practice their careers" (ibid., p. 85).

In terms of family patterns, the data revealed a higher marriage rate and lower rates of separation and divorce among both male and female Jews in Providence than was the case for the total population of Providence as indicated in the 1960 United States census data (ibid., pp. 102–3), and that these rates "reflect the greater stability of Jewish marriages, the traditional Jewish value of family cohesion, and the emphasis on marriage and family life in the Jewish cultural heritage" (ibid., p. 104). This pattern is similar to that which Lenski found in his study of Detroit, where Jews had a lower divorce rate than did both Protestants and Catholics (Lenski, 1963, p. 219). However, when Goldstein and Goldscheider analyzed the Jewish divorce rates in Providence intergenerationally, they found it to be higher among those born in the United States than among the foreign born, and higher among Reform than among Conservative and Orthodox Jews (Goldstein and Goldscheider, 1968, p. 113). Also, in contrast to a number of studies at the time which indicated that in the general population the more educated have lower divorce

rates than the less educated, they found divorce and separation to be more common among more highly educated Jews.
They suggested that this may be attributed to the more highly
educated Jews being more secularized and acculturated and,
therefore, their rates tend to be more similar to those of non-
Jews (ibid., p. 112).

The patterns of Jewish intermarriage in Providence also
tended to be different from those reported elsewhere, especially Washington, D.C. Goldstein and Goldscheider suggest
several reasons for the relatively low intermarriage rates in
Providence: the community is relatively large, numbering
approximately 20,000 Jews; it is longstanding with strong
roots and a strong organizational structure; and it has a stable
population with a relatively high proportion of first- and
second-generation Americans. Even the third generation,
which has a higher rate of intermarriage than the other two
generations, has a lower rate than was found among third-
generation Jews in Washington, D.C. (ibid., p. 169). Furthermore, even though the rate of intermarriage in Providence did
show definite signs of increase among third-generation
American Jews, and among those who live in the suburbs,
those groups also have a higher proportion of conversions
among their intermarriages than among the other segments
of the Jewish population in the city (ibid., p. 170). Goldstein
and Goldscheider were not therefore seriously concerned
about the impact of intermarriage, especially because a large
proportion of the children of intermarriage were being raised
as Jews. They asserted too that Jewish education played a
considerable role in the decreasing probability of intermarriage, and that Jewish education among the younger members
of the third generation was on the rise. The extent to which
these researchers were accurate in their perception of the
impact of intermarriage, or the extent to which the patterns in
Providence were representative of the larger American Jewish
population, will be discussed in light of the contemporary
patterns of Jewish intermarriage in American society, in a
later chapter.

Analysis of the religiocultural patterns in Providence

indicated that although the traditional Jewish values had been abandoned by the third generation, complete structural assimilation did not result. While the third generation increasingly held memberships in and affiliations with non-Jewish organizations and associations, it also maintained its Jewish affiliations, especially in synagogue memberships, and it continued to retain those religious rituals with a family and/or social orientation. Thus, while there have been declines in Orthodoxy and in such rituals and practices as observance of traditional dietary and Sabbath regulations and synagogue attendance, Jewish values have been retained in the observance of the holidays of Chanukah and Passover, synagogue membership, and affiliation with one of the three branches of American Judaism, and there has been a strengthening of Jewish education (ibid., p. 229).

Goldstein and Goldscheider therefore are reluctant to interpret the patterns in Providence as indicative of religious decline, revival, or stability. To them, the patterns are manifestations of "an over-all development of new forms of Jewish identity and expression, with an emphasis on those aspects that are congruent with Americanization. Religious commitments are retained when they are functionally integrated within a secular context and where retention of Jewish identity is possible in a form that is expected and conditioned by the majority community" (pp. 229–30). Essentially, they concluded that, as Gans found in Park Forest and Sklare and Vosk found in Riverton, a new and uniquely *American* Judaism was being developed in the third generation. Although this new American Judaism was very different from traditional Judaism and was rather secularized, it did provide a sufficient basis for group cohesion and did not signify an impending total assimilation and absorption into the larger society to the point of identificational assimilation.

In contrast to the generally optimistic conclusion of the authors of the Riverton and Providence studies, and even to the slightly more cautious conclusions of Gans in his study of Park Forest, Sklare and Greenblum were rather skeptical of the long-range viability and holding power of this new brand of American Judaism after having completed an in-depth study of Jewish identity and continuity in an affluent suburb of a large midwestern American city, which they call "Lakeville" (Sklare and Greenblum, 1967). The data for the study were gathered during 1957 and 1958 by interviewing a sample of 432 of Lakeville's 8,000 or so Jewish population. In each case, one adult per household unit was interviewed. The total population in Lakeville was approximately 25,000.

The authors do not claim that the community was representative of the American Jewish community at that time, 1957, because that would have rendered the work out of date in a very short time. It would have minimized "certain important demographic and sociological trends in American Jewish life." Rather, they sought "to locate a place where the Jew who would be increasingly encountered in tomorrow's Jewish community was presently widely represented" (ibid., p. 7).

Socioeconomically, the Jews of Lakeville were highly affluent, virtually all professionals or technicians, managers, officials, or proprietors, or salespeople. None were clerks, operatives, service workers, or laborers. Not only were almost all in white-collar occupations, the majority worked for themselves: "61 percent are either self-employed or the owner or part-owner of a business" (ibid., p. 25). The median family income for the 1950s was relatively high, $18,112, and 85 percent or more had at least some college education. The majority of the respondents were of Eastern European descent; only about 20 percent were of German descent. The Germans tended to have higher levels of income and lower levels of education than the Eastern Europeans, and some Germans did manifest hostile attitudes toward the Eastern Europeans in Lakeville because of their status anxiety (ibid., p. 38). As a community, Lakeville Jews were younger, more highly educated, and more affluent than most of their non-Jewish neighbors.

Since historically religion has been a basic element in Jewish identity and because within the context of American pluralism Jews conceive of themselves as a religious group,

Sklare and Greenblum began their analysis by measuring the religiosity of Lakeville's Jews. Respondents were presented with a list of eleven basic rituals and observances of Jewish tradition and were asked to indicate how many they practiced and how many had been practiced in their parents' homes. The mean number observed by the respondents was 2.8, and only 10 percent observed seven or more. This was considerably lower than the rate of observance for their parents, where the mean was 5.2, and 41 percent observed seven or more of the rituals. The only two rituals practiced by a majority of the respondents were the lighting of candles on Chanukah and having a *seder*, the traditional festive meal on Passover. In an analysis based on the rate of observance of specific rituals by the respondents as compared to their parents, Sklare and Greenblum determine that the rate of retention in ritual observance is highest when a ritual "(1) is capable of effective redefinition in modern terms, (2) does not demand social isolation or the adoption of a unique life style, (3) accords with the religious culture of the larger community and provides a "Jewish" alternative when such is felt to be needed, (4) is centered on the child, and (5) is performed annually or infrequently" (p. 57).

If "the majority of Jewish homes in Lakeville lack a distinctive religious character" (Sklare and Greenblum, p. 60), the focus of "sacramentalism" perhaps has shifted from the home to the synagogue. And yet 74 percent of the respondents are irregular attendants at synagogue services; 13 percent do not attend at all. Only 3 percent attend Sabbath services every week or almost every week. As with the observance of rituals, there was a marked decline in synagogue attendance from parents to respondents.

The declines of "sacramentalism," observance of rituals, do not however mean that the Jews of Lakeville did not place much emphasis on the role of religion in their conception of themselves as Jews. Rather, there has been a shift from defining religion in terms of observance of rituals to defining religion in terms of belief in God, feeling religious, and moralism. On the basis of these criteria, only 27 percent of those who observed none of the rituals defined themselves as "not at all religious." Most of the completely nonobservant did consider themselves religious to some extent, 30 percent somewhat so, 27 percent moderately, and 16 percent very religious (ibid., p. 91).

Although neither ritual observance nor attendance at synagogue services are prerequisites to being a "good Jew," membership in a synagogue apparently is. Thus, more than 80 percent of the families in Lakeville are or were members of either the one Conservative or four Reform congregations in the community. Among those who were at least minimally observant, there was a greater affiliation when their children were in their school years. The totally nonobservant, on the other hand, were not affected by the ages of their children, and their rate of affiliation remained constant, at about 50 percent (ibid., p. 186).

Sklare and Greenblum then provide one of the first studies of the relationship between American Jews and the state of Israel. Even as early as the 1950s, the Jews of Lakeville professed a deep attachment to Israel. When asked how they would feel were Israel to be destroyed, 90 percent stated that they would feel a sense of loss, 65 percent "very deeply," and this sense of loss would relate primarily to their feelings of Jewish identity, rather than in terms of their humanitarianism. Also, among the 65 percent who would experience a "very deep" sense of loss, almost 80 percent believed that Israel has had a positive effect on the status and security of American Jews, while more than half of the 10 percent who said they would experience no sense of loss believed that Israel has had a harmful effect upon American Jews. From an evaluation of their opinions about various types of support and activity on behalf of Israel, however, a somewhat different picture emerges. More than 90 percent approve of raising money for Israel, but hardly any believe that American Jews should emigrate to Israel, nor do they encourage their children to do so. Less than 15 percent believe that giving financial support to Israel should take priority over local Jewish needs, and less than one-third approve of affiliation with a Zionist organization. And, 20 percent of those who state that they would feel a "very deep" sense of loss were Israel destroyed limit their favorable support of Israel to fund raising. Nor is the Jewish communal life in Lakeville permeated with an Israel orientation. Except for those who are affiliated with the Classical Reform congregation, the David Einhorn Temple, which still retains the anti-Zionist ideology of pre-World War II Reform, there is a clear correlation between synagogue attendance and support for Israel and between religious observance and support for Israel. Other kinds of Jewish organizational involvement, however, are inconsistently related to favorable support for Israel (Sklare and Greenblum, pp. 214–49).

In most other ways, such as their organizational involvements, friendship ties, desire to transmit Jewish identity to their children, and concern about intermarriage, the Jews of Lakeville are quite similar to those of Providence and Riverton. Lakeville's Jews have a sense of being comfortable with and feeling good about their Jewishness. But Sklare and Greenblum perceive that all is not as well in that Jewish community as its members think. The authors, in the final analysis, are skeptical of the ability of this community and, by implication, American Jewry as a whole, to transmit the kind of Jewishness they have developed to future generations. They conclude:

> Over the generations the families of the present-day Lakeville Jews have increased their financial resources, their general level of education, and their mastery of the environment many times over. While some have multiplied their Jewish resources, many have dissipated them to a lesser or greater degree. It is indisputable that the majority of Lakeville's Jews would like to conserve their Jewish resources. But unless an aggressive policy of growth is pursued the Jewish resources of a previous generation inevitably decline. The press of the general environment is so compelling that instead of being conserved the inheritance from earlier generations inevitably diminishes. In sum, the long-range viability of the pattern of Jewish adjustment characteristic of Lakeville's Jews is in question [p. 331].

The question raised by Sklare and Greenblum becomes even more significant when considered with the findings in the second volume of the Lakeville studies, dealing with Jewish-Gentile relationships, by Benjamin B. Ringer. Ringer documents the increasing status consciousness among Lakeville's Jews as they become culturally assimilated. The social and cultural lives that they lead clearly reflect their attempt to maintain a semblance of balance between pulls in opposite directions. They want to lead the life-styles of affluent non-Jews, but they want to lead them with other Jews. They desperately want to become firmly rooted in the value system of the larger society, but they also desperately want to maintain their distinctly Jewish identity. In their desire for social acceptance, there is great pressure to conform (Ringer, 1967, pp. 96–113).

The tensions between the desire on the one hand for assimilation and for maintenance of group identity on the other are clearly manifested in the leisure activities of the Lakeville Jews. Those who are most status conscious join country clubs, the facilities and activities of which reflect elite status, but these country clubs are Jewish. Even when they join nonsectarian organizations, as many do, those organizations often turn out to have mostly Jewish members (ibid., pp. 114–19). But they often deny that this is by design or desire. Thus half of those who live in neighborhoods in which Jews are the majority, for example, stated that they would prefer to live in mixed neighborhoods. They want to be able to live among non-Jews, see how they live, and acculturate even further; but even so they do not want to live in an entirely non-Jewish neighborhood (ibid., pp. 123–26).

The extent to which the Jewishness of Lakeville's Jews is "symbolic ethnicity," as Herbert Gans uses the concept (Gans, 1979) is apparent in the conflict over the issue of how and whether they should celebrate Christmas. Since no one is clear as to what Jewish identity means, some feel no qualms at having a Christmas tree in their homes, while others feel that having a tree goes beyond the limits of acceptable participation in non-Jewish life-styles (Ringer, pp. 132–34).

If the authors of the Lakeville studies were correct in their hypothesis that Lakeville represented American Jewry of the future, American Jewry as a whole predictably would be experiencing increasing tensions between the desires for assimilation and the maintenance of group identity, with the conception of the latter becoming more and more vague. In fact, Charles S. Liebman arrived at precisely this conclusion, based not only upon his reading of the Lakeville studies but also upon his analyses of "politics, religion, and family in American Jewish life" (Liebman, 1973). His basic thesis was that the "American Jew is torn between two sets of values— those of integration and acceptance into American society and those of Jewish group survival. These values appear . . . to be incompatible. But most American Jews do not view them in this way" (ibid., p. vii).

Liebman was so convinced that these values were incompatible and that integration would ultimately be victorious over group survival that he felt that he and his family had no Jewish future in American society, and they emigrated to Israel. His personal decisions aside, his basic thesis was based upon many developments that have been discussed in this chapter and the preceding, and upon the emergence of a phenomenon that became pronounced during the period of the third generation, namely, the political liberalism of American Jews.

Numerous studies appeared during the 1950s and 1960s which demonstrated conclusively that American Jews supported liberal and left policies, parties, and candidates in a manner highly disproportionate to their numbers and very uncharacteristic of their social class. The political liberalism of American Jews manifested itself on both domestic and foreign policy issues and could not be explained in terms of vested economic interests because it manifested itself even when the issues were not in the economic interest of American Jews. Between the mid-1950s and late 1960s three major theories or approaches were presented to explain the political liberalism of American Jews, and Liebman has systematically and critically analyzed each of them.

Lawrence Fuchs has argued that Jewish political liberalism has its roots in specific intrinsic Jewish values: *Torah* learning; *zedakah*, charity and philanthropy, which are based upon a religious ideology of communal as well as individual responsibility for the welfare of others; and "life's pleasures," or nonasceticism. Based on a study of the culture consciousness of Jewish youth by Werner J. Cahnman (1952) and the growing literature on American Jewish culture, Fuchs suggested that American Jews have selected these three Jewish values as their highest priorities, and that the American Jewish subculture is unique in the degree to which it manifests an intense allegiance to them. Translated politically, the value of *zedakah*, Fuchs maintains, led American Jews to enthusiastically support President Franklin D. Roosevelt's New Deal policies because they entailed not sympathy for the poor and the downtrodden but their political rights. To Fuchs, American Jews defined *zedakah* as a redistribution of power and they saw Roosevelt as the advocate of the political program through which that would be accomplished. The Jewish value of *Torah*, manifested in the American Jewish love of learning and intellectuality, led to the strong American Jewish support for Roosevelt's "brain trust," social planning, and civil liberties which are a prerequisite for intellectual independence. Finally, the nonasceticism of Jews meant that they were more concerned with creating a better world on this earth, rather than waiting for either Divine intervention or a better life in the world to come (Fuchs, 1956, pp. 177–91). The combination of these three values helped to create the unique American Jewish political style, basically that of political liberalism.

Liebman refutes Fuch's theory indirectly, on several grounds. He argues that since Jewish religious values are not unambiguously liberal and one can find conservative as well as liberal, particularistic as well as universalistic, anti-intellectual as well as intellectual tendencies within Judaism, the question remains why American Jews choose the values that support their liberalism rather than their conservatism. Moreover, if Fuchs were correct, we would expect to find those Jews who are manifestly more religious to be more politically liberal than those who are less religious. Various studies indicate, however, that quite the opposite is true (Liebman, 1973, pp. 140–44). Liebman's own study of Jews in the

Washington Heights section of Manhattan, for example, "found that Jews who classified themselves as Orthodox were consistently less liberal than those who classified themselves as non-Orthodox on all measures except attitudes toward Negroes" (ibid., p. 144).

Further evidence in support of Liebman's arguments comes from a major study of American Jewish academics by Seymour Martin Lipset and Everett Carl Ladd, Jr. Lipset and Ladd analyzed the responses to interviews of more than 5,000 Jewish academics in 1969, and found, among many other things, that those professors, born of Jewish parents, who defined their own religious status as "none" had the greatest likelihood of defining themselves as "Left." Among those who identified themselves as "Jewish," there was an inverse relationship between frequency of synagogue attendance and the likelihood of defining oneself as "Left"; the least frequent attenders at synagogue services were more likely to define themselves as "Left," while the more frequent attenders were less likely to do so. Even the more frequent attenders, however, were almost twice as likely to define themselves as "Left" (4 percent) that to define themselves as "Strongly Conservative" (2.2 percent). The majority even of the more frequent synagogue attenders (56.4 percent) defined themselves as "Liberal" (Lipset and Ladd, 1971, p. 121).

A second explanation of Jewish liberalism is that it is rooted in the status inconsistency of American Jews. The phenomenon of status inconsistency and one of its effects upon economically well-to-do members of the second-generation community have been discussed above at the end of Chapter 2. Lenski suggests another reaction directly related to the political liberalism of American Jews in the third generation. Studies comparing the voting patterns of minority and dominant group members, with class held constant (Lipset, 1963, pp. 255–56), show that middle- and upper-middle class minorities, because they occupy inconsistent statuses, "are more likely to support liberal and radical movements designed to alter the political status quo," which supports the social order in which they experience status inconsistency and its

stresses, "than are persons of consistent status" (Lenski, 1966, p. 88). With respect to the liberal voting patterns of American Jews in particular, Lipset suggests that they may be explained "as flowing from their inferior status position [social discrimination] rather than from elements inherent in their religious creed" (Lipset, 1963, p. 256).

Liebman argues that while the theory of status inconsistency may explain why some American Jews turn to the radical left, it does not explain the much more prevalent attraction of Jews to parties of the liberal left of center (Liebman, 1973, p. 145). Moreover, he cites a study by Edgar Litt which shows that those Jews who most experienced ethnic subordination held the least liberal attitudes, were "least likely to be tolerant of political non-conformists and altruistic toward other deprived groups" (Litt, 1961, p. 280). A later study by Olsen and Tully casts doubts on any significant relationship between status inconsistency and desire for political change. Their analysis of data from the 1967-68 Indianapolis Area Project found a negligible relationship between status inconsistency and desire for political change and, where such a relationship did exist, it was "in the opposite direction from that predicted—status consistent people were more active than inconsistents" (Olsen and Tully, 1972, p. 571).

The third major theory of Jewish liberalism is that it is rooted in the unique historical condition of Jews in Europe after the French Revolution and emancipation. According to Werner Cohn, the French Revolution entailed a division of European politics in which the parties of the left argued for citizenship based solely upon nationhood, regardless of religious affiliation, whereas the parties of the right staunchly defended the notion that citizenship and the state must be Christian. Jews were naturally attracted to the left, therefore, but only the moderate left, because the radical left, which clung to its revolutionary ideology and demanded total commitment to it, was as threatening to the Jewish self-definition as were the parties of the right. Since then, Cohn maintains, Jews have remained liberal left in their politics, in the United States as well, because of their insecurity about the Gentile environment (Cohn, 1958, pp. 614–26).

Although Liebman believes that this theory has much merit, he finds a number of weaknesses in it as well. With respect to American Jewish political behavior in particular, Liebman points to Cohn's failure to account for variations among Jews. New York's Orthodox Yiddish press, for example, did not support either the Democratic or Socialist parties at the turn of the century; it supported the Republican party. Nor does Cohn's theory explain why Jews wanted emancipation, especially since it was a threat to traditional religious and communal values. Also, Liebman argues, Cohn does not account for Jewish liberalism that preceded their attraction to the parties of the left (Liebman, 1973, p. 147).

Liebman himself explains Jewish liberalism, which includes much more than merely voting for liberal issues and candidates and involves such enlightenment notions as universal humanism and cosmopolitanism, as an attempt to "Judaize" society, to make the rest of society experience the same alienation to which Jews have been subjected.

> But this Judaization does not stem from intrinsic Jewish values. Of course, cosmopolitanism, universalism, liberalism, and even socialism can be found in traditional Judaism. But so can ethnic particularism, nationalism, and political conservatism. The modern Jew chooses that part of the tradition which is compatible with his special interests. He raises these interests to the level of ideology and presses them upon society in universalistic terms. Thus, the Jew fights for separation of church and state in the name of a secular ideal, not in the name of a Jewish ideal. From a parochial traditional Jewish point of view, one must be blind not to see the danger of secularization to Judaism. But the Judaization of society is not the quest to universalize Jewish values; it is the desire to impose the Jewish condition of estrangement upon society [Liebman, 1973, p. 158].

Liebman concludes with a bleak prognosis for the future of American Jewish liberalism because of its dependence on the continued state of Jewish estrangement, which in turn is dependent on the nature of Jewish commitment and the ability of Jews to redefine Judaism, the Jews' desire for survival, the terms by which non-Jews will accept Jews, and the degree to which America reflects its Christian experience (ibid., p. 159).

One problem with Liebman's prognosis, as with those of others (compare Dawidowicz and Goldstein, 1963), is the assumption that liberalism is related to estrangement and insecurity. If that in fact were the case, we should have found a higher degree of liberalism among those who are most estranged. Yet Liebman himself cites evidence to the contrary. Also, the Olsen and Tully study does not bear that out.

While a satisfactory explanation of American Jewish political liberalism, especially from the Depression until the 1970s, may still elude us, virtually all those who sought to explain it foresaw its decline because they foresaw the continued assimilation of American Jewry into American society and culture and the increasing detachment of American Jews from their Jewish group identification. The politics of American Jews in the 1970s and 1980s will be analyzed in a later chapter. None of the observers of American Jewry in the mid-1960s predicted, however, nor could they have, a whole series of events that had dramatic impact upon Jewish identity and identification during the 1960s and early 1970s. It is to these events and their impact upon the fourth-generation community that we now turn.

5. The Pendulum Shifts, 1965–1975

American Jews were rather comfortable with themselves and their position in American society during the latter half of the 1950s and the early 1960s. Whatever misgivings individual American Jews may have entertained about the decline in the quality and intensity of Judaism in the third-generation community, the group and its constituent organizations appeared convinced that the adoption and internalization of American norms and values and the removal of all barriers to structural assimilation were the keys to guaranteeing the continued well-being of America's Jews. Perceiving that they had successfully integrated into the "triple melting pot" (Kennedy, 1944, 1952; Herberg, 1960), American Jews and the organizations became active in reforming and perfecting American society, especially through the dismantling of the institutionalized segregation that had perpetuated the political and social disenfranchisement of blacks and other deprived minorities for so long. In contrast to the impressions of David Boroff—whose views are fairly typical of many Jewish intellectual critics—that American Jews were growing more conservative because "as the doors of American society swing open hospitably to talented Jews, the impulse to castigate and criticize becomes attenuated" (Boroff, 1961, p. 90), American Jews remained politically liberal to left and they became increasingly involved in organizations actively engaged in promoting social and political change. Nor did the events of the 1960s support Boroff's prediction that "as Jews

increasingly become part of the 'Establishment,' intellectual teenagers will merely see themselves as apprentices rather than critics" (ibid. p. 90).

To assign a specific date to the founding of the New Left is difficult because it never was a specific body; but its origins are in the issuance of the Port Huron Statement in June 1962, a statement seen as the guiding principles and handbook for radical action of the Students for a Democratic Society, and SDS was to become the core group within the movement. While most Jewish students were neither leaders nor members of New Left organizations, Jews did play a very significant role in the leadership and membership of those organizations. Arthur Liebman has estimated that during the first half of the 1960s the number of Jews in SDS ranged from 30 to 50 percent (Liebman, 1979, p. 67). Likewise, "a majority of the leadership of the Free Speech Movement in Berkeley in 1964 was Jewish, and it was Jewish students within the student body at Berkeley who gave the FSM its strongest base of support" (ibid., p. 68; see also Feuer, 1969, p. 423; Somers, 1965, p. 548).

Coinciding with and giving purpose to the student organizations of the New Left were the "long hot summers"— the series of race riots, accompanied by looting and violence, which erupted in many American urban centers during the 1960s. The New Left immediately took up the cause of the oppressed black population, especially since many early founders of the movement had been involved in the civil rights cause as nonviolent protesters in the South during the late 1950s and early 1960s. The civil rights and black protest movements affected Jews in several ways. Jews were overwhelmingly liberal and played a significant role in the movement to eradicate the institutionalized injustices under which blacks had been economically, politically, and socially deprived for so long. As Liebman points out, "in the summer of 1961 Jews made up two-thirds of the white Freedom Riders that traveled into the South to desegregate interstate transportation. Three years later Jews comprised from one-third to one-half of the Mississippi Summer volunteers. Two of the white youths martyred during this experience, Michael Schwerner and Andrew Goodman, were Jews" (Liebman, 1979, p. 68).

Adult Jews, too, played important roles in civil rights organizations, some as national leaders, others as local leaders, and many as members. For a large segment of the American Jewish population, as well as for many of its organizations, civil rights was an issue, if not *the* issue, of highest priority.

The racial situation and its ramifications, on the other hand, began to affect American Jews in ways that began to erode the Jewish-black alliance that had existed until the middle of the 1960s. The summer of 1964 witnessed violent racial disturbances in many American cities. Although virtually all disturbances were limited to the black ghettos of the cities, many Jews were affected, and disproportionally so among non-blacks because invariably these slums had previously been Jewish neighborhoods and many Jewish business people continued their businesses even after the neighborhoods had become black. Despite the findings of several surveys which minimized black anti-Semitism as a factor in the disproportionate looting and destruction of Jewish businesses (e.g., Marx, 1967), many Jews did perceive a definite and threatening increase in black anti-Semitism. Also, regardless of motivation and intent, the Jews were directly and negatively affected.

As race relations became more turbulent, the alliance between Jews and blacks became increasingly precarious. Then in July 1966 Stokley Carmichael, leader of the Student Nonviolent Coordinating Committee (SNCC), issued a call for "Black Power." His intentions and the subsequent development of this slogan aside (Carmichael, 1966; Carmichael and Hamilton, 1967), many took it to mean that only blacks could participate in the movement for black "liberation in America." In cities around the country Jews felt rejected by a movement to which they had devoted so much of themselves. Activists that they were, some Jews decided that they would

now direct their energies toward overtly Jewish causes, since they were no longer welcome in civil rights organizations.

With the escalation of the Vietnam War, following the Gulf of Tonkin Resolution in August 1964, the New Left gained wider respectability and new recruits. As it became more self-confident, the movement increasingly escalated the level of its tactics and objectives. Leaving peaceful resistance and nonviolent change behind, it rapidly espoused and engaged in militance, violence, and terrorism under a revolutionary banner. Only a minority, of course, espoused and engaged in these objectives and activities, but it was a vocal minority, prepared to use "any means necessary," both within and without the movement, to achieve its ends, and the activities and objectives of this minority symbolized the New Left in the eyes of the larger American public. American adults, including Jews, became increasingly wary and fearful of the New Left precisely at the time when the movement itself was in the process of disintegration, the result of its lack of a coherent ideological framework, structure, and leadership.

The precise reasons why Jewish youth were disproportionally involved with the New Left have not been any more satisfactorily explained than was the more general phenomenon of Jewish political liberalism. Two of the more prominent efforts at explaining the radicalism of American Jewish youth during the 1960s, however, are worthy of discussion especially because of their vastly different evaluations of the significance of this phenomenon. To supply some background, two most notable explanations of the New Left in general will be discussed.

On the basis of numerous surveys of student activists which he conducted, Richard Flacks found that the student activists tended "to have above average academic records. . . . Student protestors come from families with high income and occupational status; they tend to be most prevalent at the top schools; they have above average aptitude for academic work, and perform at above average levels"

(Flacks, 1970, p. 345). Their socioeconomic backgrounds are particularly significant, Flacks argues, and he summarizes them as follows:

> Activists are disproportionately the sons and daughters of highly educated parents; in a large proportion of cases, their parents have advanced graduate and professional degrees; a very high percentage of the activists' mothers are college graduates; the parents tend to be in occupations for which higher education is a central prerequisite: professions, education, social service, public service, the arts; . . . family interests—as they are expressed in recreation, or in dinner-table conversation, or in formal interviews—tend to be intellectual and "cultural" and relatively highbrow; these are families in which books were read, discussed, and taken seriously, in which family outings involved museums and concert-halls rather than ball-parks and movies, etc. They were families in which "values" were taken seriously—conventional religion and morality were treated with considerable skepticism, while at the same time strong emphasis was placed on leading a principled, socially useful, morally consistent life. They were, finally, families in which education was regarded with considerable reverence and valued for its own sake, rather than in utilitarian terms [ibid., p. 346].

The parents of the protestors thus were a unique part of the middle class. They were part of its "intellectual" or "humanist" subculture. Among the distinctive characteristics of this subculture were:

1. "a strong commitment to intellectuality and "culture" and a considerable disdain for mass culture and mass leisure. Their children were expected to be intellectually aware and serious, artistically creative or at least appreciative, serious about education and self-development."

2. The "parents were unusual in their political awareness and their political liberalism."

3. They "were overtly skeptical about conventional middle-class values, life-styles, and religious orientations."

4. They "tended to express those values implicitly through the structure of the family and the styles of child rearing which they adopted; . . . they rather consciously organized family life to

support anti-authoritarian and self-assertive impulses on the part of their children and rather clearly instructed them in attitudes favoring skepticism toward authority, egalitarianism and personal autonomy" (ibid., pp. 347–48).

The roots of student activism are to be found, according to Flacks, in this humanist subculture and its norms and values: "This new humanist youth culture embodies norms concerning sex-role behavior, worthwhile activity, and personal style which are quite opposed to those which prevail in conventional adolescent society; it expresses values which seem quite subversive of conventional middle-class aspirations, and an attitude toward adult authority which is clearly defiant. The American student movement is an expression of that new youth culture" (ibid., p. 348).

This approach, considers that the activism of the students, to the extent that it was rebellion, was not rebellion against their own parents but against the conventional middle-class society, the "Establishment." With respect to their parents, on the contrary, they were acting upon precisely what the parents had taught them.

In contrast to this view, Lewis A. Feuer argues that the student movement was a special type of social movement, that it was a manifestation of a "conflict of generations." He defines the student movement as "a combination of students inspired by aims which they try to explicate in a political ideology, and moved by an emotional rebellion in which there is always present a disillusionment with and rejection of the values of the older generation; moreover, the members of a student movement have the conviction that their generation has a special historical mission to fulfill where the older generation, other elites, and other classes have failed" (Feuer, 1965, p. 11).

Feuer maintains that student movements arise in a society characterized by "gerontocracy"—that is, where the older generation disproportionally possesses the political and economic power—and social status, if there is a sudden "deauthorization" of the older generation in that society. When such "de-authorization" occurs, usually as the result of dramatic events, the youth will be inspired by a spirit of "juvenocracy" and a desire for "filiarchy" to wrest power from their elders. Even as the New Left attempted to present itself as a strong social force, Feuer maintains that it was, as it ultimately showed itself to be, a movement based essentially upon abnormal psychological motivations: "The psychological origin of student movements puts its impress on both their choice of political means and underlying ends. Wherever a set of alternative possible routes toward achieving a given end presents itself, a student movement will usually tend to choose the one which involves a higher measure of violence or humiliation directed against the older generation" (ibid., p. 531).

Thus to Feuer, in contrast to Flacks, it was not in the social structural conditions of American society but in the psyches of the activists themselves that the "conflict of generations" was rooted. (Certain similarities however exist between the contrasting structural and psychological-cultural explanations of Flacks and Feuer and the contrasting structural and cultural explanations of the persistence of poverty in American society during the 1960s [Waxman, 1977a]).

As for the disproportional Jewish participation in student activism, likewise we find Nathan Glazer providing a structural explanation and Feuer arguing for a much more psychological one. According to Glazer, "the fact that so many of our present Jewish students are children of radicals of the Thirties explains why the students are radical today" (Glazer, 1969, p. 126). Basing his arguments on the research of Flacks and Kenneth Keniston, he suggests that

> the war between the generations is considerably muted in just those families in which the parents *have* been liberal and radical. . . . When the parents are liberal or radical or ex-radical, there is no war between the generations. And almost all Jewish parents are at least *liberal* in political outlook. . . . These parents support, with some reservations, their children's activism. Documentation on the precise degree of such support is sparse. But the children, at least, expect it. They assume they will not be cut off without a

cent. Their bail money will be paid. Their legal costs will be paid. Their tuition and living costs will be paid—if not by their own parents, by *other* highly liberal and socialist parents, in large numbers Jewish. Mark Rudd's parents spoke proudly of him to the press, though as far as one can tell from the accounts they are only liberals, as one would expect of a well-to-do suburban Jewish couple, and not radicals. Just as the parents feel warmly and positively about their children, even if they think they somewhat go too far, so do the children feel warmly and positively about their parents, even if they feel they have not gone far enough [ibid.].

To Feuer, on the other hand, the Jewish student activists were not so much in conflict with the larger conventional middle-class society as they were in revolt against the authority and, especially, the passivity of their very own parents.

The contemporary Jewish student of liberal parents was in strange revolt against them and their heritage, even as the liberal fathers had revolted against their immigrant grandfathers. In the case of Jews in the student movement, there was no return of the third generation to the heritage of the first; Marcus Hansen's law of the immigrant generations did not hold. For the Jewish generations, it was always a negation of the negation. The basis of the revolt was always oddly much the same, and had little to do with economics. In previous generations Jewish students felt ashamed that their often cultureless parents were a persecuted people, always passive, always suffering, telling horrid stories of the indignities of pogroms. Their fathers seemed lacking in manliness. Their misfortunes lacked the heroic cast, and were therefore devoid of the nobility of tragedy. When a new generation after the Second World War heard of Jews, it was as victims, again almost always passive, of the Nazi holocaust, of those who had had torn from them the last shreds of human dignity as they were led in queues to abattoirs. The Jewish students of successive generations felt that their parents—orthodox, liberal, religious, agnostic—somehow shared in the psychology of passive acquiescence, that as the persecuted, they had been virtually deprived of their manhood, emasculated. Books, plays, films such as the *Diary of Anne Frank* or *The Deputy* probably made the Jewish would-be student activist wish all the more to repress his Jewish origins. The elder generation, for all its anti-Nazism, somehow shared in the collective guilt; it had not acted forthrightly, dramatically, to prevent such things from taking place. Thus the Jewish activist student tried to obliterate his Jewish derivation. Nevertheless, he felt he had been conceived in a world which enveloped him with injustice. The Jews were a chosen people, in that the world had chosen them for genocide and pogroms. And the Jewish student activist felt called upon to protest, without, however, drawing attention to the fact that he was a Jew—to protest against racial hatred, genocide, culturocide, while repressing at the same time the fact that he came from a people which had experienced all these demonic forces. . . . Thus, the basic reason for the continued high involvement of Jewish students in the small American student movement has been the successive de-authorization of the older generation by successive waves and forms of historical anti-Semitism. It was not in their case a revolt against middle-class values, any more than the earlier movement of City College men had been a revolt against their fathers' proletarian situation. What was involved was the peculiar de-authorization of a generation associated with the passive recipience of persecution (Feuer, pp. 429-30).

Whatever the correct interpretation may be, as the violence and militancy of the New Left grew, the American Jewish community became increasingly wary of the movement and concerned about the Jewish role in it. But the American Jewish community probably would not have denounced it so rapidly and forcefully had not the traumatic events of the spring and summer of 1967 taken place.

The Six-Day War between Israel and her Arab neighbors had a completely unanticipated and unpredicated impact upon American Jews. Many had been spurred to various activities on Israel's behalf during the three weeks preceding the actual outbreak of fighting, when President Nasser of Egypt had closed the Straits of Tiran to ships carrying cargo to and from Israel and when various Arab spokesmen vowed to battle with Israel and drive Israel into the sea. Then on Monday morning, June 5, the news came that war had actually broken out and that aircraft from Egypt, Jordan, Syria, and Iraq had bombed Israel; Radio Cairo reported that Tel Aviv was in flames and that Haifa's oil refinery had been destroyed, and virtually every Arab country proclaimed war on Israel. There was only silence from the Israeli government and American Jewry was panic stricken. Deep-seated but hitherto dormant attachments to Israel were awakened, and there was acute fear of another Holocaust. Whatever their previous sentiments concerning Israel, American Jewry was overwhelmingly supportive of Israel in the Six-Day War. Even the anti-Zionist Jewish organization, the American Council for Judaism, felt that its director, Dr. Elmer Berger, had gone too far in assisting in the speechwriting for the Syrian ambassador to the United Nations during the Security Council deliberations and in issuing public statements critical of Israel. One Lakeville resident, "a long-time member" of the Council, "wrote Berger a long and blistering letter," and later told Marshall Sklare: "What Berger said was right but it was bad timing. I hate negativism. If he couldn't say anything good about Israel, why couldn't he have kept his big yap shut" (Sklare, 1968, p. 6). As a result of the crisis and war, even this individual, who retained his philosophical opposition to Zionism, considered himself pro-Israel. He was now in the interesting position of being "pro-Israel and anti-Zionist." The overwhelming majority of American Jews, who did not share this individual's philosophical struggles with the notion of Zionism, "were unambiguously pro-Israel. There was no doubt in their minds as to which side was right" (ibid.). Obviously American governmental policy and public opinion being clearly supportive of Israel's position made it relatively easy for American Jews to be pro-Israel. Nevertheless the strength and intensity of the American Jewish commitment to Israel was unexpected. From the very onset of the crisis in May,

> American Jews did not wait for organizational directives. Even as they sat glued to radios and TVs or put in long-distance calls to friends in Israel, they fretted over what they could do. They organized meetings on the synagogue or neighborhood level, and they donated food, blood, and medical supplies. Doctors and teachers volunteered to serve if Israel called upon them. On campuses special lectures and "teach-ins" were held as the traditionally alienated intellectuals stood up and were counted. The attendance at synagogue services soared, equaling the High Holy Day mark, as Jews congregated to pray for Israel's survival.
> The funds poured in, surpassing all previous campaigns.

Organizations called a moratorium on their usual money-raising drives, and all concentrated on the Israel Emergency Fund run by the United Jewish Appeal. Many communities launched their own campaigns even before they were approached. Illustrations abound on the magnitude and even sacrificial elements of the campaign. . . . The results amazed the professional fund-raisers and caused a log-jam in tabulating the receipts. By the end of the war [i.e., less than a month's time] over $100,000,000 was raised, and the figure climbed to $180,000,000 before the campaign was closed [Cohen 1975, pp. 138–39].

The Six-Day War dramatically altered the self-conceptions of American Jews as Jews, both individually and collectively. Both the despair during the crisis and the euphoria that followed Israel's swift victory evoked a spirit of unity with Israel and a sense of commonality among American Jews which had not been previously evident. The result, was a slowing in the assimilatory trend that had been evident during the eras of the first three generations of Eastern European Jewry in the United States. The threat to Israel aroused the fear of another Holocaust in American Jewry and awakened a strong desire for survival within that community. Israel's victory was perceived as a Jewish victory and reenforced the determination to survive. That survival could not be assured by will alone, of course. The leadership of American Jewry and Israel, as we shall see later, undertook major efforts to retain the strong sense of unity which had been sparked by the war. As Arthur Hertzberg observed, the crisis and war "united those with deep Jewish commitments as they have never been united before, and it has evoked such commitments in many Jews who previously seemed untouched by them. Very large numbers of American Jews now feel their Jewish identity more intensely than they have for at least a generation" (Hertzberg, 1967, p. 72).

Just two months after the war, the New Politics Convention was convened in Chicago. Although many aspired that this gathering would unite the variety of black and white liberal-left and radical groups and create a new, leftist political party, the convention was taken over by a group of black militants who made no secret of their contempt for whites in general and the "imperialistic Zionists" in particular. Rather than promoting unity, the convention turned into a "public spectacle" which did "not deserve to be taken seriously by anyone" as even SDS's John Maher, Jr., proclaimed (*Ramparts*, 1967, p. 108).

It was taken seriously by many Jews, however. Already by 1965 many liberal intellectual Jews had become wary of the New Left. *Commentary* magazine, one of the most prestigious liberal intellectual publications in the country and sponsored by the American Jewish Committee, published a number of critiques of the new radicalism by the magazine's editor, Norman Podhoretz, and such well-known social critics as Nathan Glazer, Robert A. Nisbet, and Dennis Wrong. After the New Politics debacle of August 1967, *Commentary* became the strongest critic of the New Left within the intellectual community in the United States.

The liberal Jewish reaction was, perhaps, to be expected. Even more significant, possibly, was the reaction of many radical Jews who defected from the New Left because of the overtly anti-Zionist resolutions adopted at the National Conference on New Politics and because of the explicitly anti-Zionist and implicitly anti-Semitic pronouncements that were increasingly heard from leaders of the Black Panthers. Some of these Jewish radicals had been products of the socialist Zionist youth movements; some had been reared in homes that espoused Yiddish secular socialism; others were former members of Conservative Judaism's youth movement—United Synagogue Youth (USY)—and had attended USY's Camp Ramah which, while being structurally upper-middle class, placed great emphasis on the value of community and tended toward a counter-culture position; and still others had had intensive formal Jewish education on the elementary, day school level, but were not marginal individuals because they were strongly influenced also by the larger American youth culture. For many, the Six-Day War and their alienation from the New Left precipitated a heightened sense of Jewishness and the redirection of their activism to Jewish concerns and issues, especially those of Israel, Soviet Jewry, the quality of leadership in American Jewish organizational life, and Jewish culture and community (Porter and Dreier, 1973, pp. xxix–xxxii; Dreier and Porter, 1975). The activism of the young Jews, in many instances, forced the Jewish communal leadership to recognize the consequences of its ambivalence (see above, end of Chapter 4) and to adopt more explicitly survivalist stances.

The groundwork for the more conscious and explicit survivalism of the American Jewish communal leadership was laid, ironically, by the spokesmen for black nationalism. The blacks were the first to openly and loudly reject the ideology of the melting pot and argue instead for cultural pluralism. Although the liberal Jewish philosopher, Horace M. Kallen, had expounded the social philosophy of cultural pluralism years earlier (Kallen, 1924, 1956), it was not publicly adopted as a political ideology until black nationalists espoused the cause. Only then did white ethnic groups, including Jews, begin to publicly assert their own ethnicity and group interests. This was evident on the campuses of colleges and universities across the country. Until the mid-1960s, there were very few programs in Jewish studies in secular universities. For the most part, where courses of Jewish content were taught, they were offered by departments of languages, religion, or Near East history. It was, to a large degree, in reaction to the establishment of black studies programs that Jewish studies programs were introduced at many colleges and universities during the very late 1960s and the 1970s. The new ideology of pluralism provided the legitimacy and the heightened religio-ethnic consciousness that generated the introduction of these programs which were but one manifestation of the broader survivalist trend.

A further contributor to the growing survivalist stance of the organized American Jewish community was the founding, in the spring of 1968, of the Jewish Defense League. Following a discussion of the problems facing Jews in New York among Meir Kahane, Bertram Zweibon, and Morton Dolinsky, who met one Sabbath afternoon in May 1968 in their changing neighborhood in Laurelton, Queens, the three decided to form a new organization. Kahane, who was a writer for *The Jewish Press*, a relatively new Anglo-Jewish weekly which was gaining wide circulation among Orthodox and strongly ethnic Jews, placed an ad in that paper calling upon Jews who care about Jewish survival to join the new Jewish Defense Corps (later, League). The paper gave very wide and favorable coverage to the new group, and the leaders of JDL grew ever more bold and creative in gaining publicity for the organization. Created to protect Jewish interests through the courts, the league also engaged in patrolling Jewish neighborhoods and protecting poor and elderly Jews who remained in previously Jewish, now black neighborhoods because they were too poor and/or tired to relocate. But Kahane also had a flair for notoriety, and whatever he did appeared designed to antagonize not only his overt, immediate targets—invariably black militants—but also the larger liberal public and especially the leadership and membership of the organized Jewish community. The New York City Board of Education experiment with community control and the teachers' strike in the fall of 1968 almost divided the entire city along racial lines and, particularly, along black-Jewish lines (Mayer, 1969), and the JDL emerged as a force to be reckoned with. Subsequently, Kahane and the JDL went on to what they perceived to be world Jewish issues, such as Israel, Arab terrorism, and the plight of Soviet Jewry. In 1974, after having moved to Israel and lost an election to Israel's parliament, Kahane resigned from the JDL and, although he subsequently tried to regain control of the organization, neither he nor it was able to maintain the movement and momentum that had been achieved earlier (Russ, 1981).

The significance of the Jewish Defense League, in terms of the thesis of this chapter, was that in its initial stages it brazenly highlighted issues of great concern to many Jews in their local neighborhoods, such as safety and the excesses of black militancy. The national Jewish organizations, for a variety of reasons, were unaware of the intensity of these concerns, and it took the escapades of the JDL to bring the organizations back in touch with a significant segment of the grass roots. As Haskell Lazere, director of the New York City chapter of the American Jewish Committee, states:

> Jewish agencies have lost touch with the rank and file of the Jewish community. . . . Jewish agencies have shown a willingness to accommodate and adjust to the needs of others. . . . But the Jewish Establishment has been dealing with issues at top levels, not in the neighborhoods or the streets. Jewish leadership deals with the Wilkinses, the Youngs, and the Rustins . . . while the people in the neighborhoods, especially the transitional ones, are confronted daily with extremists. . . . What's coming through to those attracted by JDL is that we care about others more than we care about our own. . . . Without turning away from the broader community—locally or nationally—we have to turn our attention inward to the troubled neighborhood level. We have to know what goes on in neighborhoods most of us don't live in. . . . While we are pushing for equity capital for black businessmen, we should simultaneously be seeking or creating relocation equity for Jewish businessmen who will go under unless it is forthcoming. . . . My point of reference is that the approach should stem from Jewish concern for themselves, not Jewish concern for others (quoted in Russ, p. 23).

Although the majority of American Jewry, even those in the volatile neighborhoods, disapproved of many of the tactics of the JDL, there was a growing sense that if it had not been for Kahane and his group, the concerns might never have received attention. Likewise the plight of Soviet Jewry became a priority on the Jewish communal agenda owing in no small measure to the tactics of the JDL and other militants. And the plight of the Jewish poor in many American cities might never have reached communal attention had it not been for the few critics who were willing to risk challenging the establishment (Levine and Hochbaum, 1974; Waxman 1979a). The issue of institutional and communal inertia will be discussed later. For the present discussion, the militancy of the minority, such as the JDL and others, forced the national Jewish organizations to realign their priorities in accordance with the concerns of local Jews.

In the third-generation community, it will be recalled,

communal life was not permeated with an Israel orientation
(above, chapter 4). The Six-Day War and its aftermath,
however, put Israel in the spotlight of American Jewish
communal life to the point where at times it appeared to be the
sole focus of the organized community. The Israel orientation
is readily apparent, for example, in the list of National Jewish
Organizations which appears in the annual edition of the
American Jewish Year Book, the almanac of American Jewry
published by the American Jewish Committee and the Jewish
Publication Society of America. More than thirty of the
largest and most active national Jewish organizations are
affiliated with the Conference of Presidents of Major Jewish
Organizations, for which Zionist and pro-Israel activity is the
major emphasis. The Conference of Presidents is housed at
the American headquarters of the Jewish Agency for Israel
and the World Zionist Organization in New York City, and
one of its first presidents was the founder and first president
of the American Zionist Federation also. Since 1967, as Elazar
points out, "insuring the survival of Israel has become the
heart of the defense function of the American Jewish community. Even the community-relations agencies are now
spending a high proportion of their time and resources trying
to increase support for Israel in the United States. As a result,
the most important decision-makers in the community are
those who are related to the defense of Israel, namely the
federation and UJA leadership, voluntary and professional"
(Elazar, 1974, pp. 103–4).

Another indication of the central role of Israel in
American Jewish communal life since 1967 is provided by
Yakir Eventov and Cvi Rotem, two Israeli observers of the
American Jewish communal scene:

American Jews showed themselves more willing and ready to be
identified as Jews, to affiliate with Jewish organizations and
institutions, and to send their children to Jewish schools as a result
of their ties with Israel. Israel occupies an important place in
synagogue activities, sermons, and various religious celebrations,
and Israel's Independence Day assumes an important place in the
American Jewish calendar. The Israel flag is frequently displayed

in synagogues and community centers. In many synagogues prayers for the welfare of the State of Israel and world Jewry are recited on Sabbaths and holidays following that for the welfare of the United States. Both the Conservative and Reform branches attempt to establish themselves in Israel through rabbinical schools and various educational programs.

Another impact of Israel has been the use of the Hebrew language in contrast to the decline of Yiddish. Hebrew songs and Israel folk dances have become American Jewish popular culture: at weddings, bar mitzvot, and on many college campuses. Jewish art, which traditionally concentrated on East European themes, expanded to include Israel symbols; Israel crafts find a wide market among American Jews. Fiction on Israel life increases rapidly and an extensive periodical literature is directed from Israel institutions toward American Jewry [*Encyclopedia Judaica*, 1971, XVI, 1147].

Some correctives, as will be indicated, must be applied to the portrait provided by Eventov and Rotem. The situation in the early 1980s is not quite the same as it was in 1971. Moreover, they were describing the impact of Israel on the life of the organized community, but not necessarily American Jewry as a whole. Within the context of the present discussion—namely, the dramatic changes that took place in the American Jewish community at the end of the era of the third-generation community and the beginning of the fourth—their description is, essentially, valid. Since 1967 the American Jewish community has become much more explicitly survival oriented, and Israel plays a central, if not *the* central role in that orientation. Not only has support for Israel been incorporated into the religious behavior of American Jews, as Charles Liebman indicates (Liebman, 1973, pp. 88–108), in large measure Glazer is correct when he asserts that "Israel has become *the* religion for American Jews" (Glazer, 1979, p. 233). Leaving aside the question of the genuine transcendental quality and character of American Judaism, Israel has become part of the core of American Jewish "civil religion" (cf. Bellah, 1967), or American "civil Judaism" (Woocher, 1978, 1979, 1981). Jewish group survival has become a "sacred" value in Jewish communal life, and Israel has become the sacred

symbol of the unity of the Jewish people (Woocher, 1981, p. 149). None of this was evident in the communal life of the third generation.

The extent to which group survival has become a sacred value in American Jewish communal life in the fourth generation is evident also in the role and significance that the destruction of European Jewry, the Holocaust, have taken on in that communal life. During the period of the third-generation community, especially during the 1950s and early 1960s, there was very little public discussion of the massacre of European Jewry during the Nazi era. Few books and articles were written on the subject, nor was it a prominent topic on the American Jewish lecture circuit, as is evident from the brochures of the Jewish Welfare Board Lecture Bureau. Nor were there community-wide annual commemorations of the Holocaust. No prominent American Jewish Holocaust centers existed, and virtually no periodicals devoted to the dissemination of information on the subject existed. There was almost a deafening silence on the entire subject.

The first awakening to the Holocaust as a symbol, as an issue of contemporary and future significance, came as the result of the Israeli capture and trial of Adolph Eichmann in 1959 and 1960. But even then, much of the discussion was on the legitimacy of Israel's actions rather than the Holocaust itself. Several years later, Hannah Arendt sparked deeper probing of some of the issues with the publication of her book, *Eichmann in Jerusalem* (Arendt 1963), which became a source of great controversy in the American Jewish community and beyond.

It was not until after the Six-Day War, ironically enough, that the Holocaust became incorporated into American Jewish civil religion. Apparently the fear and anxiety for Israel, created by the crisis and the war, forced American Jews to confront the possibilities of another Holocaust. This fear and anxiety made them question their own security, especially when they perceived that much of the world was not as concerned as Jews felt they should be. The victory of Israel was perceived as the birth of an entirely new era. The slogan

"Never Again," which the JDL was to adopt, became the central value of American Judaism, even as it rejected the actions of the JDL. The Holocaust thus became the point of reference from which the rebirth began. Symbolically, if not necessarily theologically, the Holocaust was the Armageddon, and Israel was the symbol of the Messianic Era. The philosopher of religion, Emil Fackenheim, averred that the "commanding Voice of the Holocaust" demands that Jews persevere against all obstacles and threats, that they "are not permitted to hand Hitler any posthumous victories" (Fackenheim, 1968, p. 20), and American Jewry acknowledged with a loud "Amen" and the subsequent transformation of the Holocaust into the core of both the ritualism and symbolism of American Judaism.

Not only in America, moreover, did the Holocaust become a central part of civil Judaism during this period. Charles Liebman has convincingly shown that in Israel as well this process has taken place and that it happened after the statist period, particularly after the leadership of David Ben-Gurion and most decisively during the leadership of Menahem Begin (Liebman, 1978). With the passing of the government that was imbued with the ideology of Zionist-Socialism, the Holocaust understandably has become the central legitimating myth, as the term is used in the study of religions, of the state of Israel. The Holocaust legitimizes the very existence of the state, its character and actions, which are to be supported and defended even at the sacrifice of individual life and limb.

In a similar manner, the Holocaust for American Jewry has become the symbol and legitimating myth of the corporate unity of Jewry and has served to validate the actions taken by the corporate leadership of the American Jewish community. Moreover, it is the symbol not only of unity but also for some of the uniqueness upon which that unity is based. For many children of the third-generation community to whom Judaism was rather nebulous and who had an ambiguous conception of what being Jewish means, the Holocaust has become a very important symbol that provides meaning to Jewish unique-

ness and hence unity. Perhaps this is why so many American Jews who otherwise manifest little commitment to specifically Jewish norms and values are so adamant about the uniqueness of the Holocaust. They insist not only that the Holocaust was a solely Jewish tragedy, but that no other group has ever experienced anything remotely resembling it. For them, to minimize even one iota of the uniquely Jewish character of the Holocaust would be to deprive them of what they perceive to be their uniqueness as Jews. Whereas in traditional Jewish religious thought Jews are a covenantal community, a community based upon the belief in the covenant made with Abraham and confirmed at Sinai, and to others Jews are a peoplehood, bound together by a common history and cultural system, many American Jews who experienced an emotional awareness of being Jewish but who lacked both the religious and cultural sense of community and peoplehood sought to legitimize their essentially nonrational Jewish consciousness in the Holocaust. While for other Jews the Holocaust was another confirmation of Jewish uniqueness, for these Jews the Holocaust is the source of Jewish uniqueness.

After 1967 the Holocaust, therefore, became a central symbol for American Jews. It became part of the core of civil Judaism in America which not only symbolized but reinforced Jewish unity. As such it played a major role in altering the previous process of assimilation.

One further factor that had great impact upon the shift in the Jewish communal pendulum between the eras of the third and fourth generation was the coming of age of a new, distinctly American Orthodoxy. As was discussed previously, during the period of mass immigration the Jewish communities in Eastern Europe were already experiencing a traditional as well as religious upheaval. While most of those who came to the United States during the years 1881–1924 did establish and affiliate with Orthodox synagogues, they were not necessarily ideologically committed to Orthodoxy, and their children readily departed from Orthodox affiliation. During the years of the second and third generations, Orthodoxy was perceived as the religious branch of lower-class Jews (Leventman, 1969, p. 46), and to most observers it was a relic with no future in American society. In the first edition of his study of Conservative Judaism published in 1955, for example, Marshall Sklare declared that "Orthodox adherents have succeeded in achieving the goal of institutional perpetuation to only a limited extent; the history of their movement in this country can be written in terms of a case study of institutional decay" (Sklare, 1972, p. 43).

By the era of the fourth generation it was readily apparent that a "renaissance of American Orthodoxy" was taking place and that Orthodoxy had "transformed itself into a growing force in American Jewish life" (ibid., p. 264). While the "full story of" that renaissance "has yet to be written" (ibid.), some of its major variables can be delineated. Foremost among them appear to be: patterns of immigration, education, and changes in the larger American technology and culture.

It will be recalled that during the years of peak Jewish immigration from Eastern Europe, the Orthodox rabbinic-intellectual elite remained in Europe. They were opposed to immigration to the United States because they viewed America as a *treifeneh medineh*, an impure and secular society in which Judaism could have no future. Even with the rise of the Nazi menace, many of those rabbis who did ultimately leave Eastern Europe were frequently the last who managed to get out. The rabbis were among the last to leave because they felt that they had an obligation, as leaders, to care for their followers.

During the years 1937–1948, an estimated two hundred thousand to one-quarter million Jewish refugees from Eastern Europe arrived in the United States (Wischnitzer, 1948, p. 289), of which a significant number were Orthodox rabbis and their followers. Although they resisted coming to the United States in earlier years, now they had no choice, and they decided to come and transplant their religious culture in this country. This new infusion of ideologically committed Orthodox provided the numbers and manpower for the renaissance that was to manifest itself more than a quarter of a century later.

Numbers alone, however, would not have provided for that renaissance. Obviously, there had to be some major changes in the prevailing operations of American Orthodox institutions; otherwise, the process of institutional decay which Orthodoxy was experiencing would have been merely slowed at best. Its basic prognosis would not have been altered. The rabbinic and educational elite of Orthodoxy, therefore, undertook to radically alter both the system of Jewish education and the status of sacred learning in the United States.

As a first step, the National Society for Hebrew Day Schools (*Torah Umesorah*), was formed to encourage and assist in the founding of Jewish day schools—elementary and high schools that would provide intensive traditional Jewish education along with a quality secular curriculum—in cities and neighborhoods across the country. While, as was indicated previously (above, Chapter 2), a number of such day schools were founded early in this century, their numbers and hence their impact were relatively small. With the efforts of the leadership of this new immigration, the picture changed significantly. In terms of the numbers of schools, there has been a virtual boom in of the day school movement since World War II.

As Table 2 indicates, the number of day schools grew from 35 to 323 and enrollments grew from 7,700 to 63,500 between the years 1940 and 1965. By 1975, there were 425 day

Table 2. Hebrew Day Schools: Numbers, Types, and Enrollments

Year	Total Day Schools	High Schools	Total Enrollments	Number of Communities
1940	35		7,700	7
1945	69	9	10,200	31
1955	180		35,500	68
1965	323	83	63,500	117
1970			72,000	
1975	425	138	82,200	160

SOURCE: Mayer and Waxman, 1977, p. 99

schools and 138 high schools with an enrollment of 82,200. These schools are located not only in the New York metropolitan area, but in 33 states across the country. By 1975 every city in the United States with a Jewish population of 7,500 had at least one day school, as did four out of five of the cities with a Jewish population of between 5,000 and 7,500. Among cities with smaller Jewish populations, one out of four with a population of 1,000 Jews had a Jewish day school (Mayer and Waxman, 1977 pp. 99–100).

The impact of intensive formal Jewish education upon adult religious behavior and attitudes is the subject of several empirical studies conducted during the early 1970s (Lazerwitz, 1973; Cohen, 1974; Dashefsky and Shapiro, 1974; Himmelfarb, 1974). Himmelfarb's study bears most directly on this issue, and he found that supplementary schools of Jewish education, such as Sunday schools and afternoon schools, do not have any long-lasting impact upon Jewish involvement, whereas day schools do have impact for those students who have had more than six years of such schooling (Himmelfarb, 1974). Of course, years of schooling is not the sole determinant; other factors, such as age, parents, spouse among others, are important variables. But, when all of those are controlled, the intensity of the education does reveal itself as a most significant variable.

A number of the newly arrived Orthodox leaders had been heads of advanced rabbinical seminaries in Eastern Europe and, immediately upon their arrival in the United States, they set out to reconstruct those seminaries on American soil. Such leaders as Aharon Kotler, Abraham Kalmanowitz, Elijah Meir Bloch, and Mordecai Katz, all rabbis, reestablished their advanced seminaries in Lakewood, Brooklyn, Cleveland, and elsewhere, in the Eastern European mold, and helped cultivate a generation of knowledgeable and ideologically committed Orthodox Jews, many of whom were later to establish other such advanced seminaries in dozens of American cities (Helmreich, 1982). While some graduates of these institutions went on to occupations and professions within the field of the rabbinate and Jewish education, many others entered secular professions, such as law, teaching, government, and business, while remaining highly supportive of Orthodox institutions and retaining their Orthodox behavior (ibid., p. 310).

In a recent study of the largest and apparently still thriving Orthodox Jewish community in the United States, located in Brooklyn, New York, Egon Mayer analyzes how Boro Park Jewry, which numbers approximately 55,000, has in large measure reversed the assimilation process which Leventman characterized as "from *shtetl* to suburb" (Leventman, 1969), and learned to make use of the material advantages of modernization without experiencing its cultural consequences. The Jews of Boro Park were able to "avoid the magnetic pull of cultural assimilation even as their community was becoming structurally more similar to the larger society," Mayer argues, because they emphasized the values of separateness and sanctity. Their values are perpetuated through a normative structure within which the observance of the Sabbath and dietary and "family purity" laws are most pervasive and concretized by a highly organized system of institutions, including the family, the yeshiva, the large and small synagogues, and a variety of youth organizations. As members of a "cognitive minority" with highly developed value and normative structures, Mayer suggests, the Jews of Boro Park do not experience the "cognitive dissonance" which the traditional Jew in modern society is supposed to experience (Mayer, 1979).

Mayer's analysis of the growth of Orthodoxy in Boro Park, which implies the resurgence of Orthodoxy in the fourth generation as a whole, is a unique contribution to our understanding of some variables that have caused the shift in the process of assimilation which was manifest during the first three generations. Ironically, this very shift seems to have escaped Mayer, for he argues that Boro Park proves that Sklare, Leventman, and others were incorrect in their generational theses. What he fails to perceive is that although the patterns they analyzed in the first three generations have not persisted in the fourth, this does not mean that the analyses were incorrect at the time of being written. Rather, basic changes in the fourth generation render it essentially different from previous ones. Many of these changes within Orthodoxy are attributable to the educational efforts of the leadership of the World War II Orthodox immigration.

Because of their socioeconomic status, moreover, many graduates of these institutions by the 1970s were in a position to become involved with Jewish communal life, in both professional and lay capacities, beyond solely the Orthodox community. Increasing numbers of Orthodox Jews have assumed leadership roles in Jewish federations and other institutions of the American Jewish community, with the result that these institutions have become more sensitive to Jewish tradition and explicitly Jewish concerns. As Liebman has shown in his study of the changes in the leadership and decision making in the New York Federation of Jewish Philanthropies between the years 1968 and 1978, the increased involvement of the Orthodox is an important factor in the federation's recent tendency "to view itself as an institution with responsibilities to the total Jewish community" (Liebman, 1979, p. 76).

In addition to the efforts of the immigrant leadership, a number of important social and technological developments in American society facilitated the Orthodox renaissance in the fourth-generation community. As to enrollments in day schools, for example, it is naive to think that all parents who sent their children to these schools were motivated solely by a commitment to intensive Jewish education. Unquestionably, some had other reasons, such as avoiding public school systems that were becoming increasingly plagued by a variety of problems, especially the racial one. Even for those parents, however, their sending their children to Jewish day schools, rather than to secular, nondenominational, private schools does indicate some sensitivity to their Jewishness and their desire to have Jewish continuity for their children.

More important and rarely acknowledged are such structural changes in American society as the five-day work week and the technological advances in the food industry. One major factor accounting for the defection from Orthodox affiliation during the second generation was the restrictiveness of Orthodoxy. For those who strongly aspired to socioeconomic mobility, Orthodox restrictions that prohibited working on the Sabbath and required eating only kosher foods—foods prepared in a ritually correct manner—were too much of a burden to bear. They inhibited both economic mobility and social intercourse with those in the larger society. By the era of the fourth generation, much of that had changed. The five-day work week was the norm for the majority of American Jews. Thus, Orthodoxy has been able to become more assertive in its demand for Sabbath observance (Waxman, 1982).

Technological developments in the food-processing industry have largely removed the restricting and thus stigmatizing nature of kosher food. Whereas in earlier generations the availability and selection of kosher food was limited, today there is a wide variety available in every large supermarket, and those foods not readily available locally can be easily shipped in from elsewhere in the country. Kosher meals are available on most airlines and in many hotels. To observe dietary laws, therefore, does not restrict one's mobility. Moreover, the more densely populated Jewish communities have an assortment of kosher foods which was inconceivable in earlier generations, such as kosher pizza, Chinese, French and Italian cooking of high quality, and even nondairy cheesecake and cheeseburgers. If you can't "have your cake and eat it too," you can at least eat almost any type of cake and still remain loyal to traditional Jewish dietary norms.

As a result of these and other structural and technological changes, Orthodox Jews have been able to enjoy many comforts of the larger middle- and upper-middle class life-style while adhering to Orthodox Jewish norms. They have thus been able to reduce the rate of defection from Orthodoxy and develop a rather sophisticated institutional power base, and these factors have dramatically enhanced the influence that Orthodox Jews have within the American Jewish communal structure.

Orthodoxy would probably not have become so influential as it has were it not for a number of significant changes in the larger American culture too. Many of the other changes discussed as part of the shift in the pendulum during the late 1960s and 1970s are also tied to these larger cultural changes. Within the context of this chapter, the rise of religious consciousness and the rise of public ethnicity are most relevant.

While much of the discussion concerning the secularization of American society in the mid-1960s was largely academic, the early 1960s were years of relatively little interest and activity in religion in the country. It certainly would have been preposterous in 1965 to predict that religious consciousness would significantly rise in the country, that "new religions," cults, and Eastern religions which emphasize mysticism would dramatically increase, and that nationwide church and synagogue attendance would go up several years hence (Carroll, Johnson, and Marty, 1979). Nor would it have seemed likely that a presidential candidate from one of the two major political parties would in the following decade include conservative religious notions as part of his campaign and that he would win the election, as did Jimmy Carter in 1976. Whereas, as was cited earlier (above, Introduction), in 1968 Peter Berger was predicting that institutional religion would almost disappear in the country by the year 2000, by 1977 he was able to foresee "a massive reaction" to secularization, "something of the nature of a great religious revival. I can't tell you when, I can't tell you what form it will take. It may well be something within the churches. This has happened before . . . " (Berger 1977b, p. 70).

Various explanations have been given for the rise of religious consciousness, including cults and "new" religions. Two major elements in most of them concern the loss of legitimacy in the dominant institutions and the loss of community in American society in the 1960s and early 1970s. According to Charles Glock, the rise of religious consciousness among youth was in response to the disenchantment of the scientific world.

The effect of a scientific world view is to undermine the underlying assumptions of the old imageries, the cultural values and social arrangements informed by them, and the inherent ability of these world views to give life meaning and purpose. At the same time, by virtue of its uncertainty and ambiguity, a scientific world view offers no clear alternative formula either for organizing society or for living one's life. . . . As a consequence of its ambiguity in these respects, a scientific world view, as it diffuses and becomes the lens from which increasing numbers of people view their world, has the potential for creating crises both for the society and for individuals" (Glock, 1976, p. 362).

Modernity, including utilitarian individualism and technological rationality, was repudiated by a new generation of educated youth who felt a loss of meaning, and the new religious consciousness succeeded in filling the void (Bellah, 1976, pp. 333–52). Neither the mainline religious nor civic values and authority figures were able to fill the void, the former because of their increasing involvement in social activism and their increasing reliance upon secular rationalism, and the latter because of such debacles as the Vietnam War and Watergate.

Not only does modernity promote a crisis of meaning, it also precipitates a loss of and subsequent search for community. The impact of modernity upon community forms the theme of many major works of most classical sociological theorists in Europe and America in the nineteenth and early twentieth centuries, and most prominently in the work of Ferdinand Tönnies. Tönnies analyzed social change in terms of the transition from *Gemeinschaft* (community) to *Gesellschaft* (society), and he foresaw efforts to recapture some of the securities of the former within the latter (Tönnies, 1957 [1887]. See also Cahnman and Heberle, 1971; Cahnman, 1973). Among the contemporary American sociologists, Robert Nisbet and Peter Berger have both pointed to the loss of community in modern American society as the result of structural developments and public policy. Writing of "the loss of community," Nisbet argues that "in the process of modern industrial and political development, established social contexts have become weak, and fewer individuals have the secure interpersonal relations which formerly gave meaning and stability to existence" (Nisbet, 1953, p. 15). Along similar lines Berger suggests:

> Modernization brings about a novel dichotomization of social life. The dichotomy is between the huge and immensely powerful institutions of the public sphere (the state, the large economic agglomerates that we know as corporations and labor unions, and the ever-growing bureaucracies that administer sectors of society not properly political or economic, such as education or the organized professions) and the private sphere, which is a curious interstitial area "left over," as it were, by the large institutions and indeed . . . marked by "underinstitutionalization." Put more simply, the dichotomy is between the megastructures and private life. . . . As long as the individual can indeed find meaning and identity in his private life, he can manage to put up with the meaningless and disidentifying world of the megastructures [Berger, 1977, pp. 133-4, See also Berger, Berger and Kellner, 1973; Berger and Neuhaus, 1977].

The problem, according to Berger, is that social policy in America has tended to undermine the important mediating structures, such as family, neighborhood, religious group and ethnic group, which provided the individual with a buffer against the megastructures and gave him or her a sense of rootedness. As a result of the weakening of the traditional mediating structures, when youth leave the confines of the nuclear family and are confronted with only large and impersonal bureaucracies, they are attracted to either the new religions or the more conservative denominations of the traditional religions because these provide structure, meaning, and warmth similar to that which family provides. In essence, their quest is a quest for community (Anthony and Robbins, 1981, p. 26).

With the rise of religious consciousness in American society, and as a result of many of the very same forces, came a rise of public ethnicity and an attempt to retrieve some qualities of the ethnic community. Once blacks had publicly rejected the ideology of the melting pot and adopted the ideology of cultural pluralism, white ethnic groups were quick to follow suit. Ethnicity burst into the American scene with a passion. The mass media and the advertising industry soon caught on, and the public was being told that "every American had two homelands," and that a certain airline has a strong desire to fly people to their other homelands. Meltable or not, ethnics were rising and flaunting their ethnicity. For many, the assertion of ethnicity in the public sphere coincided with an increasing assimilation in the private sphere. Several keen observers of the American Jewish scene remarked that many American Jews were turning the Jewish Enlightenment dictum to "be a Jew in the home and gentleman in the street" on its head; in the street they were asserting their Jewish ethnicity while in their homes, in the private sphere, they were manifesting increasing cultural assimilation. Be that as it may, to a large degree these Jews were reflecting patterns characteristic of American society as a whole and not unique to American Jews.

The implications of this "rise of ethnicity" will be discussed in a later chapter. For the present, while a variety of factors precipitated the phenomenon—including for some a "reactionary impulse" (Patterson, 1977), that is, the reactionary utilization of ethnicity as a political counter to the gains of blacks—it was also another response to the loss of meaning and identity produced by modernity. It is not simply a coincidence that the rise of religious consciousness and the rise of ethnicity occurred almost simultaneously in American society. In no small measure they were responses to the same predicaments, the loss of community, meaning, and identity. Initiated for blacks by Alex Haley and then diffused throughout the society, the "roots" phenomenon was a glaring example of the search for identity. While it may have been a fetish for some, for many others it became a serious enterprise, an avocation or hobby.

It is misleading, therefore, to view the heightening of Jewish consciousness in the fourth generation as solely an American Jewish phenomenon. While there were a variety of factors within the Jewish community which promoted the shift away from further assimilation and toward greater group self-consciousness, these factors were present at a time when there was broad, society-wide heightening of both religious and ethnic consciousness. The larger structural and cultural changes made it much more acceptable for American Jews to become more conscious of their Jewishness.

In the final analysis the heightening of Jewish consciousness was not a break with the norms and values of American society. On the contrary, it was the realization or operationalization of larger American social and cultural patterns. Paradoxical as it may appear, it was not a manifestation of the rejection of cultural assimilation; it was the realization of its persistence.

Does this mean that the assimilationist theorists were correct and that identificational assimilation is inevitable, remote as it may appear today? Before I attempt to deal with that question, I shall make a careful and extensive analysis of the social patterns of the fourth-generation community.

6. Taking Stock: Contemporary America's Jews

Reliable data on the American Jewish population are very difficult to obtain. The doctrine of separation of church and state has been interpreted to preclude questions concerning religious affiliation in surveys conducted by the United States Bureau of the Census. In the mid-1950s the Bureau of the Census did conduct a survey of about 35,000 households in which respondents were given the opportunity to respond to a question concerning religious affiliation, and a brief report of that survey was subsequently issued (U. S. Bureau of the Census, 1958). This report and two later studies derived from data in the report were, for many years, the only sources of national information on the religious characteristics of the American population. Given the many changes in American society and culture during the last quarter of a century, it is doubtful that these data can be utilized at the present time for anything more than broad speculation about the religion of the American population in general and American Jews in particular. Also, since the bureau does not identify Jews as an ethnic group, its data cannot be utilized as a source of information about Jews.

For more or less current information on the Jewish population in the United States, there are three main sources. The most widely used and quoted, and probably the most reliable for the decade of the 1970s, is the National Jewish Population Study (NJPS), sponsored by the Council of Jewish Federations and Welfare Funds. This study, the most scientifically valid national sample of American Jews ever obtained, provided a wealth of previously unavailable information. A complete report of the findings was never published, however. For a variety of reasons, only a series of brief reports that summarized data of concern in community planning within local Jewish federations was issued. Since the data for the study were collected during the late 1960s and very early 1970s, there is some question as to their current reliability. It seems reasonable to assume that significant changes have taken place in the characteristics of American Jewry during the 1970s.

Another source of information on the American Jewish population is in the series of community surveys periodically conducted by local Jewish federations. The quality of these surveys, in terms of social research techniques, varies widely. Also, how representative they are, even for the local community, has been questioned in many cases, since they frequently survey only those Jews affiliated with local Jewish institutions. Questions have also been raised about the degree to which a particular community is representative of American Jewry as a whole. Yet in this respect Goldstein reported that his review of the community surveys revealed surprisingly uniform patterns (Goldstein, 1971).

A final source of information is the limited number of specialized studies conducted by social scientists and reported in academic journals. Many criticisms directed at the community surveys are applicable here as well, especially since the number of Jewish cases in many of the samples is extremely small. Given the limitations of reliable data, the following composite portrait should be taken as tentative. Yet, since the data come from a variety of sources and many findings are more or less similar, we can assume that the picture that emerges is close to being true.

Size

The most educated estimates of the Jewish population in the United States place it between 5,500,000 and 5,690,000 in 1981. These estimates are based upon the 1970–71 National

Jewish Population Study estimates of the number of non-Jews in "Jewish households," which are then deducted from the estimates of persons in Jewish households (Chenkin and Miran, 1982, p. 165; Schmelz and Della Pergola, 1982, p. 283). Accordingly, Jews were between 2.39 and 2.47 percent of the total United States population which in 1981 was estimated at 230,000,000. When these figures are compared with those of the 1930s, when the Jewish population was 3.7 percent of the total population, obviously the Jewish component of the American population is becoming smaller. Not only is it decreasing relative to the total population, it is decreasing in absolute terms as well, because the estimated American Jewish birth rate is even lower than the 2.1 that is generally accepted to be replacement level. The reasons for the negative Jewish population growth and its consequences will be considered later, in a discussion of American Jewish family patterns. In addition, the American Jewish population would have been even smaller had it not been for the estimated 90,000 Jewish immigrants who arrived in the country between 1971 and 1981, primarily from the Soviet Union and Israel (Schmelz and Della Pergola, p. 283). The nature of that immigration and its impact upon American Jewry will be discussed below.

Geographic Distribution

Until relatively recently, Jews in the United States were concentrated in the major urban centers, and in the northeastern part of the country. Sklare reported that as recently as 1962, 77.8 percent of the Jewish population lived in ten population centers, 46.5 percent lived in the New York/northeastern New Jersey Standard Consolidated Area, and as many as 95 percent of America's Jews lived in urban areas (Sklare, 1971, pp. 44–45). Using the 1957 census data, Goldstein found similar patterns, namely, that 96 percent of all Jews in the United States aged fourteen and over lived in urban areas, compared with 64 percent for the general population (Goldstein, 1971, p. 38). In fact, Jews were so urban that the

phenomenon of Jews in small towns was unique enough to be
a subject worthy of a doctoral disseration in 1958 and a follow-
up study in 1977 (Rose, 1977). Moreover, the evidence
indicated that, as recently as 1968, 64 percent of the American
Jewish population lived in the Northeast (Chenkin, 1970, p.
347, Table 2).

During the 1970s, however, the residential patterns of
Jews in the United States underwent significant change. By
1981 the percentage of American Jews residing in the Northeast declined to 56.9, while the percentage residing in the
South increased from 10.3 in 1968 to 16.3 in 1981. In the West
the increase was from 13.2 percent in 1968 to 15.1 percent in
1981. Table 3 shows the changes in the geographic distribution of America's Jews from 1968 to 1981.

The pace of the geographic mobility of American Jews is
further indicated by a report—based upon data from the

*Table 3. Percentage of U.S. Jewish Population, Distributed by
Regions: 1968, 1974–5, 1981*

Region	Years		
	1968	*1974–5*	*1981*
Northeast	64.0	60.0	56.9
New England	6.8	7.1	6.4
Middle Atlantic	57.1	53.0	50.5
North Central	12.5	12.6	11.6
East North Central	10.2	10.1	9.4
West North Central	2.3	2.4	2.3
South	10.3	14.1	16.3
South Atlantic	8.1	9.4	14.0
East South Central	0.7	0.7	0.7
West South Central	1.5	1.6	1.7
West	13.2	13.0	15.1
Mountain	0.9	1.3	1.7
Pacific	12.2	12.1	13.4

SOURCE: *American Jewish Year Book*, 71 (1970), 347; 75 (1974/75), 306; 82 (1982),
169.

National Jewish Population Study—which found that only 42·
percent of those aged 30 to 34 years were, in 1970, living in the
same city in which they resided in 1965. For those aged 35 to
39, the percentage was somewhat higher, 49 percent, but 19
percent of that group stated that they were planning to move,
and 9 percent said that their plans were immediate. When the
figures for several age cohorts were combined, the data
revealed that only 62 percent of the Jews in the United States
aged 20 and over were, in 1970, living in the same city in which
they resided in 1965. For those aged 25 to 39, it was less than 50
percent, and more than 20 percent were living in a different
state altogether (Massarik, 1974).

These patterns of dispersion are reflected also in a study
of the geographic distribution and change of the American
Jewish population between the years 1952 and 1971, by
counties. Newman and Halvorson found that while the Jewish
population in 1971 was still much more concentrated than the
general population, they were also much more dispersed than
they had been in 1952. Jews increasingly tend to locate in
counties characterized by high degrees of denominational
pluralism, regardless of the size of the Jewish community in
those counties. They "feel accepted in America and are less
concerned about venturing out into more traditionally conservative culturally homogeneous enclaves" (Newman and
Halvorson, 1979, p. 192).

The geographic mobility of American Jews has implications, both qualitatively and quantitatively, for the Jewish
character of the larger American Jewish community and its
organizational structure. There is a difference, it should be
pointed out, between American Jews and the American Jewish
community. Not all of the former are part of the latter. Of the
approximately five and one-half million Americans who
identify themselves as Jews, only about 60 percent are
affiliated with the organized Jewish community—that is, they
belong to a synagogue, Jewish organizations, and/or contribute annually to a local Jewish federation or any other
recognized Jewish philanthropic fund-raising campaign
(Elazar, 1976, pp. 70–75). It is this 60 percent or less of

America's Jews, basically, which are involved with and support the many national and local religious, educational, cultural, and social organizations dealing with community relations, overseas aid, social welfare, mutual benefits, as well as Zionist and pro-Israel causes which make up the American Jewish community.

If, as is assumed, one's ethno-religious identification and the likely transmission of that identification and identity from one generation to the next are inextricably related to one's involvement with the ethno-religious community, then the high rate of geographic mobility is significant in that it may upset, if not rupture, the patterns of communal involvements and may lead to a weakening of community ties. Moreover, since many probably anticipate moving again within a relatively short period of time, they may not care to invest their energies in a community which for them is only temporary. Nor will the local community seek to exert itself and reach out to many who may be seen as transients.

That geographic mobility weakens ethnic group ties has been the predominant assumption among sociologists of ethnic groups in general (e.g., Park, 1928; Wirth, 1938 and of American Jews in particular (e.g., Goldstein, 1971, p. 50). Jaret's data suggest however that, as far as Jews are concerned, geographic mobility has different implications for two different subgroups. For the Reform/Nonaffiliated subgroup, geographic mobility does weaken ethnic group ties. For the Orthodox/Conservative subgroup, however, mobility does not appear to have this effect. In some cases it even promotes ethnic participation (Jaret, 1978). But, since the overwhelming majority of American Jews are represented by the Reform/Nonaffiliated subgroup, as a later discussion of denominational patterns will indicate, the increasing rate of geographic mobility will probably lead to greater weakening of ethno-religious group ties, barring, of course, any outreach activities by the organized community. The implications in terms of communal policy should be obvious and will be elaborated upon in the final chapter.

Geographic mobility also places heavy strains on institutional structures which were developed at a time when the Jewish population was centrally located within limited densely populated areas. Population dispersion requires that institutions and organizations branch out to establish new facilities and provide services in many new and different areas, as compared to the more or less centralized structures of the past. This new reality requires major policy decisions, in terms of both design and financial feasibility.

Occupational Patterns

At the turn of the twentieth century, approximately 34 percent of New York's male, Eastern European Jews were machine operators in the clothing industry and an additional 23 percent were blue-collar workers in other industries, for a total of 57 percent in blue-collar occupations. By 1963 only 26.9 percent of the Jewish population of New York City were blue-collar workers, and this figure was considerably higher than those in other cities. In Boston, Detroit, Milwaukee, and Providence, for example, there was a maximum of 15 percent of adult Jewish males in the working class during the mid-1960s, as compared to more than 50 percent of the general male population who were blue-collar workers (Sklare, 1971, pp. 60–65). Since the beginning of the century, Jews have been moving relatively rapidly out of the blue-collar occupations and into managerial, proprietory, professional, and technical occupations. As Sklare points out, however, it cannot be assumed that Jews are randomly distributed throughout any occupational category, and it is not known precisely what ranks they hold within those occupational spheres. While discrimination against Jews has, apparently, declined in law as well as in other fields, there is no evidence to indicate whether Jews are well-represented in the more prestigious law firms. The same holds for the world of corporate executives (ibid.).

While it has been found that in the country as a whole "the level of self-employment among males has fallen by over 55% in the last three decades, from over one-fourth of the labor force in 1940 to one-ninth in 1970" (Goldscheider and

Kobrin, 1980, p. 256), a study of ethnic variation and change in self-employment in Providence found that a marked difference remains in the self-employment patterns of Jews and non-Jews. Specifically, "over half of the Jewish males are self-employed, three-and-a-half times the Protestant-Catholic level and two-and-a-half times the Italian level" (ibid., p. 261). Moreover, the high self-employment among Jewish males is not solely the consequence of the self-employment patterns of their fathers. The study of Goldscheider and Kobrin suggests that ethnicity and ethnic factors continue to be important:

> Self-employment may be viewed as an indicator of access to social and economic resources and is distinct from those aspects of occupational attainment associated with achievement through education. The ethnic variation in self-employment may be related, therefore, to differential access to those opportunity structures which are unrelated directly to the traditional determinants of occupational status. While the self-employment of fathers has an effect on the self-employment of sons, this effect is differential by ethnicity. Hence the inheritance of self-employment, directly and indirectly, is more characteristic of some ethnic groups than others and may be limited to particular occupations and industries [ibid., p. 276].

Since the early 1960s a new trend in the occupational patterns of American Jews has emerged, namely, an increase in the professional categories and a decline in the managerial and proprietory occupations. A comparison between the 1965 and 1975 surveys of the Jewish community of Boston, for example, indicates that in 1965 one-third of Boston's employed Jewish males were professionals and 37 percent were in managerial and proprietory occupations; in 1975, the percentage of professionals had risen to 40 percent while those in managerial and proprietory occupations had declined to 27 percent (Axelrod, Fowler, and Gurin, 1967; Fowler, 1977, p. 47). The patterns for women, interestingly enough, were not quite the same as those for men. Women showed increasing percentages in both the professional and managerial categories, a result, no doubt, of the higher levels of educational attainment and greater participation of women in labor during those ten years.

While the rates in Boston may be unique, evidence from other cities indicates that they reflect the patterns in the rest of the country, and some observers have expressed concern about the impact that these new occupational trends will have upon the American Jewish community. Sklare, for example, has expressed concern that as Jews enter the professions, they will increasingly adopt new professional life-styles and relinquish the old ethnic ones (Sklare, 1971, p. 66). Apparently he did not envisage that many of these professionals might be able to integrate traditional Jewish norms with their new life-styles, even though the potential for such integration seems greater today than it was in the past due to such changes in American culture as a greater tolerance for cultural pluralism, and technological changes that make traditional Jewish norms somewhat less of an impediment to the advantages of the professional life-styles.

Another effect of the rising professional status of American Jewry has implications not so much for the individual and his or her life style as for the communal and organizational structure of the American Jewish community. On the basis of his secondary analysis of data from the 1965 and 1975 Boston Jewish community studies, Steven Cohen suggests that the shift from entrepreneurial to professional status has resulted in a smaller number of millionaire donors, who have played a major role in the ability of Jewish organizations to raise large sums of money, since millionaires are much more likely to be businessmen than professionals. Also salaried people do not have access to the many different methods of hiding their income which are open to businessmen, with the result that the former have less to contribute to philanthropic ventures. Finally, there is less social and economic pressure upon professionals to contribute, and they have less of a need to identify with the Jewish community (Cohen, 1980).

These trends in Jewish philanthropy are not inevitable however. While the Boston data confirm an increasing professional status among its Jews, this need not necessarily mean a decline in self-employment. If the Goldscheider and Kobrin findings of a persistence of self-employment among the Jews of Providence are representative of those of other cities, it seems reasonable to predict an increase in the numbers of self-employed professionals. Perhaps they will turn out as wealthy as the business entrepreneurs. Also, Jewish fund raisers seem increasingly adept at creating social pressures among professionals in order to elicit contributions from them. Finally, the Boston Jewish community is hardly representative of American Jewry, as Cohen himself points out when he indicates the growing number of self-employed professionals who do contribute quite substantially to the Combined Jewish Philanthropies of Greater Boston (ibid., p. 45).

Educational Patterns

While some questions have been raised as to the precise nature of the relationship, the occupational patterns of American Jews are not independent of educational patterns. A study conducted through Columbia University in the mid-1960s compared the educational mobility of eight different ethnic and religious groups in New York City and showed that 89 percent of the native-born Jews surveyed had significantly exceeded their fathers' levels of education. Furthermore, the difference between sons' and fathers' levels of education was far greater among native-born Jews than for any other group (Sklare, 1971, p. 57).

Similarly an analysis of data derived from the United States Bureau of the Census in 1965 indicated that the educational plans of Jews were significantly different from those of non-Jews. For example, 86 percent of the Jews and 53 percent of the non-Jewish students interviewed indicated that they planned to go to college. When intelligence, mother's education, occupation of head of household, and family income were held constant, the findings showed that 70 percent of the Jewish students and only 53 percent of the non-Jewish students planned to go to college (Goldstein, 1971, pp. 60–68; Rhodes and Nam, 1970).

The persistence of these patterns during the past decade

and into the present is indicated by Goldstein's comparison of data from the National Jewish Population Study with that of the Bureau of the Census for the white population in 1970. Of those aged 25 and older, 45.5 percent of the total white population but only 15.6 percent of the Jewish population had less than twelve years of schooling. On the other hand, only 4.9 percent of the total white population and 18.2 percent of the Jewish population had five or more years of college education. When different age cohorts are examined, the data reveal that for those Jews between the ages of 30 and 39, 83 percent had some college, 70 percent had graduated from college, and only 4 percent had no high school education. While differentials persist between the educational levels of Jewish males and females, the educational levels of Jewish females are also quite high, especially in the younger age cohorts. For the 30 to 39 year age cohort, 75 percent of the Jewish women had some college, whereas only 2.4 percent did not complete high school (Goldstein, 1981a, pp. 48–49).

In addition to the implications for Jewish occupational patterns Goldstein suggests that these educational patterns may have consequences in terms of the individual's attachments to the Jewish community:

> Jews with higher education may have significantly higher rates of intermarriage and become more alienated from the Jewish community. This development involves not only the possible impact of physical separation from home and the weakening of parental control in dating and courtship patterns, but also the general liberalizing effect a college education may have on religious values and Jewish identity. It would be ironic if the very strong positive value which Jews have traditionally placed on education, and that now has manifested itself in a very high proportion of Jewish youth attending college, turns out to be an important factor in the general weakening of the individual's ties to the Jewish community [ibid., p. 51].

The educational patterns may also have consequences upon family in a variety of ways. As Goldstein points out, higher education, especially at the postgraduate level, results in many young Jews leaving home and probably not returning permanently once they have completed their education. Also the rising levels of education among young Jewish women are likely to have some impact upon rates of marriage, fertility, and marital stability (ibid., p. 50). The implications of these changes for the American Jewish community will be discussed in the next chapter.

Income Patterns

According to the most recent data available, which admittedly are dated since they are based upon information that is about ten years old, the median family income of American Jews is significantly higher than that of the total U.S. population, and is the highest of all the white and non-white ethnic groups for which such information is available (cf. Sowell, 1981, p. 5). Also, on the basis of data from samples obtained by the National Opinion Research Center in 1972 and 1976, Wade Clark Roof found that the income of Jews ranks very high when compared with that of other religious groups. The median income of Jews is higher than the eight Protestant and nine Catholic groups when the mean is unadjusted; when the mean is adjusted for age, region, and size of city, only Episcopalians have a higher median family income (Roof, 1979, pp. 286–87). Whereas the median family income in 1971 for the total population was $10,285, that of Jews was $12,630 (Chenkin, 1972, p. 10). This fact should not be surprising, given the high educational and occupational levels of Jews. Since we do not have sufficient data to make comparisons based on the number of household members employed however, that part of the difference in median family income possibly may lie in the disproportionate number of dual-career families among American Jews (Ruderman, 1968, pp. 134–35).

To give a more accurate picture of the income patterns of American Jews, two more points must be made. First, while American Jews as a group do have higher median family incomes than the national median, a relatively substantial number of Jews still fall below the Bureau of Labor Statistics "moderate income" level, such as the aged, single-parent families, and recent immigrants from the Soviet Union, Iran, and Israel (Levine and Hochbaum, 1974; Waxman, 1979a). This is especially the case in the nation's major metropolitan centers and, as was indicated earlier, these are still the areas with substantial Jewish populations. A preliminary analysis of a recent survey of the Jewish population in Los Angeles, for example, indicates that 40 percent "is economically marginal having total family incomes of $15,000 a year or less. Half of these, 20 percent of the population, are at the poverty level or below, a figure that seriously challenges the notion of universal Jewish affluence" (Sandberg and Levine, 1981, p. 6). Furthermore, while Jews have moved up the income ladder, and some have entered the category of millionaires, it would appear that very few Jews have made it to the top rung, which Dye refers to as "America's Centimillionaires," or those who have fortunes of over $100 million (Dye, 1976, pp. 40–42).

Political Attitudes and Behavior

The political liberalism of American Jews in the twentieth century and attempts to explain it were discussed in the last chapter. Despite the perennial spate of empirical data showing that Jews hold liberal political attitudes and vote liberally to a degree that is very inconsistent with their socioeconomic status, every few years the rumor spreads that American Jews are becoming politically conservative (e.g., Patterson, 1977, p. 165; Kilson, 1975, pp. 259–60). That if indeed they are, they would be only conforming to patterns that long have been characteristics of the general American population, is invariably overlooked by many who foretell of a Jewish swing to political conservatism. Among the data of the past decade one finds for example in 1972, despite George McGovern's mishandling of the so-called Jewish issues and Richard Nixon's strong support for Israel, approximately two-thirds of the Jews who voted, voted for McGovern for president. While this represented a decline from 1968 in Jewish Democratic voting, when more than 80 percent of

Jewish voters chose Hubert Humphrey over Richard Nixon, two facts must be considered. First, in the 1968 election an unusually high percentage of Jews voted for the Democratic candidate, Humphrey, as they had done throughout the decade of the 1960s. Whereas in 1952, 64 percent and in 1956, 60 percent of the Jewish vote went to the Democratic candidate, in 1960, 82 percent, in 1964, 90 percent, and in 1968, 83 percent of the Jewish vote went to the Democratic candidates (Levy and Kramer, 1973, p. 103). Moreover, despite the decrease of Jewish support from 1968, the Jewish vote for McGovern in 1972 was much greater than that of any other white group in the electorate (ibid., p. 241).

In 1976 Jews as a rule voted for Jimmy Carter and in New York about 80 percent did so, whereas whites in the country as a whole, especially those of similar income and education, moved to the right. In a nationwide *New York Times*-CBS survey in the autumn of 1978, which questioned close to 9,000 voters on both domestic and foreign policy issues, Jews were found to be more liberal than any other white group (Clymer, 1978). In local elections as well, a study of the 1978 "Vote White" City Charter campaign in Philadelphia found that both more prosperous and less prosperous Jews aligned themselves with blacks to help defeat Mayor Rizzo's Charter change proposal (Featherman and Rosenberg, 1979).

Even in the 1980 election, when the Jewish vote for the Democratic candidate sank much lower than since the New Deal, the voting patterns did not indicate a swing to the right. While Jimmy Carter received only between 42 and 47 percent of the Jewish vote, Ronald Reagan received even less, 35 to 39 percent. An estimated 14 to 21 percent of the Jewish vote went to the Independent candidate, John Anderson. The combined Carter-Anderson total of Jewish votes was about 65 percent, which was approximately the same percentage of Jews who voted for McGovern in 1972. What apparently happened in 1980 was that many Jews were dissatisfied with Carter, but they still would not vote for a conservative Republican candidate. Throughout the campaign, there were clear indications that the Jewish vote was going to be very different from what it had traditionally been. In the ethnic Jewish press an unprecedented number of articles and advertisements came out in support of a candidate other than the Democratic one, and much of this output was more anti-Carter than pro-Reagan or pro-Anderson. The Orthodox-oriented *Jewish Press* was a rare example of a Jewish weekly newspaper that was staunchly pro-Reagan. There were many reasons for the anti-Carter sentiment among American Jews, his perceived weakness in foreign policy matters, including Israel, for example, but they did not result in any significant shift to the right.

Virtually all the evidence, from both national and local elections, belies what Michael Ledeen refers to as "a major hoax in the conventional wisdom" (Ledeen, 1979), namely, the projection that American Jews are rapidly moving to the political right and that they have weakened in their commitments to peace and social justice as they have moved socioeconomically upward. To the contrary, on issues concerning welfare, civil rights, women's rights, civil liberties, and even internationalism—except in support for the United Nations because of its overt hostility toward Israel—American Jews have remained liberal (Fisher, 1979a, 1979b). When asked on an NBC Exit Poll on November 4, 1980, for their position on the Equal Rights Amendment, for example, 69 percent of the Jews were in favor of it, as compared to 45 percent of the total population interviewed; 17 percent of the Jews and 36 percent of the total interviewed opposed ERA. Asked whether the decision about abortion should be left to the woman and her doctor, 89 percent of the Jews interviewed responded affirmatively, while 74 percent of the Protestants and 61 percent of the Catholics did so. Nor have Jews turned their backs on their commitment to civil rights even though there has been strong resistance to affirmative action defined as quotas within the American Jewish community (cf., Glazer, 1979; Rose, 1981). While the country as a whole has moved to the right, Jews remain "off the graph" (Himmelfarb, 1973, pp. 65–116), that is, they maintain their left-of-center position on the American political spectrum.

At the present time, on the other hand, no evidence

supports Arthur Liebman's prediction of a major swing to the left by American Jews in the next few decades (Liebman, 1979, pp. 600–613). As Liebman sees it, the major reasons for this leftward swing will not be Jewish history and tradition—such as concern for the underpriviledged—although these factors may play a minor role. The move or "return" to the left, as he sees it, will be pragmatic; because of external social forces, it will be the most rational option. Liebman assumes that the American economic crisis will deepen and that there will be a corresponding Jewish economic decline. Because Jews are relatively absent from the key positions in the core sectors of the economy and are present in the more competitive sectors, they are much more vulnerable during a period of economic decline. Moreover, in such a situation Jews are particularly subject to financial decisions of the non-Jewish core capitalists, and those decisions probably will not be favorable to Jewish interests and many Jewish businesses will likely go under. Jewish professionals and others who supply goods and services to Jewish firms will be affected by the contraction, while the opportunities for Jews in the educational and governmental spheres will decline. Anti-Semitism will probably increase in the economic crisis, Liebman assumes, and Jews will be excluded from professional and middle-class careers. The growing cadre of Jewish low-paid workers, petty merchants, frustrated intellectuals, and others—angry because of their downward mobility or their inability to rise socioeconomically—will find that their only alternative is to align with other exploited groups to bring about democratic socialism.

While Liebman is correct in that Jews are relatively absent from the core positions in the economy, there is no evidence to support his prediction of a significant decline in opportunities for American Jews. While they are undoubtedly experiencing the effects of the current national economic decline, there is no empirical reason to assume it is having a disproportionate impact upon them. Liebman is correct that the opportunities in academia have been shrinking and are projected to continue so. On the other hand, many occupations—engineers, scientists, mathematical specialists, science technicians, medical workers, computer specialists, social scientists, lawyers, accountants, and even social workers—are expected to experience growth during the current decade, according to the Bureau of Labor Statistics of the U. S. Department of Labor (*New York Times*, 1980). These are all occupations in which Jews are disproportionally represented, and there is no evidence of any increasing restrictions preventing Jews from entering them. Nor is there any evidence of an increase in anti-Semitic attitudes and behavior that would have a negative impact upon the economic condition and opportunities of American Jews, as the following discussion indicates. Finally, given the increasing discord in the past several decades between the concerns of American Jews as they see them and those of the socialist and Communist countries and their supporters in the United States, it seems highly unlikely that American Jews would align themselves with the champions of socialism even if Liebman's other predictions were to be realized.

Patterns of Anti-Semitism

In 1966 Charles Herbert Stember identified a clear trend of gradually declining anti-Semitism in the United States from the end of World War II to 1962, the last date for which data was available to him (Stember, 1966). Between 1963 and 1975 a series of nine studies on different aspects of anti-Semitism, sponsored by the Anti-Defamation League (ADL) of B'nai B'rith and carried out by the Survey Research Center of the University of California at Berkeley under the direction of Charles Y. Glock, generally found the continuation of that trend (Glock and Stark, 1966; Glock, Selznick, and Spaeth, 1966; Marx 1967; Selznick and Steinberg, 1969; Lipset and Raab, 1970; Stark, Foster, Glock, and Quinley, 1971; Glock, Wuthnow, Piliavin, and Spencer, 1975. See also Glock, 1979). Perhaps the most consistent finding was that those of lower socioeconomic status—in terms of education, occupation, and income—invariably scored higher on questions measuring anti-Semitic beliefs and discriminatory attitudes than did those of higher status, and of the three variables, education is the most predictive. The rather conclusive finding with respect to the inverse relationship between education and anti-Semitism is in sharp contrast with Stember's more tentative finding, several decades ago, that the impact of education is limited. His findings suggested that education tends to reduce the more blatant kinds of discrimination and expressions of hostility, but that it does not really have any significant impact upon the more subtle kinds. As he put it, "the impact of education is limited. Its chief effect is to reduce traditional provincialism—to counteract the notion that members of minorities are strange creatures with exotic ways, and to diminish fear of casual personal contact. But the limits of acceptance are sharply drawn; while legal equality is supported, full social participation is not" (Stember, 1961, p. 171).

This finding of Stember, prior to the ADL studies, is one of the issues which Lucy Dawidowicz raised in her critique of the entire series of studies (Dawidowicz, 1977). In fact, where Stember saw education at least as reducing "traditional provincialism," if not bringing about real attitude change, Dawidowicz is skeptical of contemporary formal education's having any impact:

> Indeed, the emphasis on education as *the* countervailing force to prejudice exposes the weakness of this method of relying exclusively on attitudes and opinions without referring to ancillary or supplementary considerations, such as the capacity of social and political institutions to absorb and neutralize group conflict. Moreover, nothing that one has learned from contemporary and historical sources supports confidence in the healing properties of education in overcoming prejudice. Especially nowadays, when a college education is no longer a bulwark against the superstitutions of astrology, when propaganda of the Third World and the Palestine Liberation Organization can flourish on college campuses as the New Received Truth, and when rationalism on the campuses is not only straight and square but dead, we can scarcely depend on educational institutions to provide defenses against the blandishments of ethnic prejudice [ibid., p. 205].

Dawidowicz is critical also of the volume in the ADL series by Gary Marx, which deals with anti-Semitism among blacks. Marx found that blacks score higher than white non-Jews on an index of anti-Semitic beliefs when the indicators deal with economic practices of Jews. On noneconomic indicators, less of a difference was found between black and white non-Jewish beliefs. Moreover, contrary to what many believe, especially Jews, blacks were not found to selectively, or specifically, evaluate Jews any more negatively than they do whites in general. In addition to denouncing Gary Marx as an apologist for black militancy, Dawidowicz's most serious criticism is that the questions Marx asked in order to measure militancy were rendered "ancient history" by the changes in the civil rights movement in the mid-1960s. Had he conducted his study in 1968 rather than in 1964, she argues, his findings would have been entirely different.

In a more limited study in 1970 of a sample of blacks aged 20 years and older in two areas in south central Los Angeles, Tsukashima found that, in contrast to popular opinion, black anti-Semites—that is, those who are prejudiced specifically against Jews—tended to come from less ghettoized areas, to be of higher socioeconomic background, and to be characterized by a limited range of contact with Jews, as compared to those who are not prejudiced toward Jews in particular. Tsukashima interprets his findings as suggesting an emerging "class conflict between aspiring, middle-class blacks competing with middlemen Jews" (Tsukashima, 1978, p. 58).

In an extensive report on anti-Semitism prepared by William Schneider for the American Jewish Committee in 1978, an analysis of recent opinion surveys found a relatively low level on anti-Semitism, lower in fact than most Jews assume, despite the energy crisis and economic recession. In percentages Schneider found on the average about one-third of non-Jews "willing to accept anti-Semitic stereotypes or willing to say that Jews differ from others in ways that might be interpreted negatively" (Schneider, 1978, p. 18). Schneider's analysis concurs with earlier studies which found that anti-Semitism declines with higher education. He found that anti-Israel sentiment rises with increased education, however (ibid., pp. 114–27; see also Lipset and Schneider, 1979). More recent surveys—by Yankelovich, Skelly and White in December 1979 and by Gallop in October 1980, indicate a slightly different pattern with respect to attitudes toward Israel. Their surveys suggest that the more educated are both more pro-Israel and pro-Arab than the less educated, and that the difference between pro-Israel and pro-Arab sentiment is greater among the educated (Rosenfeld, 1980a, 1980b).

Schneider's findings concerning black anti-Semitism were similar to those of previous studies, namely, that it is most pronounced in economic stereotypes and that it has seen an apparent gradual decline. He also found significant differences between young blacks and older blacks and young blacks and young whites. His data indicated a higher rate of anti-Semitism among young blacks than among older blacks. Also, young blacks were significantly more anti-Semitic than young whites. Moreover, comparing survey data from 1964 and 1974, Schneider found white anti-Semitism to have decreased at a faster rate than black anti-Semitism, with the result that by 1974 blacks were relatively more anti-Semitic than whites (Schneider, pp. 88–94).

In 1981 Yankelovich, Skelly and White conducted a broad study of anti-Semitism in the United States, and they found that it has declined significantly during the past fifteen years or so. The decline "has been most evident when it comes to traditional negative images of Jewish character such as those relating to dishonesty, shrewdness, assertiveness or willingness to use shady business practices" (Yankelovich, Skelly and White, Inc., 1981, p. 3). According to them, it is not individual attitude change that has resulted in the decline of anti-Semitism, but societal changes. There has been no overall decline of anti-Semitism among those alive today who were in the 18 to 55 year cohort in 1964. Rather, many of those who were 55 and older in 1964 and were highly anti-Semitic are no longer alive, and those who were young children in the mid-

1960s are 18 to 34 today and are highly tolerant (ibid., pp. 3–4). These findings reconfirmed the relationship between education and anti-Semitism (see Table 4). Thus, whereas 28 percent of those who were not high school graduates and 26 percent of those who were high school graduates were among "The Prejudiced," only 14 percent of those who were college graduates or postgraduates were in that category.

With respect to anti-Semitism among blacks, the findings of Yankelovich et al. were closest to those of Schneider, although not quite the same. The 1981 data revealed that anti-Semitism among blacks has essentially remained at the same level as it was in 1964, in contrast to a decline among whites, and indications are that "anti-Semitism among blacks is, at least in part, a specific expression of a more general conflict between "the haves" and the "have nots" (ibid., p. 32). Specifically, 20 percent of the whites surveyed were among "The Prejudiced" and 37 percent of the blacks (ibid., pp. 31–34).

The theme of several studies in the ADL series on anti-Semitism was the close association between religion— especially Christian beliefs—and anti-Semitism. Yankelovich et al. found that, in contrast to impressions frequently conveyed in the popular media, "Christian Orthodoxy and

Table 4. Education and Anti-Semitism

	Total % Non-Jews	% Prejudiced	% Neutrals	% Unprejudiced
Total % Non-Jews	(100)	23	32	45
Respondent's Education				
Less than high school graduate	(100)	28	37	33
High school graduate	(100)	26	35	38
Some college	(100)	15	22	58
College graduate/ postgraduate	(100)	14	18	61

SOURCE: Yankelovich, Skelly and White, 1981, p. 28.

religiosity have declined significantly since 1964" (ibid. p. 117). Also, while there is some connection between Christian fundamentalism and anti-Semitism, it is "due to the effects of age, education and race. After controlling for these three demographic factors, the association of religion and anti-Semitism disappears" (ibid.).

These findings concerning the patterns of anti-Semitism in the United States are in stark contrast with the American Jews' perception of them. As Yankelovich et al. found, most Jews feel that non-Jews hold much more negative attitudes toward them than the findings on the non-Jews indicate; Jews are much more aware of anti-Semitic incidents and believe that the number of such incidents is on the rise; and most Jews believe that an increase of anti-Semitism in the country is a possibility (ibid., pp. 49–69). If one reads the Anglo-Jewish press in the country, it is evident that Jews are very sensitive to anti-Semitism. After all, it is the role of the Jewish press to report all events affecting Jews. It is also evident that certain sectors of the American Jewish population perceive an anti-Semitic threat in the country today more than others. In the New York City area, for example, some publications such as *The Jewish Press*, published in New York, and *The Jerusalem Post* contain regular notices of the "Museum of the Potential Holocaust" in New York, with a branch in Jerusalem, which proclaim: "Hate-motivated movements . . . are growing quickly in membership and influence in America. They are gaining the sympathy and support of many of your neighbors. Hitler is their patron saint. Learn about them. The lesson might save your life."

The Jewish Defense League and other organizations espouse the same theme. Many others, who might not quite agree, do nevertheless cite evidence of an increase in anti-Semitic incidents recently. The Anti-Defamation League of B'nai B'rith, for example, issued an audit of anti-Semitic incidents for the year 1981, which was widely reported in the Jewish press, according to which "the number of episodes of vandalism against Jewish institutions, private Jewish property such as homes and stores, and anti-Semitic vandalism of public property, increased substantially in 1981—an increase for the third straight year. The audit also shows a substantial increase in bodily assaults against Jews, in mail or phone threats to Jews and Jewish institutions, and in the harassment of such targets (ADL, 1982, p. 1).

How can we interpret the glaring discrepancy between the perceptions of so many American Jews about anti-Semitism and attitude studies that document a steady and significant decline in anti-Semitism in the United States? It would be tempting simply to say that Jews are paranoid were it not for the incidents to which so many Jews can personally attest as evidence of anti-Semitism. Also, as a sage colleague who was both a Catholic priest and a sociologist once remarked, any Jew who is not "paranoid" has no sense of history. And yet the survey research so consistently indicates a steady decline in anti-Semitism that it would be difficult to reject the findings out of hand. Perhaps the best conclusion is that at the present time the position of Jews in American society appears to be relatively secure, certainly in the sense that there is no immediate threat to their physical survival or their socioeconomic survival. Further interpretations of the evidence on anti-Semitism must depend upon, as Wuthnow suggests,

what implicit comparisons are being made. Four options are possible: comparisons with the past, comparisons with other social groups, comparisons with an idealized state of affairs, and comparisons with what is considered reasonably attainable. Comparisons with the past typically lead to inferences that current levels of anti-Semitism are relatively benign. Comparisons with other social groups are more difficult to make, since various such comparisons are possible. As the survey research has shown, Jews tend to elicit more dislike than Protestants or Catholics, but less dislike (generally) than blacks. Comparisons with an idealized state of affairs are most likely to inflate the seriousness with which anti-Semitism is regarded. Many who have studied it have likened it to a disease that should be eradicated completely. As long as 10 percent of the population is afflicted, there is cause for concern. Comparisons with what is reasonably attainable tend to produce mixed evaluations. . . . Perhaps the main thing to be said is that both caution and introspection need to be exercised in interpreting statistics on anti-Semitism (Wuthnow, 1982, pp. 166–67).

7. The Contemporary American Jewish Family

One major social issue which was widely debated during the 1970s was the future of the family in modern society. The issue was probed from a variety of perspectives and involved spokespersons from such fields as sociology, social welfare, social history, religion, and politics; indeed, Sussman (1978) has suggested that the 1970s may well come to be known as the decade of "The Great Family Debate." The sources of that debate and an evaluation of the various prognoses will not be discussed here. For the purposes of this chapter it is sufficient to point out that within the American Jewish community as well there was (and is) widespread concern over the future of the American Jewish family. As to the larger societal issue of the future of the family, however, some were not overly concerned about the implications of the decline of the family within the Jewish community, although there has been a virtual consensus that the decline of the American Jewish family presents a serious challenge to the future of the American Jewish community. The focus of concern has been upon individuals as members of the American Jewish community and the implications for the continuity of that community, and not solely upon the well-being of individuals qua individuals. Why is American Jewry so uniquely concerned about the future of the American Jewish family? In this chapter I shall attempt to explain this concern, first by pointing to the role of the family in Jewish socialization and continuity and then by analyzing the empirical data concerning the contemporary American Jewish family.

The well-being of the Jewish family is a primary concern because it plays a central, if not the central, role in defining and transmitting Jewish identity and identification. A vast body of literature describes and explains the socialization of children by the family, the more relevant parts of which have been reviewed elsewhere (Waxman, 1979b). Certainly within the history and tradition of Jews, the family has been the most prominent institution involved in ethnoreligious identity formation and the transmission of ethnoreligious norms and values. (For a detailed, though idealized, description of the role of the Jewish family in Eastern European small towns and villages, see Zborowski and Herzog, 1962, pp. 269–380.) It is, thus, no coincidence that the home and the synagogue are the two, and the only two, institutions in Jewish life which are referred to in traditional Jewish literature as *mikdash me'at* or "sanctuary in miniature." The family and the synagogue— which historically was not a "house of worship" solely but equally the center for education, study, and learning—were the two major institutions through which both Judaism and "Jewishness" (Glazer, 1972) were transmitted. The family in addition has been the stage, if not the focal point, for much of Jewish religious tradition. Observers both past and contemporary have viewed the family as the institution responsible for Jewish continuity (cf. Vitz, 1977, p. 89). Accordingly, the contemporary condition of the American Jewish family will be examined as well as the implications of this condition for the future of the American Jewish community. The focus of this analysis will be upon five structural variables: marriage, divorce, fertility, intermarriage, and extended familism.

Marriage

Jews and Judaism have traditionally placed a high priority on marriage as an intrinsic value, and data indicate that a high proportion of America's Jews are married, and that the vast majority marry at least once. In their study of Providence, Rhode Island, Goldstein and Goldscheider found that Jews had a higher rate of marriage than non-Jews (1968, pp. 102–3). In a more recent study of Rhode Island, Kobrin and Goldscheider found marriage to be virtually universal among Jews, with the proportion of ever married increasing over the years (1978, p. 38). That those findings are fairly representative is evident when compared with figures reported from the National Jewish Population Study (NJPS). In the table, "Percent Distribution of Households' Age of Head, by Marital Status, U.S. Jewish Population—1971," less than 5 percent of respondents aged 30 and over are single. More than 95 percent are listed as married, separated or divorced, or widowed (Chenkin 1972, p. 16). This high rate of ever married would seem to indicate that American Jewish continue to abide by the biblical dictum that "it is not good for man to be alone" (Genesis 2:18).

Andrew Greeley (1974, p. 45) reports different findings in data derived from seven National Opinion Research Center (NORC) surveys. He found that "among the three major religious bodies, the Jews (at least if they are Eastern European and 'Other') are rather surprisingly less likely to be married than the Catholics, and the Catholics are less likely to be married than the Protestants." His figures show a somewhat higher rate of never married than reported by Chenkin. Without specifying age cohort, Greeley found that for American Jews of German background 3.2 percent were never married, for those of East European background the percentage rose to 11.3, and for "Other" American Jews 15.7 percent were never married (p. 46, Table 6). The discrepancy between the NORC and NJPS data cannot be explained at this point. Nevertheless, Greeley's data are more commensurate with the preceptions of many observers of American Jewry that the rate of marriage is now considerably lower than reported in studies before the 1970s (cf. Goldscheider, 1978).

One source of relatively recent data, which also provides for comparison with data collected a decade earlier, is the study of the Boston Jewish population sponsored by the Combined Jewish Philanthropies of Greater Boston (Fowler, 1977). Recognizing that the Jewish population of Boston is atypical of American Jewry as a whole in that the Boston population has a disproportionately high number of Jews involved in academia, its trends may nevertheless indicate patterns that will spread to other American Jewish communities in time. A number of changes in family patterns from the mid-1960s to the mid-1970s are significant. Whereas in 1965, 73 percent of the adult Jewish population of Greater Boston was married, by 1975 this figure had declined to 56 percent (p. 13). More specifically, in the 21–29 age cohort the percentage of those married dropped from 58 percent in 1965 to 42 percent in 1975 (p. 14). Overall, Jewish population remaining single rose from 14 percent in 1965 to 32 percent in 1975, and those currently divorced or separated rose from 1 percent in 1965 to 4 percent in 1975 (p. 13).

Preliminary data from a more recent study of the Jewish community in Greater Los Angeles suggest different patterns. While 35.8 percent of respondents ages 18-39 remained single, less than 4 percent of those aged 40–59 and 3 percent of those 60 and older remained so (Phillips, 1980). While there are no data from the previous decade with which these figures can be compared, they may suggest a tendency toward later marriage, rather than nonmarriage. If this were the case, it would simply be a continuation and extension of pattern which, as discussed below, has been evident since the early 1960s—that American Jews marry later than non-Jews.

As to age at first marriage, most evidence suggests that Jews marry later than their non-Jewish neighbors. Kobrin and Goldscheider found "that only a very small proportion of Jewish males marry at age 20 or younger compared to Protestants and Catholics" (1978, p. 78), and that "Jewish women marry at older ages on average than Protestants and Catholics in both age cohorts" (ibid., p. 83). Sklare cites a study conducted in New York City during 1963–64 from which he concludes that "native-born Jews marry later than their peers but when they reach what they consider an appropriate age they out-distance all others" (1971, p. 75). While this finding is borne out by every study of American Jews, Greeley's studies of American Catholics produced somewhat different findings. He reports data showing that "Catholics are much less likely than either Protestants or Jews to be married before their twenty-first birthday" (1977, p. 187). Since he does not provide precise information on the source of his data and the number of Jews in his sample, Greeley's findings cannot really be reconciled with the majority of studies that uniformly report later marriages for Jews than for non-Jews.

Divorce

Despite the high priority on marriage in the Jewish tradition, Judaism has never viewed marriage as an absolutely permanent and indissoluble bond during the lifetime of both spouses. Though betrothal is defined as a sacred bond—the Hebrew word is *kidushin*, from the term *kodesh* which translates as "sacred"—Judaism provides for an institutionalized ceremony through which people can dissolve that bond, should remaining together become intolerable. In considering divorce rates, therefore, and especially when analyzing the comparative rates of different groups, it must be emphasized that the absence or infrequency of divorce is not necessarily an indication of strong and positive relationships between spouses. As Goldberg (1968) points out in his survey of Jewish and non-Jewish divorce rates since the nineteenth century in Europe, in parts of Africa and Asia including Israel, and in the United States and Canada, attitudes toward divorce vary from society to society and group to group. In societies where Jews had a larger percentage of divorce than non-Jews, the reason was frequently Jewish emphasis on human dignity, rather than the marital bliss of the non-Jewish population. In examining data from various communities in the United States, Goldberg found that "separation and divorce are less prevalent among Jews than among the general white population" (1968, p. 8). In his Detroit sample, Lenski (1963, p. 219) found a lower divorce rate for Jews than for Protestants and Catholics, as did Goldstein and Goldscheider (1968) and Kobrin and Goldscheider (1978) in their studies of Providence, Rhode Island. Among Jews themselves, Goldstein and Goldscheider found the divorce rate to be higher among those born in the United States than among those born elsewhere, and higher among Reform than among Conservatives and Orthodox Jews (1968, p. 113). In contrast to a number of studies indicating that among the general American population the more educated have lower divorce rates, Goldstein and Goldscheider found divorce and separation to be higher among the more highly educated. They suggest that this may be attributed to more highly educated Jews being more secularized and acculturated, and that the rates of these Jews would therefore be more similar to those of non-Jews (p. 112). If their data are representative of national Jewish patterns, one could predict a growing divorce rate among Jews.

While no reliable data are available on current divorce rates among American Jews, there is consensus among rabbis and other Jewish communal workers that the American Jewish divorce rate has risen dramatically in recent years. Some have gone so far as to claim that the American Jewish divorce rate is identical with the general divorce rate (Smolar, 1979; Postal, 1979). When pressed for reliable evidence, most will admit that their conclusion is based on intuition and personal observation rather than data. Preliminary data from Greater Los Angeles do not support their claim. The data indicate a doubling of the divorce rate between 1968 and 1979, but in 1979 the Jewish divorce rate was still significantly lower than the general divorce rate (Phillips, 1980).

While it has been an article of faith until recently that the Orthodox Jewish divorce rate is very low (both relatively and absolutely), some claim that it too is rapidly changing. For three consecutive years, 1977–79 for example, the leaders of the largest Orthodox rabbinic organization, the Rabbinical Council of America, highlighted the issue of the rapidly increasing Orthodox Jewish divorce rate at the organization's annual convention (*The Jewish Week*, January 30, 1977, p. 4; February 5, 1978, p. 17; June 24, 1979, p. 22). These reports are based on intuition and personal observation, with no reliable supporting data (see the exchange of letters on this subject between Mayer and Waxman, *The Jewish Week*, July 1, 1979, p. 38; July 15, 1979, p. 22). The sole item approximating empirical data is the report by Kranzler (1978) of a girls' day high school in Boro Park, Brooklyn, the largest Orthodox Jewish neighborhood in the United States. The guidance counselor at the school estimated that about 8 percent of the approximately one thousand students came from homes in which the parents were divorced. Given that this is a highly traditional Orthodox school in an intensely Orthodox neighborhood, the 8 percent figure comes as a surprise. Since these data relate to cases of divorce in which there are children of high school age, it seems reasonable to assume that if younger and/or childless divorced Orthodox Jews were included the percentage would be even higher.

Single-Parent Families

A related aspect of American Jewish life, which has recently become an issue of concern to survivalists within the community, is that of single-parent families (Waxman, 1980). There are no solid data on the number or increase of such families. Nevertheless, there are indices within the community of significant increases and reliable data showing sharp increases within the American middle class. Such information strongly suggests that there has been a significant increase in the number of American Jewish single-parent families in the 1970s.

From the standpoint of the Jewish community, the causes for concern lie in the central role that the family, in its two-parent form, has played in Jewish socialization and in the evident disaffiliation and alienation from community among American Jewish single parents. Concerned as they are about the rate of increase, leaders of institutionally affiliated American Jewry have not yet resolved the dilemma of successfully integrating single-parent families into a two-parent, family-centered communal life. There are structural and cultural elements to this dilemma. The main structural component of Jewish communal life is the two-parent family, and there is a dialectical relationship between the structure and the religious-cultural value of the centrality of that family form. The perception of alienation on the part of many single parents derives from the structure that implicitly excludes single parents, the religious-cultural value which does likewise, and from the rejection of the demand by some single parents that the Jewish community not only accept and integrate them as individuals, but that the community legitimize single parenthood as an equal and viable alternative to the two-parent form. With increasing numbers of Jewish single-parent families, there will undoubtedly be increasing pressure on the organized Jewish community to take cognizance of and accommodate the needs of such families.

Fertility

All self-conscious minority groups are concerned about group size, presumably, since it is anticipated that the larger the size of the group, the greater its chances for survival in the majority/minority situation. The areas among America's Jews where this is most clearly articulated, if not acted upon, are fertility and intermarriage. Both these facets of Jewish family life are perceived by some as determining the very survival of the Jewish community in the United States; this fact is evident from even the titles of many of the most quoted writings on the subject, such as "The Vanishing American Jew" (Morgan, 1964) and "Intermarriage and the Jewish Future" (Sklare, 1964). A former president of the New York Board of Rabbis is quoted as having urged the American Jewish community to exempt itself from the nationwide trend toward zero population growth and to increase its numbers. Otherwise "it will grow weaker and will face a threat to its existence. . . . Three children should be the minimum number for Jewish families," he asserted, "but the larger the better" (Spiegel, 1974).

Most demographers would probably view this perception as alarmist, if not downright paranoid (cf. Jaffe, 1978; Berelson, 1978). But others feel these fears about American Jewish population decline are well founded. Goldscheider (1978) has summarized two contrasting perspectives on the issue:

To an outsider, the concern about the disappearance of American Jewry or the vanishing American Jew appears exaggerated or alarmist, if not ludicrous. At best the issue appears rhetorical or artificially created, to be rejected with the obvious retorts about the strength of American life. One does not have to go beyond a regular reading of the press to know that Jews are conspicuously present in a wide range of political and social activities. . . . An insider who knows the strength and weaknesses of the Jewish community goes beyond the superficial indicators and below the surface, however. Other signs appear, more powerful and challenging, subtle and destructive, which provide an alternative perspective [Goldscheider 1978, pp. 121, 123].

A look at a number of demographic variables of American Jewry provides substance to the "insider" fears.

According to the *American Jewish Year Book* (Chenkin and Miran, 1979, p. 177), the size of the American Jewish population numbers 5,781,000, or about 2.67 percent of the total population of the United States. When these figures are compared with those of the past, the 1930s for example, when Jews were 3.7 percent of the total population, it can be readily seen that American Jewry is becoming an increasingly smaller part of the overall American population. This does not necessarily mean that American Jewry is shrinking. These figures may reflect the traditional pattern of Jews maintaining a lower birthrate than their non-Jewish counterparts. As Goldscheider (1967) has demonstrated, the lower birthrate of Jews is not only characteristic of contemporary American Jewry but has been the pattern in the United States since the nineteenth century. This pattern is found in Europe as well, as Goldstein states: "Already in the late nineteenth century, the Jewish birthrate was lower than that of the non-Jewish population. This differential has persisted to the present. Jews marry later than the average, desire and expect to have the smallest families, have had the most favorable attitudes toward the use of contraceptives, have used birth control to a greater extent than other groups, and have been among its most efficient users" (1981b, p. 163).

Closer inspection reveals that American Jewry is not only becoming a smaller proportion of the total population, but that the American Jewish birthrate is at and possibly below the replacement level, which is generally accepted to be an average of 2.1 children per family. For American Jewry the issue is not that of zero population growth, but of negative population growth. Studies of the fertility expectations of women of childbearing age, which suggest a narrowing of the gap between the birthrates of Jewish and non-Jewish women, leave no room for optimism about the Jewish birthrate, because the projected decline in the differential is not due to a rise in the Jewish birthrate but to an anticipated decline in the non-Jewish birthrate (Goldstein, 1981b; Cohen and Ritterband, 1981). If current trends of religious intermarriage continue, the rate of Jewish fertility seems likely to decline even more significantly, since, as Goldstein indicates, couples in which one of the spouses is Jewish have significantly fewer children than couples where both spouses are Jewish. For Jewish women married to Jewish husbands, the average is 2.1 children, whereas for Jewish women married to non-Jewish husbands the average is 1.6. Similar patterns prevail in the case of Jewish husbands married to Jewish and non-Jewish wives. The reasons for this differential are beyond the scope of this chapter. The significant issue here is that the differential exists and that intermarriage is increasing.

There are a number of qualifications to these projections and predictions. First, there are the limitations inherent to demography. Second, as most demographers of American Jewry caution, the limitations of those studies whose samples are significantly Jewish and the small number of Jews represented in national surveys, make for an even greater risk in predicting Jewish demographic patterns. A third limitation is the serious bias in the samples in all the surveys and studies upon which the predictions are based. There are groups of American Jews, such as Hasidim and other Orthodox Jews, who live not only in Brooklyn but in sections of practically every large city in the United States who are not represented in the samples. Because they are not inclined to talk about private family matters, because they live in highly insular communities and would probably not talk about such matters with outsiders, because they have a greater tendency to remain within their own primary groups—their chances of being queried as respondents and interviewees in demographic studies are remote, if not nil. But these groups' demographic patterns may be radically different from the mainstream, sufficiently so as to offset the trends of the majority. It has been suggested, for example, that families with more than a half-dozen children are common among these groups. If that continues to be the case, their high birthrate could compensate for the low birthrate of the majority and thus curtail the American Jewish population decline. This is merely a highly speculative point within a discussion of the limitations of demographic prediction.

A number of ideological movements in American society have arisen which have had a direct impact on the family and fertility and in which there appear to be a proportional number of Jews affiliated, but about which there are little reliable data. Included among these are the "gay" movement, the radical feminists, and those who favor marriage without children. The organized Jewish community is not quite certain of the way to deal with these movements, although the Union of American Hebrew Congregations, the national agency of the Reform synagogues, has accepted gay congregations into its ranks. Whether and how these movements will affect mainstream American Jewry and its pattern of family life remains to be seen. This area calls for extensive empirical analysis.

One contemporary social movement has had enormous impact upon family life in general and American Jewish family life in particular—the women's movement. Although the Equal Rights Amendment did not pass, the women's movement—which was spawned by the many social and cultural changes in American society, especially after World War II—and the place of women within those changes have made a broad imprint within American society. But there is a tendency, among both critics and supporters of the women's movement, to exaggerate the direct impact of that movement on the fertility rate of American Jews. On the one hand, some portray feminism as the arch villain responsible for the declining birthrate and many other ills affecting the American Jewish community. If it were not for feminism, they argue, American Jewish wives would be home where they belong having and raising good Jewish children. To them, "Women's Lib" is the curse of our day. On the other hand, it has been argued that the only reason American Jewish men are concerned with the issue of fertility is that they are male chauvinists, and they are trying to use the issue of fertility as a rationale for maintaining Jewish women in subordinate positions (see Bulka, 1979, and Frank, 1977/78, for example). The issue is much more complex, of course; the declining birthrate and other American Jewish family matters may be only tangentially related to the women's movement and are much more directly related to participation of women in the labor force.

The dramatic increase in the participation of women in the labor force in the United States during the twentieth century borders on the revolutionary. Since 1960 women have accounted for fully 60 percent of the labor force growth in the country. Moreover, there has been an even more dramatic increase in the labor force of married women with young children. Since 1960 the rate has doubled, and the rate for women with preschool children has tripled (Kamerman, 1982, p. 149). Sheila Kamerman has succinctly summarized the relevant data of American women in the contemporary labor force:

> The most rapid growth in the labor force participation rates since 1970 has been among married women under age 35, with children under age 3. Mothers have higher labor force participation rates than women without children, and married women with children are as likely to work as those with none. Half of all adult women work today (60 percent of those who are nonaged)—about two-thirds full-time. Close to 60 percent of those with school-age children, 50 percent of those with children aged 3–6, and 40 percent of those with children under age 3 are in the labor force today. In contrast, labor force participation rates for married men,

historically the status with the highest rates, has been declining
steadily, although those with children continue to have rates over
90 percent, the highest for any group [ibid.].

Although we have no precise data for the labor force
participation rates of American Jewish women, we can assume
that they are at least as high as the general rates, especially
when the relationship between education and female labor
force participation is taken into account. According to Kamerman, "regardless of whether a wife has children, the more
highly educated she is the more likely she is to be in the labor
force. Over two-thirds of the wives who are college graduates
were in the labor force in 1978. The largest single family type
today in the United States is the two-earner, husband-wife
family" (Kamerman, 1982, pp. 149–50). Given the high educational levels of American Jewish women, it is certain that
they have very high rates of labor force participation.

This increase in the labor force participation rates of
American Jewish women to a large extent accounts for the
declining birthrate of American Jews. As Kamerman points
out, when one analyzes fertility trends and the available
evidence on decisions concerning fertility, clearly a major
factor in the decision to have more than one child is dealing
with the conflicts and struggles between the demands of work
and those of maintaining responsibilities to family (ibid., p.
153). While the tensions between work and family are not
new, somehow they were managed more easily when only one
parent was at work and the other parent, invariably the
mother, remained at home. Today however, with the rapid
increase of working wives and mothers, the tensions between
work and family for both parents are magnified.

Since women today are in the labor force for the very
same economic and noneconomic reasons that men are, and
the evidence shows that women are in the work force to stay
and that their numbers will continue to increase, it seems
inane to make the fertility issue a focus for debates on
feminism. Rather, only by removing the fertility issue from

polarizing rhetoric and by subjecting it to careful empirical analysis will it and its central needs be addressed.

Along these lines, students of social policy have made recommendations to American Jewish communal organizations for the creation of communal support systems aimed at alleviating the many economic and social pressures experienced by American Jewish families today and viewed as being at the heart of the declining fertility rate and many other vicissitudes of Jewish family life in modern American society (Kamerman, 1981; Waxman, 1979b; Rosen, 1979). There appears to be a growing consensus that the American Jewish communal institutions should adopt an explicit posture in favor of larger families and provide supports—reduced or free tuition in Jewish schools for families with three or more children, quality Jewish day-care facilities, among many others—aimed at encouraging Jewish couples to have more children.

The significant impact of these recommendations is, highly questionable, however. Given that there is no broad pronatalist ideological posture in American society as a whole—on the contrary, the general American ideological stance at best is anatalist, if not antinatalist—and given that American Jews are so highly acculturated in American society, it seems rather farfetched to hope that the American Jewish communal organizations would adopt a pronatalist stance to begin with. Moreover, even if the community had the resolve to adopt this stance, its impact is in doubt. While it is not difficult to point to the variety of ways in which the American Jewish communal organization inhibits an increased birthrate, there is no evidence that changes in those arrangements would result in a higher one. While it seems reasonable to suggest, for example, that the absence of quality Jewish day-care facilities has a negative impact on the Jewish birthrate, the experience in countries that do provide quality day care indicates that the birthrate has not increased accordingly, even in those countries that take an offical pronatalist stance. The same is true with other social services in countries seeking to increase the birthrate. In virtually every industrialized country the birthrate continues to decline in the face of expanding social services. There is a universal inverse relationship between social class and fertility, with those who ostensibly have the greatest need for family policies having the largest families. Increasing the birthrate, apparently, involves much more than changing institutional arrangements to reduce economic burdens.

Goldscheider has argued that minority status has been the source of the low birthrate among American Jews: "The aspirations of Jews for social mobility, their desire for acceptance in American society, and the insecurity of their minority status tended to encourage small families" (Goldscheider, 1967, p. 207). This suggests that if the American Jewish community wishes to increase the birthrate, it must make much stronger efforts to change the minority status and economic insecurity of American Jewry. Only when Jews have become more acculturated, integrated, and economically secure in American society, this implies, will the birthrate increase. Yet, the reality of the American Jewish experience indicates quite the reverse. American Jewry has been disproportionally successful economically, has become increasingly acculturated and integrated into American society, and the birthrate has continued to decline. Conversely, the birthrate is higher among the more strictly Orthodox who invariably are less acculturated and less affluent than less Orthodox and non-Orthodox Jews. If, as this suggests, there is a causal relationship between secularization and declining birth rates, it is difficult to envision any significant changes in the fertility patterns of American Jews in the foreseeable future.

Intermarriage

As is the case for all social groups, Jews reserve one of the most severe sanctions—intense ostracism—for those members who reject and deny the group. Historically apostasy has been deemed an even more serious affront than the violation of religious codes. The former is perceived as a rejection of both the religion and the group, whereas the latter is limited to the Jewish religion.

Until recently intermarriage was considered such an act of rejection. Among traditionalists not only was intermarriage not condoned, but the Jewish spouse was considered "dead" and his or her family observed many of the traditional rites of mourning. Even in the minority of cases where the non-Jewish spouse converted to Judaism—in which situation the evidence of rejection, if any, was not clearly present—there was strong disapproval from the Jewish community. The community feared that the conversion was religiously insincere and that, while the couple may not have explicitly rejected the Jewish community, their children would surely be lost to it. It was inconceivable that the offspring of such parents would be socialized as Jews. Intermarriage, even when involving conversion, was perceived as harmful to the Jewish people, which has a strong sense of corporate identity.

With the modern era the socioeconomic position of Jews in the United States and in the urban centers of Europe improved. Along with rising political and social equality there were increased informal social contacts and interpersonal relationships between Jews and non-Jews. Predictably, the intermarriage rate of Jews increased somewhat (Barron, 1946, pp. 177–89), but the group as a whole remained highly endogamous. In his review of studies of Jewish intermarriage Rosenthal (1963) reported that data from a study of Washington, D.C., by Stanley Bigman indicated an overall Jewish intermarriage rate of 13.1 percent, with that rate rising to about 18 percent for third-generation American Jews. "The Washington data revealed that children in at least 70 percent of mixed families are lost to the Jewish group" (p. 32). By 1965, the National Jewish Population Study estimated the intermarriage rate to be 29.1 percent and rising. As of 1972, it estimated that the rate of intermarriage had risen to 48.1 percent (Massarik, 1973, p. 11).*

---

*It should be noted that this rate is based upon couples, not individuals. The difference may be clarified through the following example. Suppose there were ten Jewish males marrying ten females, five of whom were Jewish

As evidence of rising intermarriage rates mounted during the 1960s, public expressions of concern for the Jewish future of intermarriage couples and their children grew louder. In 1964 Marshall Sklare (1964, p. 48), widely regarded as the foremost authority on the sociology of American Jewry and whose analyses emanate from a survivalist perspective (Waxman, 1977–78), decried "Jewish complacency about the rate of intermarriage." Contrary to prevalent arguments used by those attempting to dissuade couples from intermarrying by suggesting that intermarriage is a symptom of psychological maladies and invariably leads to marital instability, Sklare asserted that "it is precisely the 'healthy' modern intermarriage which raises the most troubling questions of all to the Jewish community." He warned that the rising intermarriage rate posed a formidable threat to "the Jewish future." In 1970 he reiterated his warning, asserting that this threat overshadowed recent positive developments in the American Jewish community. "It strikes," he argued, "at the very core of Jewish group existence" (Sklare, 1970, p. 51).

Despite the stern warnings and dire predictions of Sklare and many others, no strategy for dealing with the issue has appeared on the Jewish communal agenda. An attitude of inevitability seems to have developed—that the community will have to reconcile itself to "living with intermarriage" (Singer, 1979) and making the best of it. In an attempt to resolve the tensions of the resulting "cognitive dissonance" (Festinger, 1957), a number of students of Jewish intermarriage now argue that what appeared as a threat may actually be a blessing in disguise. Fred Massarik, who was scientific director of the National Jewish Population Study,

---

and five not. Using an intermarriage rate based on couples, there would be a 50 percent intermarriage rate; half of the couples are endogamous—both spouses are Jewish, and half are exogamous—they involve intermarriage. However, if the intermarriage rate were based upon individuals, then only five of the fifteen Jews, or 33.3 percent, are marrying non-Jews. This needs to be stressed because of the frequent popular reports which misinterpret the data and state that one out of every two Jews who marries at the present time marries a non-Jew. In actuality, if the data are accurate, the figures are one out of every three.

has reconsidered the data and suggests that the issue for Jewish survival is not intermarriage but fertility, and that "the net effect of intermarriage may be an increase in Jewish population rather than a decrease" (1978, p. 33). While not arriving at an unequivocal conclusion, Massarik argues that the issue of intermarriage as it affects the Jewish future is more complex than it has previously appeared. It is only one variable which itself has many complex features, such as whether the non-Jewish spouse undertakes conversion, or whether the Jewish spouse is male or female. Each of these variants has a differential impact on the future identification and plans for involvement of the intermarried couple and their children with the Jewish community and Jewish religious-cultural life. While Massarik is correct in his contention that the issue of intermarriage is complex, the available evidence does not support his tentative suggestion that intermarriage may increase Jewish population. As discussed below, the available data strongly suggest that the conversion rate in intermarriages is approximately 20 to 25 percent. The vast majority of non-Jewish spouses do not convert and, of those who do, many do so only perfunctorily. For the children of those who do not convert, Jewish socialization, according to available evidence, ranges from negligible to nil and therefore it is highly doubtful that they can be counted as part of the next generation's Jewish population pool.

In their summary report of a national study (Mayer, 1978) sponsored by the American Jewish Committee (AJC) on "Intermarriage and the Jewish Future," Mayer and Sheingold (1979) argue that the rate of Jewish intermarriage will continue to increase in the foreseeable future. Their study confirmed earlier findings by Lazerwitz (1971) that what they term "conversionary marriages," in which the previously non-Jewish spouse converts to Judaism, compare favorably in terms of religious affiliation and observance not only with "mixed Marriages," in which the non-Jewish spouse does not convert, but also with endogamous Jewish marriages. "The Jewish community would do well to examine what steps it can take to encourage" conversion (Mayer and Sheingold, 1979, p. 32). While they accept the inevitability of increasing intermarriage and call for steps to encourage conversion, they do not go so far as to say that intermarriage is not a threat. On the contrary, they conclude that the data "tend to reinforce the fear that intermarriage represents a threat to Jewish continuity," primarily because "most non-Jewish spouses do not convert to Judaism; the level of Jewish content and practice in mixed marriages is low; only about one-third of the Jewish partners in such marriages view their children as Jewish; and most such children are exposed to little by way of Jewish culture or religion" (p. 30).

In two subsequent publications Egon Mayer, director of the AJC study, focuses and elaborates on his outreach proposal. In the lengthier of the two written for the National Jewish Conference Center (Mayer, 1979b), he urges that the Jewish community change its traditional stance of discouraging prospective converts and establish "conversion outreach centers" which "should bridge the gap betwen the religious Jewish community and the potential convert" (p. 7). He maintains, however, that most spouses of mixed marriages are probably not receptive to conversion in any case, and so there is virtually no chance that they will ever become wholly integrated into the Jewish community. Moreover, their Jewish spouses, who may serve as their Jewish role models, rarely if ever mainfest any religious behavior. To the extent that they are active Jews they are so within secular rather than religious frameworks. Mayer maintains that there are many non-Jewish spouses in mixed marriages who identify as Jews in that they have positive feelings toward Jewry and participate in secular Jewish activities, such as serving on committees of Jewish community centers, on the boards of local Hadassah chapters, and in federation fund-raising activities. Given this growing group of mixed-marriage spouses who, according to Jewish religious law, *halachah,* are not Jewish but feel themselves to be somewhat Jewish in a secular and perhaps even ethnic sense, Mayer recommends that a new category of Jew be created—those who are members of the "people" but not of the "faith" (p. 7). In a second article on this subject, Mayer (1979c) is even more explicit in calling for a kind of "ethnic conversion," which will respond to the desire of many of the intermarried to see themselves and be seen as Jews, but without religious conviction. Motivated by a desire to improve the demographic outlook, Mayer sees hope in the minority of spouses in mixed marriages who, he claims, "are Jews through the alchemy of sociology, not of *halachah*" (p. 64).

A proposal for outreach similar to Mayer's was offered at the quarterly meeting of the board of the Union of American Hebrew Congregations on December 2, 1978, and made the front page of the *New York Times* the following day. (The proposal, together with reactions of four Jewish leaders and a discussion with a number of converts appears in *Moment*, March 1979.) A Conservative rabbi has also published a number of articles in recent years in which he advocates a change in the Jewish stance toward conversion (Friedman, 1979). At the close of 1981 the Union of American Hebrew Congregations formally approved a plan that not only undertakes major outreach efforts, but also breaks radically with the traditional identification of Jewishness through matrilineal descent (Briggs 1981). Although there have been some murmurs of opposition to both of these new approaches, the organized Jewish community has been amazingly subdued about them. Nor has it developed any strategy for stemming the rising rate of intermarriage. While the community no longer perceives intermarriage as a curse, neither does it perceive it as a blessing. The community has come to begrudgingly accept intermarriage with the implicit faith that it can be successfully endured. Empirical research on the next generation may reveal the degree to which that faith is warranted. If the five "half-Jews" interviewed by Span (1979) are in any way representative of this group, there are grounds for skepticism about the extent to which the children of mixed marriages serve as a potential source of strength for the American Jewish community.

Extended Familism

As to patterns of kinship relationships, the ideal household of the American Jew, like that of the middle class generally, consists of parents and their minor children (Sklare, 1971, p. 94), in contrast to the three-generation household typical among Jews in Eastern Europe. The American Jewish family appears to be relatively unique in maintaining strong kinship ties. This characteristic is so out of line with what one would have predicted on the basis of the group's socio-economic status, that Berman (1976) has pointed to it as "an inconsistency in theory" (see also Balswick, 1966; Westerman, 1967; Winch, Greer, and Blumberg, 1967; Sklare, 1971, p. 95; for a study of the interesting development of family clubs and cousins' clubs among Jews in New York City, see Mitchell, 1978). With the increasing rate of intermarriage, it remains to be seen to what degree the extended familism of American Jews will prevail and to what extent this kind of extended family will serve to reinforce and transmit Jewish identity and identification.

Child Rearing

One of the most popular images of the Jewish family is that it is child centered. As was discussed in a previous chapter, Gans found this to be true in Levittown and Park Forest, and Sklare (1971) pointed to the value of *nachas fun kinder*, pride from children's accomplishments, as that which motivates Jewish parents to invest so much time, effort, and money in their children's development and advancement. In a comparative religious analysis of data from the National Opinion Research Center's General Social Surveys conducted between 1972 and 1980, Cherlin and Celebuski found that it was in child rearing that Jewish families were most different from those of Protestants and Catholics:

> When asked what qualities they consider most desirable for children to have, contemporary Jewish parents were more likely than non-Jewish parents to stress qualities that reflect autonomy and self-direction; conversely, they placed a lower value on qualities associated with obedience and conformity to external authority. Thus, Jewish parents seemed more likely to instill in their children those qualities that are congruent with the more

highly-rewarded and prestigious occupations in our society. In doing so, they probably enhanced their children's chances of entering higher-status occupations [Cherlin and Celebuski, 1982, p. 7].

It remains to be seen what impact this type of child rearing has on the specifically Jewish character of the American Jewish family and what consequences, if any, it has on the Jewish identification of the children

Centrality of the Family

It was argued at the beginning of this chapter that an examination of the contemporary American Jewish family is warranted, particularly because of the central role it plays in defining and transmitting Jewish identity and identification. The foregoing examination indicates that though certain unique family patterns persist, the American Jewish family has changed significantly from the traditional Jewish patterns, and that it is increasingly manifesting the same patterns as the general American middle-class family. If that is the case, it would be appropriate to raise the question of the probability of Jewish group survival in American society. Developments within the American Jewish community during the last decade suggest that the prognosis for the survival of American Jewry is more positive than it appeared in the early 1960s. For example, in his assessment of recent changes in the suburban Jewish community of Lakeville, Sklare (Sklare and Greenblum, 1979, pp. 333–405) points to "many positive signs of Jewish survivalism," which, he implies, might mitigate the "negative signs, most obviously the rise of intermarriage" (p. 404). Do such findings support the argument of those, such as Kutzik (1977), that the family plays a subsidiary role in Jewish identification, and that communal institutions, such as the synagogue and social welfare institutions, play the more basic role? And if so, is the scarcity of data on the contemporary American Jewish family justified by its secondary nature? My response to both these questions is negative. To begin with, I have argued that although the family plays a central role in Jewish identity formation and transmission, it cannot be viewed in a vacuum, without the support of the more formal institutions of the Jewish community (Waxman, 1977b, pp. 5, 7). On this matter Kutzik agrees (1977, p. 35). His position on the primacy of communal institutions and secondary nature of the family is based on his view of "the limited . . . role of the contemporary American family in . . . enculturation or sociocultural identification." The contemporary family, "whether Jewish or not," he asserts, "is structurally incapable of carrying out enculturation on its own" (p. 11). Here Kutzik is echoing Rosenberg and Humphrey, who assert "the second-ary nature of primary groups." They argue:

> Agencies of socialization transmit culture; they do not necessarily create it. Primary groups may be the nursery of a human nature whose shapes and contours they do not determine. A sacred society will use its neighborhoods in one way, a secular society in another. The child must always be socialized within a small group, but the norms it is obliged to "interiorize" have another and a larger locus. The child is plastic, and he is molded to a large extent by his family, his play group, and his neighbors, but all these take their essential character from courses external to them [Rosen-berg and Humphrey, 1955, p. 27].

While there is no disagreement as to the family's inability to function in this manner "on its own," Kutzik underestimates the significant degree to which the family of the past and present, Jewish or not, is involved in identity formation. The family is not only a "haven in a heartless world" (Lasch, 1977); it is a "small world" (Luckmann, 1970) in which the self emerges and in which the individual acquires a stable sense of identity and reality.

In terms of Jewish identity and identification, likewise, the family plays the central role in primary socialization and provides the foundation for the complementary roles of formal communal institutions. This does not mean that strong traditional family ties will necessarily provide that founda-tion—those with no Jewish self-consciousness will not. As Rosenberg and Humphrey point out in their analogy of the primary group and the conveyor belt, "the belt is *eo ipso* a neutral object, which must be adjusted to work norms and end products impersonally thrust upon it" (1955, p. 27). We are dealing with families that have a Jewish consciousness and with the central role the family plays in defining and transmitting that consciousness to the next generation. Communal institutions are important in providing the structural context for realizing and living out that identity and for reinforcing it, but they are still secondary to the primary role of the family. Recent studies by Cohen (1978) indicate that those living in "alternate families" are considerably less Jewishly active than those living in traditional normative families. Apparently, nontraditional family forms cannot provide the framework within which the individual would acquire a stable sense of Jewish identity and Jewish reality, and therefore he or she does not seek out those structural contexts within which Jewish identity operates.

If, as the evidence suggests, changes in the American Jewish family have been most dramatic within the past two decades, it may be premature to take solace from recent positive signs of Jewish survivalism which Sklare and others have found. They may be but short-term patterns resulting from a number of events which took place within both the Jewish and general American communities during the late 1960s and early 1970s (cf. Glazer, 1972, pp. 151–86). But their staying power may be limited, especially as the American cultural milieu and the American Jewish family have changed.

Those positive signs are found among American Jewry. This is not the contradiction it appears to be. There is a basic difference between being an American Jew and being a member of the American Jewish community—between those who are nominally Jewish and those affiliated with the organized community. While it is difficult to get precise figures, indications are that the unaffiliated comprise a large portion of the American Jewish population. Elazar, for example (1976, pp. 70–74) has divided the American Jewish population into seven groups, represented as a series of seven uneven concentric circles, ranging from the hard-core "integral Jews" to those whose Jewish status is least clear, "quasi Jews." If we add up his estimates of those who are "peripherals" and beyond, we find that 25 to 30 percent of the American Jewish population is completely uninvolved in Jewish life. Another group, "contributors and consumers," who "clearly identify as Jews but are minimally associated with the Jewish community as such, comprise about 25 to 30 percent of all American Jews" (p. 73). The condition of contemporary American Jewry is one in which there is a "shrinking middle" (Goldscheider, 1978, p. 125). There is a polarization with respect to Jewish commitment. The positive signs discussed by Sklare are manifested only within that approximately 50 percent of the American Jewish population affiliated with the American Jewish community. The weakening commitment of the other half, the unaffiliated, has distinct implications for the qualitative survival and well-being of the whole.

8. Denominational Patterns, Jewish Education, and Immigration

In the era of the second-generation community, as discussed in Chapter 3, social class and time of arrival in the United States were highly significant variables in the denominational structure of American Jewry. The general pattern was for those of upper-class status and longest length of time in the country to be associated with Reform Judaism, middle-class Jews with Conservative Judaism, and working-class and lower-class Jews and those in the country for the shortest amount of time with Orthodox Judaism. Thus in the third generation, Conservative Judaism was the largest, Reform second, and Orthodox the smallest of the three major branches of American Judaism (Reconstructionism, an offshoot of Conservative Judaism founded by Mordecai M. Kaplan, has only recently developed an autonomous institutional structure and is not quite yet a branch in its own; see Kaplan, 1934; Miller, 1969; Liebman, 1970). In their analysis of data from the 1970 National Jewish Population Study, Lazerwitz and Harrison found Reform affiliates to include fewer foreign born and more third-generation Americans than Conservative affiliates, and they found Orthodox to include the largest percentage of foreign born. Socioeconomic differences between the denominations remain, but they are considerably smaller than in the past (Lazerwitz and Harrison, 1979).

In analyzing the affiliations of American Jews, Lazerwitz found that as of 1971, 11 percent identified with Orthodox, 42 percent with Conservative, 33 percent with Reform, and 14 percent had no denominational identification. With respect to membership, about 50 percent of American Jews were synagogue members (Lazerwitz, 1979). Lazerwitz's data are from the National Jewish Population Study of 1970; thus, significantly, the synagogue membership rate has dropped rather dramatically from that which Sklare and Greenblum found in Lakeville, a community assumed to be representative of American Jewish communities of the future. Whereas Sklare and Greenblum found that approximately 66 percent of their respondents were synagogue members, in shortly more than a decade later the data indicate that membership had dropped to 50 percent. It also seems reasonable to assume that the rate of synagogue membership has declined even further since 1970.

When generation was held constant, Lazerwitz found that significantly different affiliational patterns emerged between foreign-born American Jews and those with both parents having been native born. The Orthodox declined from 26 percent among foreign born to 3 percent among native born; the Conservative declined from 47 percent among foreign born to 30 percent among native born; and Reform rose from 14 percent among foreign born to 41 percent among native born. In support of the previous suggestion that synagogue membership has declined even further since 1970, note that those with no denominational identity rose from 13 to 26 percent (ibid.). While not all those with no denominational identity are necessarily nonmembers in synagogues, the data do support the assumption of a break with previous affiliational and membership patterns.

On the basis of data from both the National Jewish Population Study and the 1965 survey of the Jewish community of Greater Boston, Lazerwitz predicted that in the foreseeable future the Orthodox will decline further and become a very small denomination of only a few percentage points. The Conservatives, too, will decline because of the decline of the Orthodox, who were a major source of new members for the Conservatives, and also because of some loss to the Reform branch, which will probably become the largest branch of American Judaism (ibid.).

There does seem to be an incongruence, however,

between these data and predictions and various as yet unquantified manifestations of a resurgence of Orthodox Judaism throughout the 1970s, as was discussed above (Chapter 5, near the end). Also whether the National Jewish Population Study included a reliable sample of sectarian Orthodox is questionable (Liebman, 1965, pp. 67–85). Right-wing Orthodox, such as those affiliated with the Eastern European advanced *yeshivas*, with Agudath Israel, or the various sects of Hasidism, who—as mentioned before—have a considerably higher birthrate than the rest of American Jewry are probably much more resistant to responding to polls, questionnaires, and interviews, especially when conducted by those outside their own communities. On the other hand, Himmelfarb suggests that the impressions of a resurgence of Orthodoxy may, in reality, merely be the result of Orthodoxy's increased wealth and greater organizational sophistication and institutional proliferation, even while their actual numbers are decreasing (Himmelfarb, 1979).

The findings of a recent study of the membership of Conservative synagogues by Liebman and Shapiro suggest somewhat different future denominational patterns than those projected by Lazerwitz. Their findings supported Lazerwitz's projection of a Conservative decline because of the Orthodox decline and also because of affiliation with Conservative synagogues by only a minority of the married children of Conservative parents. Specifically, while 39 percent of the married children of Conservative parents were in 1979 affiliated with Conservative synagogues, 35 percent were nonaffiliated, 13 percent were affiliated with Reform congregations, 4 percent with Orthodox, and 0.6 percent with Reconstructionist synagogues (7 percent of those surveyed did not respond, and 1 percent gave some other answer, Liebman, 1980, p. 3; see also Liebman and Shapiro, 1979). On the basis of these findings, which indicate major membership declines in the forthcoming years for the Conservative movement, it appears feasible that, other things being equal, by the end of this century Conservative Judaism might shrink even more than Lazerwitz indicates, with large percentages not affiliating, others affiliating with Reform, and a smaller percentage affiliating with Orthodoxy.

While the ordination of women has been one of the most emotionally charged issues for Conservative Judaism in recent years, with the majority of its organizational membership strongly in support (Gordis, 1980; Gordis et al., 1981). Liebman and Shapiro find that the ordination of women would only serve to accelerate the rate of defection from the Conservative movement. Their reasoning is that the core group within Conservative synagogues is composed of those who observe Jewish dietary laws and who provide intensive Jewish education for their children. It is this group which is most strongly opposed to the ordination of women and who indicate that they would leave the Conservative synagogue and affiliate with the Orthodox were the ordination of women adopted as policy and practice. Conservative Judaism thus would be losing its strongest link with the future.

Patterns of Jewish Education

Historically, as we have seen, the formal Jewish educational system was one institution within a communal network. The goal of the educational system was to transmit Jewish knowledge. The schools were never designed to create Jewish identity or positive Jewish attitudes and values, but to intensify already existing ones. Yet a large segment of American Jewry looks to Jewish education as the creator of Jewish identity. Be that as it may, since empirical evidence and widespread belief indicate that formal Jewish education does play a primary role in enhancing if not forming Jewish identity and correlates highly with adult Jewish involvement, contemporary trends in Jewish education in the United States should be examined.

According to the most recent data available, approximately 40 percent, or 357,101, of the roughly one million Jewish children of school age, were enrolled in a formal Jewish educational program in 1978/79. In terms of actual numbers of children enrolled, this was a decline of 8.8 percent from the

1974/75 figures and a decline of 40 percent from the 1960/61 figures (American Association for Jewish Education, 1979, p. 37). In other words, about 60 percent of American Jewish children of school age receive no formal Jewish education. Among the 40 percent who do, 24.5 percent attend schools one day a week, 49.2 percent attend supplementary schools which meet two or more afternoons a week, and 26.3 percent attend schools all day (ibid., p. 22). In terms of the auspices and/or ideology of the schools, 35.6 percent of the children receiving any kind of formal Jewish education are enrolled in Reform schools, 29.5 percent in Conservative, 24.1 Orthodox, 7.1 communal (nondenominational), 3.6 independent, and 0.1 percent in Yiddish schools (ibid.).

While the number of students in Jewish schools is declining, the 1978/79 Jewish School Census indicated a trend toward the intensification of Jewish education. This trend manifested itself in several ways. While the overall student population in Jewish schools declined, for example, there was an increase in the day school population, from 77,774, or 25.4 percent of the total enrolled in 1974/75, to 90, 675, or 26.3 percent of the total enrolled in 1978/79 (ibid., p. 38). Conversely, enrollments in one-day schools have declined from 30.2 percent of the total in 1974/75 to 24.5 percent in 1978/79, and one-day education, especially in the primary grades, appears to be declining even in the Reform movement where it had been the dominant mode of education (ibid., p. 14). One further manifestation of the intensification of Jewish education is the small but clear increase in the proportion of all students who continue their Jewish education through the high school years. This group's percentage increased from 15.6 percent in 1966/67 to 16.8 percent in 1978/79 (ibid.). Thus, the emerging picture shows declining numbers and percentages of Jewish children receiving any kind of formal Jewish education, but an intensification in education for those who attend Jewish schools.

The obvious question that follows is, to what effect? The answer to this important question in turn depends upon the criteria by which effect is measured. As Walter Ackerman points out, for example, "if knowledge of the traditional

Jewish texts is to be the criterion of an educated Jew, then only the day school graduate has the background and skills to qualify" (Ackerman, 1969, p. 21). Yet, evidence indicates rather conclusively that if such knowledge is not to be the criterion but, rather, adult Jewish identification and involvement are the criteria by which the effectiveness of Jewish education is measured, day schools emerge as the most effective system of Jewish education. As mentioned above, Himmelfarb's data suggested that a minimum of 3,000 hours of Jewish instruction are necessary before Jewish schooling has any lasting impact (Himmelfarb, 1975, p. 3; see also Cohen, 1974; Sigal, August, and Beltempo, 1981). This means that at least seven years of full-time Jewish instruction are the minimum necessary for any long-range impact. Since approximately 75 percent of American Jewish children in Jewish schools do not receive that kind of Jewish education, the educational system is failing in terms of the objective set out for it by the parents who send their children to Jewish schools. The problem essentially is the one perceived by Gans in his study of Park Forest, namely, parents want the schools to provide the Jewish socialization for their children but do not wish that socialization to infringe upon their own life-styles (see above, Chapter 4, beginning). Yet all the studies confirm that the main effect of schools is to accentuate existing values and attitudes, and that encouragement and reinforcement must come experientially from the home. In the final analysis, with the best of teachers and curricula—which hardly exist at the present—the American Jewish educational system cannot meet the demands and expectations placed upon it. Given the level of Jewish commitment, as indicated by the denominational trends, little improvement in the effectiveness of Jewish education can be anticipated in the foreseeable future.

Recent Jewish Immigration

While the Jewish quality of American Jewry has diminished in some important respects in recent decades, it might be suggested that there have been other infusions from what has historically been a major ethno-religious source, namely, new groups of Jewish immigrants who have not yet been significantly exposed to the processes of acculturation and assimilation into American society. It might be anticipated that these groups would bring their traditional Jewish cultures with them and they would have an impact upon American Jewish life. The experiences, therefore, of the three major groups of recent Jewish immigration will be discussed: Soviet Jews, Israelis, and Iranian Jews in the United States.

Jews from the Soviet Union. Of the more than a quarter of a million Jews who emigrated from the Soviet Union between 1971 and 1980, 79,806 came to the United States with the assistance of the Hebrew Immigrant Aid Society (HIAS).* The Soviet Jewish emigres to the United States differ from those who go to Israel in several basic ways. Those who emigrate to the United States are much more likely to be European, rather than Central Asian or Georgian, and are highly educated and acculturated into Russian culture, although their official and social identification as Jews blocks their assimilation into Russian society. Those who emigrate to Israel, on the other hand, are largely non-Ashkenazic, more traditional and more Jewishly conscious; they tend to come from the peripheral areas of the country, such as West Ukraine, Moldavia, and the Baltic, or from Georgia and Central Asia (Gitelman, 1981, pp. 3-4).

The median age of Soviet immigrants to the United States is 35. Between 25 and 29 percent of those who immigrated between 1974 and 1980 are younger than age 20; between 8 and 19 percent are older than age 60; the trend, however, is toward a higher proportion of older people. Thus in 1980, 19 percent were above age 61 (ibid., p. 5).

More than half of the Soviet immigrants who arrived in this country between 1974 and 1979 are in the labor force and, in contrast to other contemporary American immigrant

---

*Gitelman, 1981, p. 2. These figures do not include those Soviet Jews who immigrated to the United States without the assistance of HIAS, such as those who initially went to Israel before coming to the United States, and the smaller number of those who came directly to the United States with the assistance of organizations or individuals other than HIAS.

Table 5. *Initial Settlement of HIAS-Assisted USSR Arrivals in the United States in Selected Communities, 1976–1979*

Community	Jewish Population	1976	1977	1978	1979	Total
Baltimore	92,000	88	175	238	668	1,169
Boston	170,000	105	174	355	713	1,347
Chicago	253,000	266	499	1,031	2,099	3,895
Cleveland	75,000	174	170	377	814	1,535
Detroit	75,000	116	139	283	485	1,023
Los Angeles	455,000	397	383	819	1,832	3,431
Metropolitan N.J.	95,000	123	84	219	525	951
Miami	225,000	111	101	271	528	1,011
New York City	1,998,000	2,363	2,974	5,134	12,213	22,684
Philadelphia	295,000	240	290	514	1,369	2,413
Pittsburgh	51,000	56	82	120	357	615
St. Louis	60,000	60	94	162	396	712
San Francisco	75,000	87	145	235	765	1,232
District of Columbia	160,000	49	51	97	217	414
Others	1,781,900	1,277	1,481	2,410	5,813	10,981
Total:	5,860,900	5,512	6,842	12,265	28,794	53,413

SOURCE: Edelman, 1982, p. 159.

groups, more than half of the working Soviet Jewish immigrants are professionals, engineers, and technicians. Of the
almost 10,000 professionals, for example, 3,172, or one-third
of them, are in the humanities; 25 percent, or 2,373, are in
medicine; and almost 20 percent, or 1,761 are in the arts and
entertainment. There are more males than females among
those who are in engineering and blue-collar occupations,
while there are more females than males in the professions
(ibid., p. 6). While there are no hard data, it appears that there
are problems of unemployment and especially underemploy-
ment and downward occupational mobility. A study of former
Soviet citizens who immigrated between 1977 and 1981 and
who now live in such cities as New York, Cleveland, Detroit,
and Chicago, found that—while close to 60 percent of the
sample, which included students and housewives, were employed—half of those employed reported that they were not
employed in their area of specialization (ibid., p. 8).

There are several possible reasons for the high rate of
reported downward occupational mobility. Obviously, that
there is such a high rate of professionals and technicians
among the Soviet Jewish immigrants makes them even more
dependent upon the alchemy of the occupational marketplace,
particularly in terms of the limited number of positions
available. Also, it is quite feasible that the qualifications for
professional positions in the United States are more stringent
than in the Soviet Union. Thus, in addition to learning a new
language, the immigrants may be required to undergo additional training in which they will obtain the latest knowledge
and skills in their respective fields before they will be hired in
that area. And, it is frequently the case that job titles mean
very different things in this country than they do in the Soviet
Union. As Joseph Edelman states: "Community agencies have
reported at times that, upon examination of their functions in
the Soviet Union, an engineer might be the equivalent of a
construction foreman in the United States; an accountant
might be considered a bookkeeper, and an economist might
more properly have an occupational listing of pricing
clerk. . . . There is, too, the problem that for some Soviet

occupational categories, e.g., feldsher or stomatologist, there are no American equivalents" (Edelman, 1977, pp. 174-75).

While 70 percent of Gitelman's sample of Soviet immigrants reported that they were satisfied or very satisfied with their life in the United States and that they see other immigrants equally satisfied, more than half indicated a "mildly negative evaluation" of the resettlement agencies and workers with whom they have come into contact. Many feel that the resettlement workers discriminate among the immigrants and that they "play favorites," especially in the assignment of housing and obtaining jobs and loans (Gitelman, pp. 9-11). With the meager evidence available, it is difficult to determine how accurate these perceptions are. They may, for example, stem from the inherent suspicions that Soviet citizens have of officials. Since there are no recognized private social service agencies in the Soviet Union, the immigrants may associate the resettlement workers with a government from whom they are used to experiencing discrimination. On the other hand, one could reasonably assume that many of the resettlement workers do, actually, play favorites. And yet, despite their allegations, the vast majority of those interviewed said that, with everything, were they confronted with the situation today, they would still emigrate from the Soviet Union, although about 17 percent indicated that they would choose a country of immigration other than the United States (ibid., p. 12).

As Gitelman points out, "A Russian sub-culture is developing in the United States, as is evidenced by the revival of the newspaper *Novoe Russkoe Slovo* and some Russian journals, as well as by the appearance of the weeklies *Novyi Amerkianets* and *Novaia Gazeta*, and of many original works of Russian literature published mainly by Ardis in Ann Arbor, Michigan" (ibid., p. 13). This subculture is especially visible in neighborhoods in the larger cities which have high concentrations of Soviet Jewish immigrants. One such area is the Brighton Beach section of Brooklyn, New York, which has become popularly known as "Odessa by the sea" because of its distinctly Russian character. With almost 50 percent of the

Soviet Jewish immigrants settling in New York City, this neighborhood contains between 20,000 and 23,000 of them in Greater Brighton Beach. On the main shopping street, Russian and Yiddish are common languages, Russian-style dress is commonplace, and there are many shops that specifically cater to the large Russian Jewish clientele.

In Baltimore, which has an estimated Jewish population of 92,000, more than 1,100 Soviet Jews who arrived between 1976 and 1979 settled (Edelman, 1982, p. 159). To facilitate their acculturation to both American society and the American Jewish community, HIAS of Baltimore founded a Russian-English monthly newspaper, *The News Exchange*, the first issue of which appeared in May 1978 (Hoffman, 1980). Averaging 20 pages an issue, the newspaper publishes items of practical information for the new immigrants, such as citizenship requirements, government programs for which the immigrants may be eligible, and information on medical care. Notices about programs for Soviet Jews sponsored by the Jewish community, timely articles about Jewish holidays and customs, and discussions of Jewish issues are also regular features. The Soviet Jewish readers are also asked to contribute their thoughts and feelings about their experiences, in the hope of strengthening the dialogue and developing the bond between the subcommunity and the larger Jewish community of Baltimore (ibid.). Although "there is considerable variation among the newly-arrived Soviet Jews in their reaction to Jewish communal attempts to further their Jewish knowledge," it is apparent nevertheless "that many Soviet Jews in communities throughout the country have begun to cultivate their Jewish roots" (Edelman, 1982, p. 164).

While American Jewish resettlement agencies have become more skilled and do appear to be having some success in integrating the immigrants into the American Jewish community, the enthusiasm and involvement of American Jews with the issue of Soviet Jewry seem to have waned in recent years. There are many reasons for this phenomenon, such as American Jewry's recognition of the limitations on its ability to effect any changes in the policies of the Soviet government on emigration. One other reason for the decline of the issue of Soviet Jewry within the American Jewish community appears to come from the incorrect perceptions that many American Jews had of Soviet Jews and their reasons for emigrating to the United States. In fact, for many American Jews, there probably is an inverse relationship between their dedication to the cause of Soviet Jewry and their personal contact with Soviet Jewish emigres.

During the early years of Soviet Jewish emigration, many American Jews assumed that the emigres had strong religious motivations for wanting to leave the Soviet Union and that they would look and act as the American Jews imagined that the Eastern European immigrants during the years 1880–1924 did. The reality was quite different. While they emigrated because of anti-Semitism, oppression, or economic reasons, few of the emigres who have come to the United States left for religious reasons. In Gitelman's survey, for example, he found that "only 8 percent of the Jews identify themselves as religious." While very few identify themselves as anti-religious," the overwhelming majority cluster around the intermediate categories of "traditional" and "non-religious" (Gitelman 1981, p. 17). Many American Jews were initially shocked to find that most Soviet Jewish emigres did not attend synagogue, did not send their children to Jewish schools, were largely ignorant of Jewish tradition and did not manifest a strong desire to identify with it. Even worse, as far as many American Jews were concerned, they seemed to have a strong acquisitive drive and simply wanted to be left alone to make new lives for themselves. Nor did they manifest strong appreciation for all the Jewish communal efforts on their behalf.

Since it is much more difficult to deal constructively with reality than it is to become enthusiastic about fantasy, the task of dealing with the emigres has been left to a relatively small number of dedicated professionals and volunteers who have a much firmer grasp of Soviet Jewish life. They understand that many of the emigres were raised under conditions in the Soviet Union in which there was no Jewish education, where it was very difficult to live a Jewish life, and where there were extensive measures undertaken by the government to estrange Jews from Judaism. Many of the communal workers, professionals and volunteers, have come to the realization that the integration of Soviet Jews into the American Jewish community is a difficult and slow process. Some fruits of those efforts are now beginning to manifest themselves.

Soviet Jewish immigration has become a fundamental issue for the American Jewish communal structure in another challenging respect, one involving a serious dissent from official Israeli policy. When in 1973 the Soviet government began to allow Jews to emigrate in significant numbers, it did so only for those Jews who claimed that they wished to be reunited with their families in Israel. That remains the only condition under which the Soviet Union allows Jews to emigrate. Soviet emigration laws do not provide for those who wish to emigrate to the United States or elsewhere. Thus, virtually all Jews who do emigrate do so only after they have obtained an Israeli visa. While in 1973 approximately 96 percent of those who emigrated did initially settle in Israel, the numbers have been declining rapidly since then. By 1976 more than half of the emigres opted for countries other than Israel once they arrived at the transit point in Vienna or Rome. The Israeli government, which has a number of reasons for wanting the emigres to settle in Israel, has strongly protested the services provided by HIAS at the transit points for those emigres opting to settle in the United States. The Israeli government maintains that the activities of HIAS are harmful, not only in terms of interests of the emigres themselves and the demographic interests of Israel, but also to the whole future of Soviet Jewish emigration. Israel argues that when the Soviet authorities realize that most Jewish emigrants in fact are not going to Israel, even though they were only allowed to leave with an Israeli visa, they will put a stop to all Jewish emigration under the claim that the emigres were leaving under false pretenses. Israel has brought strong pressure not only to have HIAS cease servicing the "drop-outs," or *noshrim*—as they are disparagingly referred to by

Israel, second only in antipathy to *yordim*, emigres from Israel—but to have no Jewish communal services provided for them once they arrive in this country. HIAS and the other Jewish communal organizations involved with the Soviet Jewish immigrants have steadfastly resisted Israel's cajolings, maintaining that it is their duty to help Jews who are in need, that Soviet Jewish emigres have the inherent right to choose to live where they wish, and that they are not responsible for, nor will their actions have much impact upon, the policies of the Soviet government.

In assessing the impact of Soviet Jewish immigration upon the American Jewish community, Gitelman suggests the following:

> First, it has mobilized many professionals and volunteers in efforts at resettlement. Considerable resources have been allocated by national and local organizations to immigrant resettlement. Second, it has changed the image of Soviet Jews from idealized hereos to real people, people with problems and shortcomings, like everyone else. Third, the "drop-out" issue has created tensions with the Israeli government and the Jewish Agency but has forced the American Jewish organizational leadership to take an independent stand, which I see as a generally positive, healthy development. Fourth, there may be some temporary demographic strengthening of American Jewry, badly in need of it, but in view of small Soviet immigrant family size and their potential for assimilation, one should not look to them for long-term help in reversing the decline of American Jewry. Fifth, Soviet immigrants have already made great contributions to the arts, especially in music, and will undoubtedly continue to do so. Finally, Soviet Jewish immigration has forced some American Jews to confront their own Jewishness and reexamine whether they have taken full advantage of the cultural freedoms they have [Gitelman, 1981, p. 18].

Jews from Israel. Much as the phenomenon of Soviet Jewish immigration has been a source of soul searching within the American Jewish community, that of Israeli immigration has been even more so. For both ideological-Zionist and pragmatic-demographic reasons, Israel regards emigrants from its countries as virtual traitors. As much as, if not more, the *oleh*—the one who "goes up," the immigrant—is admired, so is the *yored*—the one who "goes down," the emigrant—despised. The emigrant is stigmatized as a defector, and in 1976 Prime Minister Yitzhak Rabin labeled them *"nefolet shel nemushot,"* the fallen among the weaklings, the lowest of the low. Until recently the government of Israel treated Israelis living abroad for other than official reasons as nonpersons, and it encouraged the Jewish communities in the diaspora, outside of Israel, to do likewise. Within recent years, around 1979, the Israeli government changed its stance toward emigres at least in one respect. It began to perceive the possibility of the return of part of the emigrant population and has undertaken some measures to encourage that return. On the whole, however, the stigma remains.

While many American Jews hold ambivalent attitudes toward the Israeli emigrants in their midst—on the one hand as brethren but on the other as challenges to American Jewish fantasies about Israel—the official position of most American Jewish organizations is very similar to that of the Israeli government. As Kass and Lipset state:

> Most American Jewish organizations have, until recently, regarded the Israelis in their midst as neither Jewish immigrants to be helped and guided nor as persons whose knowledge of Hebrew and Israeli culture could contribute to raising the community's Jewish consciousness. Basically, the Jewish leadership does not wish to do anything that might encourage Israelis to remain here. HIAS, to take one example, does not help Israeli emigres to this country. As a result, some *yordim* (emigres) have turned to non-Jewish, primarily Catholic agencies dealing with immigrants, for assistance [Kass and Lipset, 1982, p. 280].

Perhaps one manifestation of their official nonexistence is that there are no reliable data on the number of Israelis living in the United States. Estimates run as high as one-half million, with some 200,000 living in New York City alone. There are neighborhoods in Brooklyn and Queens, New York, in which one can hear Hebrew spoken widely in the streets, where there are newsstands that carry a broad selection of Israeli daily papers, in which there are Israeli coffeehouses and pizza-falafel shops, and, in short in which it easy to imagine that one is in a section of Tel Aviv. Israelis in New York have their own weekly newspaper, *Yisrael Shelanu* ("Our Israel"), and their own radio shows. They remain "a people apart" for both internal and external reasons: internally, because many of them actually do retain hopes of returning to Israel and/or because they have internalized the official view of Israeli emigres as "moral lepers" (Nahshon, 1976) and, externally, because they are officially shunned. In addition, many retain the predominate Israeli view of the shallowness of American Jewish life, while some feel no sense of kinship with American Jewry.

One of the rare published empirical studies of Israelis in the United States is that of Dov Elizur, for which the research was conducted in 1972 and 1977. He found that the major reasons for emigrating were related to personal development, such as the desire for higher education, the utilization of talent and knowledge, and professional advancement, in addition to the search for suitable employment, higher income, and a higher standard of living (Elizur, 1980, pp. 56–57). While there appears to be an increasing tendency for new arrivals from Israel to maintain contacts with other Israelis here, 56 percent in 1977 as compared with 42 percent in 1972, the data also indicate a slightly increasing tendency for the more recent arrivals to have little or no contact with local Jews, 47 percent in 1977 as compared with 44 percent in 1972 (ibid., p. 58).

The religious orientation of the respondent proved to be significant in several respects. Orthodox Israelis are a minority among the respondents, and they were a smaller minority in 1977 than they were in 1972. Whereas in 1972, therefore, 29 percent of the sample were Orthodox, in 1977 only 16 percent were (ibid., p. 56). Religious observance was also found to be related to intentions to return to Israel (coefficient of 0.24, ibid., p. 62).

Elizur concludes with the recommendation that the Israeli authorities would be wise to assist not only those Israelis who have actually decided to return to Israel, but also those who have not (yet) made that decision. His reasoning is based upon the theory that return migration is more likely when migration was caused by pull factors than by push factors. Since his data indicate that there is more of a pull factor—that is, attraction to the United States, than a push factor, or rejection of Israel—motivating the emigration of Israelis, they must be viewed as a pool of potential return immigrants and encouraged to maintain their Israeli and Jewish identities by reading Israeli newspapers, listening to Hebrew-language broadcasts, and sending their children to Jewish schools (ibid., p. 67). At the present time, not only are the Israeli authorities not engaged in such efforts; neither is the leadership of the American Jewish community, which has even more reason to be. The leadership of the American Jewish community, one would think, would be interested in having the Israelis return to Israel and, if not, at least to integrate into the local Jewish community. Elizur's data indicate that this is not happening at the present time, and a recent report by Nahshon suggests that the children of the Israelis in the United States may be even more removed, not only from the local Jewish community, but from Judaism as well. He found that "of the estimated 30,000 Israeli children in the Greater New York area, only a small percentage is enrolled in Jewish schools" (Nahshon, 1981, p. 24). The American Jewish community would be remiss were it to continue to reject the Israelis living here, since the evidence indicates that the overwhelming majority of them consider themselves to be part of the Jewish people, feel good about their Jewishness, and present themselves to others as Jews (Elizur, p. 59).

Jews from Iran. Although precise numbers are unavailable, it is known that there was an accelerated immigration of Jews from Iran during the last several years, of the reign of the last shah, Riza Pahlevi, which lasted until the Iranian borders were sealed under the regime of Ayatollah Khomeini. Irani Jews are Sephradim, and they have formed two subgroups among the Sephardim, especially in the New York area. Those from the city of Meshed have tended to cluster around the neighborhoods of Kew Gardens and Forest Hills, in the borough of Queens, while those from Teheran have settled mainly in Great Neck, Long Island. Those from Meshed tend to be more traditional than those from Teheran, although the children of both manifest signs of rapid acculturation. Rabbi Isaac N. Trainin, director of the Department of Religious Affairs of the New York Federation of Jewish Philanthropies, was in charge of the project to assist Iranian Jews in New York during the period of the Iranian Revolution, and he has reported:

> Many homes which I have visited indicate that they have become as acculturated as the average American Jew. There is little evidence in homes of books on Judaica, etc. I have attended a number of bar mitzvahs and weddings in the Iranian Jewish community and have found them to be as Americanized and as lavish as are the weddings of other American Jews. There may be some food which is genuine Iranian, but certainly, in terms of music, you hear the same jazz and the same American music . . . [as in the typical American Jewish bar mitzvah or wedding.] A considerable number of Iranian Jewish families who have lived here for a number of years do send their children to day schools, but I believe that it is not for religious reasons, but rather because of the dislike of public schools. While it is too early to tell in terms of mixed marriage or divorce, . . . my prediction is that in not too long in the future, Iranian Jewish families, certainly in the second generation, will be the same as most American Jews [Trainin, 1981, p. 3].

In addition to families, there were Iranian Jewish students who had been studying in this country at the time of the revolution along with approximately 1,500 Iranian Jewish students who were brought here by two Orthodox Jewish organizations, the Lubavitch Hasidic movement and Agudath Israel of America (ibid., p. 2). Some of these students are in colleges and universities, while most of those brought over by Lubavitch and Agudath Israel are at yeshivas in New York primarily. Since they are not, officially, immigrants, none of them were processed by HIAS or NYANA, New York Association for New Americans, and their status is uncertain.

Their families are still in Iran, and it is not known whether they will ultimately return to Iran or their families will eventually emigrate to the United States. In the final analysis, it is too early to project what impact, if any, this small spurt of immigration will have upon the larger American Jewish community.

9. Leadership, Decision Making, and the Struggles for Change

American Jews as an ethno-religious group in American society are a voluntary group with no specific legal stature. In addition, while this group's organizational structure is very complex, its precise communal structure is somewhat amorphous. As we have seen, a variety of organizations operate in a variety of different spheres. Daniel Elazar has pointed to four basic categories of institutions within the American Jewish community, the relationships among which have developed by the accepted rules and principles determining their boundaries and spheres of activity. The two basic spheres are the religious and secular on the one hand and the public and private sectors on the other. Within each, leadership roles are divided into cosmopolitan and local, and professional and volunteer (Elazar, 1976, p. 257).

The division of Jewish institutions into the religious and secular spheres grows out of the Protestant milieu of American society. Those activities perceived to be related to ritual are considered the domain of the synagogue and the clergy, as "religious." Those activities and concerns involving welfare, social service, and/or an Israel orientation, are perceived as "secular," and are outside the domain of the synagogues. Educational and cultural activities fall somewhere in between; sometimes they are considered religious, while at other times they are treated as secular. In consequence, as Elazar suggests, they "often suffer because they fall between two stools" (ibid., p. 258). Although the boundaries between the religious and secular spheres are not as decisive as in Protestantism nor are they so firm as they were in the American Jewish community of the first and second generations—because of both the growth in the strength of the synagogues after World War II and the increasing sensitivity of those in the secular sphere to Jewish religious tradition—the two types of institutions remain structurally separate with professional leadership coming from very different kinds of training and background: the religious leadership comes from the seminaries, while the secular leadership tends to come from schools of social work. To some degree, the increased sensitivity to Jewish religious tradition among those in the secular spheres is an outgrowth of the approximately one-half dozen graduate programs in Jewish communal service which have been established in recent decades in New York City, Los Angeles, Boston, Baltimore, and Cleveland. Each program is designed to enhance the general professional and Jewish knowledge of its students and, although they vary in terms of Jewish ideological proclivities and quality (Weinberger, 1974), their graduates do appear to be more knowledgeable about and committed to Jewish tradition than the average Jewish graduate of non-Jewish schools of social work. In addition, a number of students in Yeshiva University's Wurzweiler School of Social Work are enrolled in joint programs in Jewish studies and social work, and most of them go on to careers in Jewish communal service. Even those who are not enrolled in such programs take four courses, required of all students at the school, in Jewish history, sociology, and social philosophy. While these have tended to bridge the ideological and functional gaps between the religious and secular spheres, however, the structural separation remains (Elazar, 1976, p. 259).

While the divisions between the private and public spheres are not as clear as are those between the religious and secular spheres, Jewish federation-related activities are generally perceived to be public, whereas lodges, fraternal associations, and country clubs are considered to be in the private sphere. Until recently, synagogues too were considered to be in the private sphere. With the growth after World War II in the membership and activities of many synagogues, however, there is an increasing perception that they as well are part of the public sphere. There appears to be a growing sense, for example, that synagogue boards have a responsibility and are accountable to a wider public than merely their own memberships. Whether synagogues will ultimately completely move into the public sphere and, indeed, whether the lines between the public and private spheres will eventually dissolve completely remains to be seen. For the present, the synagogue still retains its province within the private sphere.

The distinction between the public and private spheres is, as Elazar indicates, very similar to that between cosmopolitans and locals. As he defines them:

> Briefly, cosmopolitans regard the community as a total entity and maintain connections and involvements across all of it. While their cosmopolitanism is first defined in relation to a particular local community, after they develop a cosmopolitan outlook toward the local community they almost invariably also take a cosmopolitan view of the larger world of which that community is a part. Locals, on the other hand, are persons whose involvement and connections are confined to a small segment of the total community— a neighborhood, a particular social group, or, in Jewish life, a particular synagogue, organization, or club—and do not extend to the community as a whole, except indirectly. Moreover, their perceptions of the larger world are also quite limited, based as they are on localistic involvements [ibid., p. 260].

Generally, the institutions of the public sphere tend to represent cosmopolitan interests, while those of the private sphere tend to represent local interests. Not only does each community require both cosmopolitan and local institutions, individual institutions also frequently strive to have both types of representation. This sometimes raises problems of allocating functions and thus creates conflict between cosmopolitans and locals, as is evident in the American Jewish educational system.

With the possible exception of the New York City "Kehillah" experiment and local boards of Jewish education, the responsibility for Jewish education has been in the hands of individual synagogues or, in the case of day schools, private Orthodox individuals or boards of directors. Especially within the synagogue schools, the objective according to a pervasive localism was to foster loyalty to the particular synagogue among the children who attended these schools. The leadership of the public institutions—the federations—staunchly subscribed to the privatism of the Jewish schools. The major objective of the federation leadership was to enhance the integration of Jews into American society through acculturation. Many of the leaders had no Jewish education themselves, so they could hardly be expected to view Jewish education as an essential ingredient in Jewish survival (cf. Liebman, 1979, p. 40).

It was only with the shift in the pendulum (Chapter 5, above) that both Jewish educators and the American Jewish community have changed their positions. The events of the turbulent 1960s, the proddings of Jewish scholars and educators, and a demonstration by young activists on behalf of greater emphasis on education in federation allocations at the annual convention, the General Assembly of the Council of Jewish Federations, in Boston in 1969, have led the cosmopolitans to see a greater communal role in Jewish education. Locals, on the other hand, have come to realize that they must broaden their educational curricula, by placing much greater emphasis upon Israel, for example, if they wish to inspire and retain their children within their institutions.

The cosmopolitans as a result are demanding a larger communal voice in Jewish education, however, something the synagogue schools adamantly resist. On the other hand, the rapidly increasing costs of maintaining Jewish schools are leading many school directors to turn to federations for increased subsidies, and thus the struggle between the cosmopolitans and the locals continues and will probably persist so long as the synagogue maintains its place within the private sphere (Elazar, 1976, pp. 262–63).

Almost every Jewish organization and institution in the United States is run by salaried professionals, many though not all of whom have extensive professional training in an area related to their professional roles, as well as voluntary leaders. While the routine, day-to-day functions are the responsibility of the professionals, there are wide-ranging and time-consuming activities in which volunteers are engaged. About the nature of the voluntary leadership there have been disagreements among social scientists and debates among concerned members of the American Jewish community.

It will be recalled that the late psychologist, Kurt Lewin, took a dim view of many American Jewish leaders, whom he defined as "leaders from the periphery" (Lewin, 1948, pp. 195–96, and chapter 3, above), marginal individuals who, due to their success in the larger society, are courted by the Jewish community because of the "good connections," and who then use their place as leaders to enhance their positions in the larger society. Empirical studies of Lewin's hypothesis, however, have not borne it out, at least not since the era of the third-generation community. Thus Segalman's study of a sample of organizational leaders in El Paso, Texas, found that they were not peripheral, although the few individuals who were designated as being part of the "power elite" in both the Jewish and general communities did resemble Lewin's characterization (as cited in York, 1981, pp. 26–27). Riessman's study of the New Orleans Jewish community found that those who were more active in Jewish organizations and associations tended to place greater emphasis upon religion for their children while the less active placed greater emphasis upon their children's social adjustment (Riessman 1962). In Park Forest, as discussed previously, Gans found that those who were more active in Jewish associations attended synagogue services more frequently than did those who were inactive (see the beginning of Chapter 4, above). On the other hand, a recent study by York, based upon data from the National Jewish Population Study, found that American Jewish leaders are neither peripheral, as Lewin hypothesized, nor religiously exceptional, as the studies of Riessman and Gans indicate. York found that "Jewish leaders participate more than non-leaders in Jewish organizations, they tend to give more charity, to have higher occupational status, and to attend synagogue more frequently, but they are neither marginal in their Jewish practice and identification nor exceptional: they are as observant and as identifying as the average American Jew" (York, 1981, p. 32).

During the second half of the 1970s a number of disparate groups—ranging from student activists to Rabbi Meir Kahane, founder of the Jewish Defense League—protested the nature of American Jewish leadership and the structure of the organized American Jewish community. The basic grievance was that the communal organizations and their leadership were undemocratic because they were unrepresentative of broad segments of American Jewry, that they were deaf to dissent, and that the leadership was a self-appointed and self-perpetuating elite. Kahane's strongest attack was on the Conference of Presidents of Major American Jewish Organizations which, he charged, in frequent advertisements in the Anglo-Jewish press during 1975, undemocratically selected its constituents through "the rather ingenious trick of having as member groups, organizations that are themselves umbrella groups, thus in effect strengthening the membership of certain groups that are members of the Conference in their own right." The conference accepts only organizations and leaders who conform to its positions, he alleged, and it is undemocratic, unrepresentative, and detrimental to the interests of American Jewry. Similarly, he charged the Council of Jewish Federations and the National Jewish Community Relations Advisory Council with being undemocratic "tools of the wealthy."

Along the same lines, although from very different ideological quarters, a Jewish journal published by members and former members of the Jewish student counterculture, published a nine-point critique of American Jewish communal life. In an editorial in the journal *Response*, Steven M. Cohen, a sociologist now at Queens College in New York, asserted that Jewish communal leaders view democracy "as an impediment to efficient operation"; that Jewish life is exclusionary, in that it encourages the involvement of "the financially well-to-do, the males, the middle aged, the businessmen," but discourages the involvement of "the middle and working classes, women, young people (40 and under), intellectuals, and others"; that the communal structures reward those who assent and contribute to the smooth functioning of those structures and punish those who challenge it; that communal life is localistic, parochial, and informed by business and management philosophy; that American Jewish diplomacy is the handmaiden of Israeli foreign policy; that "the bearers of Jewish morality are slow to condemn Jewish immorality"; that "religious life is stagnant"; that "synagogues are mostly dull and cold"; that Jewish education is largely "insipid and uninspired"; and that Jewish teaching is largely "a second job and not a career" (Cohen, 1975).

Although Cohen advocated the formation of a new movement, a "Lobby for Jewish Change," and although there were (and are) many within the American Jewish community who agree with some if not all of his accusations, an organized movement has not emerged to challenge the Jewish Establishment on all the issues that Cohen cited. Rather varieties of interest groups have developed, each of which is organized under a banner that acts as a lobby to challenge the established operating procedures of the Jewish communal structure on one of the specific issues on Cohen's list. Before reviewing the activities of these organizations and movements, I shall examine the basic allegation more carefully that the American Jewish communal structure is nondemocratic.

What is democracy? Many definitions have been provided and, essentially, there is an ideological position in each. One of the ideological questions in the definition is whether elitism is compatible with democracy. On the one hand, some maintain that the only true democracy is "participatory democracy," in which

> decision-making is the process whereby people propose, discuss, decide, plan, and implement those decisions that affect their lives. This requires that the decision-making process be continuous and significant, direct rather than through representatives, and organized around issues instead of personalities. It requires that the decision-making process be set up in a functional manner, so that

constituencies significantly affected by decisions are the ones that make them and elected delegates can be recalled instantly, doing away with self-appointed elites whose decisions have a broad political impact on the society, but who are accountable only to themselves, or to interlocked groups of their peers [Benello and Roussopoulos, 1971, pp. 6–7].

According to this conception, the American Jewish communal structure is clearly not a democracy. As has been indicated, it is governed by a leadership of professionals and volunteers, some of whom are self-appointed, some who are appointed by closed boards, and some of whom are elected by the constituent members of the particular organization, but not by American Jewry at large, even though those leaders may make decisions that affect the larger community of Jews.

On the other hand, other conceptions of democracy allow for democratic elitism. Joseph Schumpeter, for example, defines democracy as "that institutional arrangement for arriving at political decisions in which individuals acquire power to decide by means of a competitive struggle for the people's vote" (Schumpeter, 1962, p. 269). According to this conception of democracy, representative democracy, the constant participation of those affected by the decisions is not required (nor is it feasible); all that is required is that the power to make decisions be gained through a competitive struggle for the vote. In fact the Italian political scientist, Gaetano Mosca, and the German sociologist, Robert Michels, have both argued that participatory democracy is inherently unfeasible. Mosca argued that there will always be rulers and ruled, and that among the factors supporting the rule of a small elite, or ruling class, is that most people simply are too busy with their own daily personal needs to become involved in politics for any length of time (Mosca, 1939, pp. 281–86). Michels argued that there is an "iron law of oligarchy" which is inherent in all organizations. On the basis of his analyses of the labor and socialist movements at the turn of the century, he concluded that as organizations grow, there is an increasing need for leadership, and that broad-based participation in every decision becomes increasingly impractical. Both the rank-and-file and the elite are more than happy with the arrangement whereby the few rule, regardless of whether the organization or party is initially conservative or radical. Revolutions, according to Michels, are nothing more than the replacement of one minority-ruled organization by another; organization means oligarchy, or rule by the few (Michels, 1949).

To return to the criticism of the American Jewish communal structure and its leadership and to the allegation that it is undemocratic, both the community and its constituent organizations, it should be emphasized, are of a voluntary nature. As to those in the private sphere, it is readily understandable that their leadership is selected only by the memberships of those organizations and their representatives. That factor is inherent in the very nature of private, voluntary organizations. If one were to examine the leadership-selection process in most local and national Jewish organizations, from synagogues to such secular organizations as B'nai B'rith and the many Zionist ones, it would be very difficult to substantiate the charge that they are undemocratic in terms of their operating procedures. On the contrary, they would pass the test of democratic procedures with high marks.

As we have seen, however, criticism of Jewish communal leadership and decision making involves more than technical democratic procedures. An even more serious criticism is that the political process is exclusive, that it caters only to the affluent. One reason for this can be found in another explanation by Mosca of how a small ruling class is able to maintain its rule over the masses, namely, that most people do not have the time or the money to afford them the opportunity for extended involvement in politics. Jewish communal leadership is very time consuming and, in other ways, demanding, and most people do not have the time, the financial resources, or the desire for such extensive involvement. As a result, the affluent are the leaders to a large degree by default.

The criticisms of Cohen and many others however, are not directed simply and solely at the communal leadership.

Perhaps an even greater fault is found with the entire communal structure that has become conservative and exclusivist. There is a widespread sense among American Jews that the organized American Jewish community has turned inward and that it does not reach out to the increasing number of Jews who, perhaps because of acculturation and assimilation, are not now affiliated or feel uncomfortable with the communal institutions. Some also feel that the organized community is not responsive to them and their needs and desires. Although there has been no successful coalition of all the segments of the American Jewish population who experience dissatisfaction with the organized community, a variety of social movements and organizations for change have emerged within the last decade or so, and some of them are having an impact. One of the most significant of these is the *Havurah* movement.

It is difficult to assign a precise date to the birth of the movement because of its heterogeneity and the fact that it sprang from various sources in different places. First introduced into American Jewish life in the early 1960s via the publications of the Jewish Reconstructionist Foundation (Reisman, 1977, pp. 7–8), the notion of *Havurah* dates back almost 2,000 years. The term means "fellowship," and was represented by two models in the ancient Palestinian Jewish community which emerged in response to the widespread decline in piety among the Jewish masses. One model, created by the Essenes, was located in the remote parts of ancient Palestine and consisted of small groups of Jews who subscribed to a rigidly ascetic Jewish life-style, whereas the other, created by the Pharisees who rejected the idea of removing themselves from the community, was located within the Jewish population centers and strove to influence the religious behavior of the larger Jewish population (Neusner, 1972, pp. 1–10). To some extent, both models are represented in the contemporary American Jewish *Havurah* movement which consists of some who have given up on the established community and especially its synagogue structure and seek to remove themselves as much as possible from it, whereas others are establishing fellowships within the community and even within existing synagogues.

A *Havurah* is a small community of like-minded families who group together as a Jewish fellowship for the purposes of providing each other with social support and pursuing their own participatory programs of Jewish study, celebration, and community service. *Havurot* (pl.) are generally small, ranging in membership from ten to twenty-four families who meet regularly, at least once a month, often in members' homes on a rotating basis. As indicated, some develop and function independently of any formal Jewish organization, while others are affiliated with synagogues.

The first unaffiliated *Havurah*, Havurat Shalom, was founded by a group of dissidents from the Jewish counterculture in the fall of 1968 in Somerville, Massachusetts. Most of the founders were young rabbis and graduate students in Boston who "felt estranged from American society, as exemplified by the Vietnam war and mass culture, and from the Jewish community, as exemplified by what they considered to be its inauthentic, bureaucratic institutions." (Reisman, 1977, p. 9) Subsequently, several other similar *Havurot* were founded in New York City and Washington, D.C. Shortly afterward, Rabbi Harold Schulweis, of Temple Valley Beth Shalom in Encino, California, experimented with a synagogue-affiliated model which proved to be highly successful and popular. During the 1970s there was a proliferation of both the independent and the synagogue-affiliated *Havurot*, and in the summer of 1980 the first National Havurah Conference was convened at Rutgers University, in New Brunswick, N.J., at which more than 350 Jews from diverse backgrounds and denominations gathered to share their *Havurah* experience (Novak, 1981).

According to a study of *Havurah* members conducted by Bernard Reisman, the overwhelming majority are married, under age 45, have somewhat larger than average American Jewish families, tend to be more politically liberal than the average American Reform Jew, have higher than average levels of secular education and occupations, have about average levels of Jewish education, as compared to other American Jews, are somewhat more religiously observant than the average American Jew, and tend to identify themselves as Reform or Conservative, with only a very small percentage identifying as Orthodox (Reisman, 1977, pp. 65–74). The reasons for the low rate of Orthodox involvement with the *Havurah* movement may be deduced from Reisman's analysis of the motivations of the joiners. He suggests that the movement is a response to the cultural conditions of American society which is characterized by loneliness, passivity, dependency, and meaninglessness, and that the *Havurah* represents a quest for community, participation, authority, and ideology (ibid., pp. 26–59). Since Orthodoxy is permeated with high levels of community, participation, authority, and ideology, predictably very few who identify as Orthodox would feel a need to join a *Havurah* (Waxman, 1982). Reisman's data indicate that, for the overwhelming majority of its members, the *Havurah* is not countercultural. Most of those who join *Havurot* do so not out of an ideological opposition to the dominant American Jewish culture but rather because they do not find that the existing institutions and their patterns of participation serve their needs. For them, the *Havurah* represents an alternative, more meaningful and satisfying avenue of Jewish expression. It is, as Schulweis suggests, an attempt "to decentralize the synagogue and deprofessionalize Jewish living so that the individual Jew is brought back into a circle of shared Jewish experience" (quoted in Wasserman, 1979, pp. 180–81).

While most American Jews are probably not very concerned with the low level and quality of Jewish education in the United States, as discussed earlier (above, Chapter 8), some who are have grouped together and formed the Coalition for Alternatives in Jewish Education (CAJE), which, in 1976, issued a proclamation calling for "substantive structural changes in our classrooms, in order to transform our schools into intellectually stimulating, open and joyful learning environments for our children and for ourselves. We also encourage such non-classroom learning as study weekends and camping programs, youth movements and *havurot*, programs in Israel and lifetime education. We welcome the emergence of alternative and parent-run schools, as indications of the ferment which is necessary for creative change" (quoted in Rossel, 1980, p. 24).

While the thousands who now attend the annual CAJE conferences come from a variety of Jewish backgrounds, there is a consensus among the conference participants that Jewish education will fail unless it breaks loose from its conservatism and incorporates dynamic new ideas and methodologies that will interest and involve the students in their own education. At the Fourth Annual CAJE Conference, held at Rutgers University in the summer of 1979, the major emphasis of the workshops was on new ways of teaching, with considerably less emphasis on content (ibid., p. 23). The annual conferences have attracted considerable interest among educators and are in indication, to some extent, of the validity of Cohen's allegation that Jewish education is largely "insipid and uninspired." Yet, it remains to be seen how much more successful the alternative teaching methods will be, given that Jewish education is not compulsory. Moreover, one of the most serious problems in Jewish education in the United States today is that it does not attract many dedicated and competent professionals. It remains, in large measure, a second job for many. Also, despite the high tuitions for children in Jewish schools, Jewish educators are not very highly paid nor is the status of a Jewish educator very high in the American Jewish community. The best and the brightest, therefore, choose other professions which offer a much higher income and/or higher status.

While the objectives of CAJE are relatively limited and its prospects for effecting change even more so, the situation is very different with respect to the Jewish feminist movement. The decade of the 1970s witnessed much turmoil and struggle with the issues of women's roles in the American Jewish community and in all branches of Judaism. Though probably not part of its agenda, the American feminist movement of the 1960s spawned a specifically Jewish feminist movement some years later. In part, this may have resulted from many leading feminists, such as Betty Friedan and Gloria Steinem, being Jewish. Also, young Jewish women have had a disproportionally high level of education which made them acutely aware of feminist issues. Some found themselves caught between two worlds, as was evident in a statement in the first issue of *Brooklyn Bridge*, a self-styled "revolutionary Jewish newspaper," in February 1971:

> Jewish daughters are thus caught in a double bind: we are expected to grow up assimilating the American image of "femininity". . . . and at the same time be the "womanly" bulwark of our people against the destruction of our culture. Now we suffer the oppression of women of both cultures and are torn by the contradictions between the two. . . . While PhDs do make Jewish parents proud of their daughters, the universities are recognized as hunting-grounds for making a "good" marriage. Grandchildren assure the race [quoted in Lerner, 1977, p. 5].

For those women whose consciousness raising involved an examination of their positions within religious beliefs and practices, the contradictions were particularly acute. Reform Judaism, which had by the 1940s lost its distinctive German character, had adopted the principal of sexual equality in the synagogue as far back as the nineteenth century with respect to having mixed pews and counting women for the quorum necessary to conduct prayers. Even within Reform, however, women's "proper" place was still regarded to be within the home. Despite official Reform ideology of sexual equality in all religious matters, it was not until 1972 that a woman, Sally Priesand, was ordained as a rabbi. Women were still not acceptable in the role of spiritual leaders. Priesand was not the first woman to study in one of the rabbinic seminaries of Reform Judaism; there were at least two others earlier in the century, but they were both refused ordination. Priesand's ordination at the now-merged Hebrew Union College–Jewish Institute of Religion on June 3, 1972, was given wide publicity in the media, and the influence of the women's movement in her achievement was clearly evident. As she herself wrote: "Ten years ago, women were much more opposed to the idea of a women rabbi than were men. Since then, however, the feminist movement has made a tremendous contribution in terms of consciousness-raising, and women now demand complete and full participation in synagogue life" (Priesand, 1975, p. xv).

Even in Reform there is some resistance to change, as is reflected in the remarks of one Reform rabbi who let it be known that women would not be called to the *Torah* in his congregation, on the grounds that "the Torah service is the last frontier of male religious functions" (quoted in Lerner, 1977, p. 17).

The ordination of women in Reform Judaism can provide the necessary title, but it does not guarantee a job. Some women have chosen to work in areas of Jewish communal service other than the rabbinate when their attempts to secure pulpits ended with frustration. Apparently, social attitudes are even more difficult to change than religious practices in Reform Judaism. As Anne Lapidus Lerner observed: "Clearly, if the Reform movement, which in many cases has abrogated such basic areas of Jewish observance as *kashrut* (dietary laws) or the use of *tallit* (prayer shawl) and *tefillin* (phylacteries), has changed dates of holidays, has held Sabbath services on Sunday, and has been equivocal about intermarriage, has taken so long to ordain a woman, the impediment was not religious in nature" (ibid., pp. 18–19).

If the impediments to change were so strong within Reform Judaism, which is explicitly based upon an ideology of change and adaptation, predictably the issue of women's equality in Conservative Judaism, which claims adherence to tradition, became volatile and threatened to split the movement. At the 1972 convention of the Rabbinic Assembly, the rabbinic organization of American Conservative rabbis, a delegation of women belonging to a Jewish feminist organization called *Ezrat Nashim*, came forth with a manifesto that included demands for the more complete participation of women in religious activities (ibid., p. 19). This was not an impulsive action. In 1971, *Ezrat Nashim*—derived from the name of the court of women in the ancient temple in Jerusalem—was founded in New York City by a small group of well-educated women from diverse backgrounds, who came together as a study group. They perceived Jewish tradition as progressive in the past, but as stagnating in recent times. Their concern derived from a deep commitment to Judaism and, simultaneously, a sense of having been utterly short-changed in religious expression as well as in the community as a whole.

The response to the *Ezrat Nashim* manifesto was loud and clear. Groups such as the Women's League for Conservative Judaism, the United Synagogue of America, the majority of the Committee on Jewish Law and Standards (CJLS) of the Rabbinical Assembly, and the faculty of the Jewish Theological Assembly all responded positively to some degree and affirmed the need to recognize "the feminist demand for increased women's rights" (ibid., p. 20). The decision of the CJLS, by a vote of nine to four, to count women equally with men toward the synagogue quorum resulted in a front-page story in the *New York Times* (Spiegel, 1973). But a heated debate continued over precisely what rights to accord women. The results of a 1975 questionnaire indicate that a majority of the Conservative synagogues who responded call women to the Torah and count women toward a quorum (Lerner, 1977, p. 21; see also Elazar and Monson, 1981). The issue of the ordination of women within Conservative Judaism, however, is not yet resolved. In 1975 the president of the Rabbinical Assembly predicted that sooner or later women would be permitted in the Conservative rabbinate. Most lay bodies of the movement have voted in favor of the ordination of women. The majority of the rabbinic faculty at the Jewish Theological Seminary is still opposed, however, and as yet they have not granted ordination to any women. Although the issue is far from resolved, the findings of the study by Liebman and Shapiro, concerning the future of Conservative Judaism (above, Chapter 8, beginning), possibly has strengthened the hand of those opposed to the ordination of women, because that study adds sociological evidence to their religious-ideological and social bases for that opposition.

Even within Orthodoxy, which is inherently much more

resistant to change, there have been strong calls for innovation and reevaluation of the woman's role, both within the synagogue per se and within religious life in general (e.g., Berman, 1973; Poupko and Wohlgelernter, 1976; Greenberg, 1981). Although the issue has not been as challenging on an institutional level within Orthodoxy as it has been within the Conservative movement, because there is both a more firmly based conception of sexual role differentiation and a much stronger tendency to submit to rabbinic authority within Orthodoxy, it seems reasonable to anticipate that the challenges to traditional modes will increase in the future. Since the levels of secular education and occupation are rising among Orthodox women, it is difficult to imagine that they will not internalize many of the prevalent middle-class American notions of women's equality, as will their male counterparts who are also increasingly acculturated in the educational and occupational structures. It seems inevitable that increasing numbers of Orthodox women and men will experience serious personal conflicts over the position of women within Orthodoxy and they will challenge the prevalent institutional arrangements unless there are indications of sensitivity to those conflicts and a receptivity to accommodation within the boundaries of Orthodox Jewish law and practice.

The religious sphere is not the only area within Jewish life which Jewish feminists have criticized for its sexism. They have challenged the exclusive domination by males of virtually all of the decision-making positions within American Jewish organizations. As Elazar observed in 1973:

> With some exceptions, women function in environments segregated from male decision-makers within the Jewish community. The exceptions are significant for what they reveal. Very wealthy women who have a record of activity in their own right, often in conjunction with their husbands, but sometimes even without them, are admitted to the governing councils of major Jewish institutions and organizations. So, too, are the top leaders of the women's groups, in an *ex officio* capacity which is sometimes translated into meaningful participation but frequently remains *ex officio* [Elazar, 1973, p. 10].

In an effort to determine the extent to which this pattern
had changed by the end of the decade of the 1970s, the listings
of "National Jewish Organizations" in the 1979 *American Jewish
Year Book* (AJYB, 1979, pp. 302–42) were examined, specifically
with respect to the proportion of women to men among the
chief executive officers of six categories of organizations:
community relations, cultural, overseas aid, religious and
educational, social/mutual benefit, and social welfare. In each
category, specifically women's organizations were excluded,
as it was assumed that their chief executive officers would be
women; although even among these were some whose
executive directors were men. The findings indicated that
seven of the twenty-four chief executive officers of community-relations organizations, or 29.1 percent, were
women; five presidents of thirty-two cultural organizations,
or 15.63 percent, were women; two of the sixteen chief
executive officers of overseas aid organizations, or 12.5
percent, were women; ten of the 137 executive officers of
religious and cultural organizations, or 7 percent, were
women; one of the chief executive officers of sixteen social/
mutual benefit organizations, or 6 percent, were women; and
three of the twenty-five executive officers of social welfare
organizations, or 12 percent, were women. The only category
in which there was any substantial difference between the
1979 percentages and those of 1969, was in community
relations organizations, where there were virtually no female
chief executive officers in 1969 (AJYB, 1969, pp. 469–90).

Undoubtedly, some will argue that the gross underre-
presentation of women in decision-making positions in
American Jewish organizations is not the result of sexism but
rather due to the lack of professionally trained women to fill
these positions. Others will argue that the underrepresenta-
tion is because women are much less career oriented than
men, and women are much less willing than men to move to
other communities when their careers so demand. These
arguments do not hold up under closer scrutiny, however.
First, many if not most men who occupy the key decision-
making positions in American Jewish organizational life did

not have specific professional training for their present positions. Rather, they came up through the ranks and gained most of their expertise on the job. Second, the results of a survey of women in Jewish communal service indicate that the majority of women who responded were very interested in career advancement and were willing to re-locate when necessary (Engel and Rogul, 1979). The available evidence strongly supports the conclusion that the pattern of moving up the ranks into key positions, which has been the typical pattern for males, has been closed to women and, to a large extent, remains so even in organizations which publicly support equal rights, including career advancement, for women. Given this pattern of exclusion, women who seek leadership positions will probably find them outside Jewish organizational life and increasing numbers of Jewish women who may not aspire to high-level executive positions will, nevertheless, feel alienated from American Jewish communal life.

None of the three movements for change discussed has become an organization; they remain social movements with relatively wide appeal among American Jews and, to some extent, with support even among many individuals and organizations in the American Jewish "Establishment." Perhaps precisely because they have not formally organized, they have avoided Michels' "iron law of oligarchy." While each challenges patterns within the established community and provides for alternative modes of Jewish expression and activity, they are, by and large, viewed as legitimate sub-communal movements by the organized community, not as deviant, countercommunal, threatening movements. They do not challenge any of the values of the organized community, even though they may challenge specific institutional arrangements.

In contrast, another movement emerged in the 1970s which, while it initially attracted many who were disturbed by what they viewed as the inflexibility and lack of creativity of American Jewish leadership with respect to the relationship between the American Jewish community and Israel, was resoundingly condemned and ostracized by the organized community. That movement, organized after the 1973 Arab-Israeli war, the Yom Kippur War, was called "*Breira*," which in Hebrew means "alternative." Founded by a group of students from the Jewish students' movement, Breira soon became a national membership organization with a paid staff and by 1975 a monthly newsletter, *Interchange*. It attracted many rabbis and intellectuals who favored a more conciliatory stance by Israel with respect to its Arab neighbors and the territories captured in the Six-Day War of 1967, and an emphasis on the creative viability and autonomy of Jewish communities outside of Israel, especially in the United States. By 1977 the organization's newsletter was publishing critical articles dealing with a wide range of Jewish issues, such as the future of the United Jewish Appeal (Goldin, 1977), the changing neighborhood of East Flatbush in Brooklyn (Koltun and Schechter, 1977), and Argentinian Jewry (Sofer, 1977). The major focus, however, remained: an interlocking sympathy and empathy with Palestinian Arabs, a critique of Israeli policies toward the Arabs, and a critique of American Jewish leadership's support of those Israeli policies.

Despite its initial popularity and success in gaining wide support from many American Jews who were dissatisfied with the leadership of the organized community, Breira was short-lived. Its demise may be attributed to both external and internal forces. Externally, the more right-wing Zionist forces within the American Jewish community launched a powerful attack upon the organization and portrayed it as an enemy of Israel. For example, an organization called "Americans for a Safe Israel" published and widely distributed a pamphlet by Rael Jean Isaac, a political sociologist, in which she alleged that Breira supported the political program of the PLO, and that a number of the founders of Breira had involvements with the PLO and other anti-Zionist activities (Isaac, 1977). Much of the Anglo Jewish press, especially the significant Anglo-Jewish weekly, *The Jewish Week*, published many of the same allegations. Given the priority of Israel's security in the

American Jewish value system, it is not surprising that many initial Breira sympathizers quickly withdrew their support of the organization.

Nor did many of the activities of Breira itself provide the assurance that it was, first and foremost, a Jewish organization dedicated to the well-being of Jews and Jewish communities both in Israel and throughout the world. As one of the founders of the organization was to subsequently observe, Breira frequently functioned in ways which left it open to question as to its *ahavat Yisrael*, love of Israel, land and people. For example, The "confident single-mindedness of the statements issued in the aftermath of the October (1973) War, . . . seemed oblivious to the enormity of the trauma in human and spiritual terms"; and likewise, "the placards and statements distributed by Breira at the time of Arafat's speech at the UN, which read essentially "Palestinians—Yes, Arafat—No, [were] an example of a decent political sentiment vitiated by a miserable sense of timing" (Mintz, 1976/77, p. 8). Also the credibility of the organization was suspect because it had "gone to lengths to court intellectuals who have hitherto had no connection with other Jewish causes" (ibid., p. 9). The organized campaign by the Zionist right to discredit Breira and its own political ineptness were sufficient to disintegrate the organization. It would, however, be wrong to assume that private dissent from establishment positions has disappeared among American Jews. On the contrary, it is very much alive, though it has not yet coalesced into an organized movement for change.

As to the initial question of this chapter, namely, the democracy of the organized Jewish community, the answer is not a simple one. It is a democracy in that most of the organizational leadership is elected by the membership of the individual organizations or their representatives. The positions of the leadership probably represent the mainstream in the community, though not always uniformly of course. But there is a significant American Jewish population—many of whom are affiliated with organizations and many more who are not—which is critical of the community leadership and structure and feels relatively impotent in effecting significant change. Nor does the communal leadership feel the need to reach out to those elements of American Jewry, to bring them within the communal structure in a meaningful way, and to engage in critical analysis for the purpose of change. It is this exclusive character of the communal structure and its leadership which poses the greatest challenge to the future of the organized American Jewish community.

10. Conclusion: Diversification without Disintegration

This work began as a challenge to one of the major perspectives in the sociological study of ethnicity which Neil Sandberg has appropriately termed "straight-line" theory (Sandberg, 1974, p. 67). The underlying assumption of the theorists who adhere to that perspective is that ethnic behavior and consciousness decline with each generation and that, inevitably, ethnic groups will disappear into the larger American culture and society. This work also set out to challenge secularization theory within the sociology of religion, according to which the forces of modernity inevitably result in the secularization of consciousness and social structure culminating in the virtual disappearance of institutionalized religion in American society. The history and sociology of American Jews do not fit into either of those theoretical perspectives.

From the evidence presented here, several divergent trends manifest themselves within American Jewry at this time. As was projected by almost all students of the third-generation community in the 1960s, there is a clear and apparently dominant trend of accelerated cultural and, to a lesser degree, structural assimilation. While some earlier theorists of ethnicity may not have realized its intensity and complexity, they were correct to some extent in predicting that rapid acculturation, cultural and structural assimilation, would invariably lead to some measure of what Milton Gordon refers to as "identificational assimilation" (Gordon, 1964, pp. 70–71), the loss of identification with the ethnic group. Thus predictably some of the fourth generation or their children will no longer be part of America's Jewish population. They will no longer perceive themselves as members of the American Jewish community nor will they consciously attempt to live their lives in any way that would identify them as Jews. Ethnic patterns persist at times, however, even when individuals are not particularly ethnically conscious. Andrew Greeley has found, for example, that different ethnic groups manifest different attitudes toward drinking alcoholic beverages and manifest different drinking patterns even when the individuals involved are unaware of the impact of their ethnicity (Greeley, McCready, and Theisen, 1980). Also, many studies indicate that Jews are much more likely than others to label mental illness and to use psychiatric facilities, and that a disproportionate number of psychiatrists are Jews (Horwitz, 1982, pp. 73, 128–29), and these attitudes toward mental illness and psychiatry probably would not disappear even if the individuals involved have undergone identificational assimilation.

The vast majority of the fourth generation, however, have not experienced identificational assimilation, nor is it predictable that their children will, especially in light of the many studies indicating the persistence of ethnicity in American society even as cultural and structural assimilation prevail. Particularly at this stage in American social history, their identification as Jewish Americans (or American Jews) is likely to prevail because the stigma of ethnicity—which had been a powerful incentive to consciously reject one's ethnic identification—has been greatly alleviated by the prevalent ideology of cultural pluralism.

The evidence does suggest divergent patterns with respect to the organized American Jewish communal structure and the American Jewish population. Specifically, on the one hand, the Jewish communal structure has become more organized, more sophisticated, and much more survivalist oriented. On the other hand, there is and there will probably continue to be a growing pattern of nonparticipation in that organized communal structure, for several reasons. To some extent, this nonparticipation will probably continue as the American Jewish occupational structure persists in its pattern of increasing professionalism, because the professional life-style inhibits extensive communal involvement. Also, as the communal structure becomes more highly organized it tends to become more conservative, more exclusive, and more subject to institutional inertia, while an increasing proportion of the American Jewish population tends to become more acculturated and cosmopolitan and seeks alternative modes of Jewish expression.

There is in addition another trend, albeit not as strong, in the opposite direction, a trend that was not anticipated even by many who do not hold to overly simple straight-line assimilation theories. Few students of the third-generation American Jewish community foresaw, or could have foreseen, the possibility of a revitalization of *"intrinsic"* Jewish cultural patterns at the same time that there has been a virtual disappearance of *"extrinsic"* Jewish cultural patterns in the fourth generation of Eastern European American Jewry. As Gordon uses these terms, *"intrinsic* cultural traits" refer to such patterns and traits as "religious beliefs and practices," "literature," and "a sense of a common past" among others, while *"extrinsic* cultural traits" refer to such patterns and traits as "dress, manner, patterns of emotional expression, and minor oddities in pronouncing and inflecting English" (Gordon 1964, p. 79).

There are, as was discussed in Chapter 5, numerous manifestations of the intensification of intrinsic Jewish culture within the contemporary American Jewish community. Marshall Sklare observed many of them when in the mid-1970s he revisited Lakeville and described the building of a Jewish day school, the movement of the community's oldest Reform temple closer to normative Judaism, an increased emphasis on Jewish survival in two temples which had originally been established with a strong classical Reform theology that denied Jewish peoplehood, a greater traditionalism in the community's newest Reform temple, the establishment of new synagogues, the teaching of Hebrew in high school, communal support for the cause of Soviet Jewry, and a much greater involvement with and support for Israel. Sklare summed up his review of the recent developments: "What has been accomplished in Lakeville in the past twenty years is an encouraging sign of Jewish affirmation" (Sklare and Greenblum, 1979, p. 405).

Nor is Lakeville unique. While there has been a decrease in the number of American Jewish children who are enrolled in Jewish schools, there has been, as has been indicated, an increase in the quality and intensity of Jewish education in Jewish schools. The publication of Jewish literature has increased, as has the quality of that literature. Rare is the Jewish organization today that will not serve kosher food at its public functions; respect for traditional Jewish dietary regulations is greater as are manifestations of Jewishness. Likewise, increasing numbers of secular Jewish organizations and institutions are closed on Jewish holidays. Also, the quantity and quality of Jewish programming in Jewish Community Centers and YM/YWHAs has increased significantly during the past several decades, and they have become much more overtly Jewishly conscious.

These developments reflect patterns in the American Jewish community that Nathan Glazer analyzed within the context of the overriding American Jewish concern with what is certainly, though not exclusively, a central Jewish value, namely survival. This central concern with survival has emerged since 1967 and is at the root of the numerous manifestations of Jewish self-consciousness which he discusses (Glazer, 1972, pp. 151–86). The revitalization of intrinsic Jewish culture in the fourth-generation community manifests itself most clearly perhaps in the explicit and virtually universal pro-Israel stance of American Jews—even though they may dissent from specific policies of the Israeli government—if for no other reason than that this support for Israel is creating a clear sense of identification with a larger common core, which in turn, intensifies a sense of a common past, present, and even future perhaps.

In a thoughtful elaboration of a notion he developed

approximately a quarter of a century ago, Herbert Gans applied the term "symbolic ethnicity" to the analysis of many patterns and traits that have herein been defined as the revitalization of intrinsic Jewish culture, as well as to many other manifestations of the so-called ethnic revival in the larger American society (Gans, 1979). While he does not say so explicitly, Gans implicitly (though unintentionally, in personal communications on April 28 and May 22, 1981) sees "symbolic ethnicity" in a pejorative light. He sees it as an ethnicity "which is worn very lightly." He explicitly considers it neither a real ethnic revival nor a "third generation return." Rather, to him it would call for some modification of straight-line assimilation theory, in that it indicates that ethnicity could continue for more generations, even into the fifth and sixth, than earlier straight-line theorists assumed.

Gans is undoubtedly correct when he says that the emergence of symbolic ethnicity has been facilitated by the prevalent ideology of cultural pluralism in the United States. What he does not explain is why that facilitating effect renders the ethnicity any less real. Concerning a significant segment of the American Jewish community, as has been indicated, a surprising number of patterns have emerged which appear to be manifestations of not only "public ethnicity," which may be no more than a passing fad, but also of a sincere return to intrinsic Jewish culture. That being Jewish in America is different than it was in the Eastern European *shtetl* is undoubtedly true, but the *shtetl* experience was unique in terms of Jewish history, and it cannot be held up as the standard by which Jewish life in America is measured. Jewish culture in America is evolving and dynamic. It is not the "world of our fathers" and mothers; neither is it superficial.

The communal life of American Jews too is very different from what it had been in Eastern Europe. As we have seen, even in Eastern Europe Jewish communal life was in a state of rapid change by the end of the nineteenth century. Contemporary American Jewish communal life, in the broadest sense of the term, is highly heterogeneous—both highly organized and highly disorganized. The organized American

Jewish community attempts to project an image of consensus by playing down the issues that divide its constituents, but that does not mean that the divisions are absent. There are broad and deep religious, political, and moral issues over which there are wide disagreements; but there is a sense of peoplehood and common purpose which override the differences. It is a community as in the distinction that the German sociologist, Ferdinand Tönnies, made between "community" (*Gemeinschaft*) and "society" (*Gesellschaft*). Though they superficially resemble each other, "in so far as the individuals live and dwell together peacefully . . . in the Gemeinschaft they remain essentially united in spite of all separating factors, whereas in the Gesellschaft they are essentially separated in spite of all uniting factors" (Tönnies, 1957 [1887], pp. 64–65). In that sense we may speak of an American Jewish community which is much broader even than the organizational structure of the formal community.

Although this work has been presented as a challenge to straight-line theory, I did not intend it as an unequivocal refutation of that theory. While that theory has been considered inappropriate as far as the American Jewish experience is concerned, it is possible that American Jews are the exception, the deviant case. For example, Talcott Parsons considered them a "distinctive case because of the religio-ethnic character of the historic Jewish community" (Parsons, 1975, p. 56). As was pointed out at the very beginning of this book, Jews cannot be neatly categorized as an ethnic group or religious group. As Glazer puts it: "As against the Christian churches—and even the non-Christian religions like Islam and Buddhism, which have some adherents in the United States—Judaism is tied up organically with a specific people, indeed, a nation. The tie is so intimate that the word 'Jew' in common usage refers ambiguously both to an adherent of the religion of Judaism and to a member of the Jewish people" (Glazer, 1972, p. 3).

While some, such as Peter Berger, have argued that the unique character of Judaism as both a religious and ethnic entity entails the "crisis of Jewish identity" (Berger, 1967, pp.

169–70), others have considered it to be an important factor in the survival of the Jewish people (cf. Silberstein, 1974). If nothing else, this unique character allows individual Jews the opportunity of emphasizing the components of group identity which ties the individual with the larger group. Even those American Jews who do not maintain active and formal association with Jewish organizations are able to maintain their group identity in a variety of other available ways. Within the organized American Jewish community and its self-conceptions, the religio-ethnic character is evident in that even the ostensibly secular Jewish organizations perceive themselves as religious to some extent. Thus the American Jewish Congress, for example, is one of the staunchest defenders of an unambiguous separation of church and state and has been at the forefront in the opposition to any form of prayer in public schools and to any form of government support of parochial schools. From their perspective, these activities in which they are involved are in defense of Jewish rights and Jewish well-being. If Jews were solely an ethnic group, it would be difficult to understand and legitimate the organization's extensive involvement in questions of religion. Likewise, the American Jewish Committee's staunch support of the separation of church and state and its extensive inter-religious activities (Cohen 1972, pp. 433–79) indicate that it perceives of itself as a religious, though nondenominational, Jewish organization.

Within this context, the fact that an increasing number of fourth-generation American Jews do not appear to have any need to affiliate with Jewish organizations may not be indicative of increasing ethnic assimilation. Nor does it suggest the increasing secularization of American Jews because, on the contrary, many in the fourth generation manifest a much greater religious quest than did their parents. An understanding of the contemporary patterns within the American Jewish community requires distinguishing between the situation in the organized community and that of those who are not part of the organized community, and viewing both within the framework of the sociology of religion, even though many of those involved are unaware of any religious component to their identity and behavior.

Tentatively, since almost all research on American Jews has been conducted from a perspective that viewed American Jews as an ethnic rather than a religious group, it appears that increasing numbers of Jews are identifying with Judaism as a folk religion and challenging the elite religion. Charles Liebman, one of the few students of American Jewry whose work is strongly informed by the sociology of religion, suggests:

> religion refers . . . to a formal organized institution with acknowledged leaders. Within the institution, symbols and rituals are acknowledged as legitimate expressions or reenactments of religious experience, and a set of beliefs is articulated as ultimate truths. Elite religion is the symbols and rituals (the cult) and beliefs which the leaders acknowledge as legitimate. But most importantly, elite religion is also the religious organization itself, its hierarchical arrangements, the authority of the leaders and their source of authority, and the rights and obligations of the followers to the organization and its leaders [Liebman, 1973, p. 46].

For a variety of reasons, there are many people who identify with the religion, but do not accept it in all of its aspects as enunciated by the elite. Moreover,

> a kind of subculture may exist within a religion which the acknowledged leaders ignore or even condemn, but in which a majority of the members participate. This is called folk religion. . . . Both share the same organization and at least nominally recognize the authoritative nature of the cults and beliefs articulated by the elite religion. Folk religion is not self-conscious; it does not articulate its own rituals and beliefs or demand recognition for its informal leaders. As far as elite religion is concerned, folk religion is not a movement but an error, or a set of errors, shared by many people [Ibid.].

Liebman analyzed the interrelationships between elite and folk religion and the extent to which they vary in each of the major American Jewish denominations, and he also described the rituals and beliefs of folk Judaism in America up to the period of the fourth-generation community. While he is correct in his observation that the strength of the folk element varies in the different denominations, it does appear that in the fourth generation the folk element has become more pronounced in each of the denominations, even in Orthodoxy, in which he suggested that the elitist element had become stronger and that the folk element had virtually disappeared (ibid., p. 83). The elite element has indeed become much more pronounced in the public sphere of American Orthodoxy, as a highly sophisticated organizational and institutional network has been developed, but not necessarily in the private sphere. Orthodoxy has, of course, always been characterized with a much stronger elite, rather than folk, element. Until World War II, the very beginning of the third-generation community, the elite was relatively weak, and the folk element was much more pronounced. With the arrival of a determined Orthodox elite and the development of its religious organization, it achieved a virtual monopoly within one generation. A pluralization of elites is now taking place even within Orthodoxy, ironically because the older elite was so successful in providing intense Jewish education to so many of the younger generation. In the younger generation many feel sufficiently knowledgeable to make their own autonomous decisions with respect to religious behavior without necessarily following precisely the decisions of a particular authority. Among the Conservative and Reform, which encompass the vast majority of religiously-identified American Jews, there even appears to have been a growing acceptance on the part of the elite of the legitimacy of folk religion to the point where folk religion is no longer a subculture which is ignored, let alone condemned. Rather, there has been an overall heightening of religious consciousness within American Judaism while, at the same time, there is much greater flexibility and acceptance of varieties of Jewish religious needs and expressions.

While one of the major functions of religion—and indeed to the Orthodox perhaps its primary function—is to provide structure, a number of sociologists and anthropologists of religion have pointed to the role of religion in providing ultimate meaning for humans (Berger, 1967; Geertz, 1976). The union of religion and culture, which so thoroughly characterizes Jewish ethnicity, is particularly relevant in terms of the way Clifford Geertz defines culture: "an historically transmitted pattern of meanings embodied in symbols, a system of inherited conceptions expressed in symbolic forms by means of which men communicate, perpetuate, and develop their knowledge and attitudes toward life" (Geertz, 1976, p. 89). Religion, in turn, is a cultural system, a complex of symbols which expresses both a world view and an ethos; that is, it formulates both an image of the world's construction and a program for human conduct and behavior which are mutually dependent and reinforcing. Religion, thus, formulates "a basic congruence between a particular style of life and a specific (if, most often, implicit) metaphysic, and in so doing sustain(s) each with the borrowed authority of the other" (ibid., p. 90).

Within this perspective, religion does not have to be institutionalized; indeed, a number of ancient religions were not. Accordingly, the increasing nonaffiliation with religious institutions within American Judaism does not necessarily indicate the decline of religion. This process may be a manifestation—and there are others as well—of the deinstitutionalization of American Judaism at this particular juncture in its history. But the process may be cyclical; it may be but a temporary one. In any event, the deinstitutionalization of Judaism is clearly not the same thing as the decline of Judaism. To draw a possibly remote analogy, in his study of the Jewish community of Boro Park in Brooklyn, Egon Mayer described the proliferation of small storefront synagogues and the decline of the older, larger, established ones. As for the older and larger synagogues, their significance has diminished. In terms of the quality of Jewish life in the community as a whole, however, there has unquestionably been an intensification (Mayer, 1979a). Similarly, the declining rates of institutional religious affiliation among American Jews may not be indicative of the decline of Judaism; rather, they may be indicative of a Judaism that is changing and in which there is a search for alternative modes of Jewish expression.

Seen in this light, what Gans refers to as "symbolic ethnicity" may entail a "new kind of ethnic involvement" and a "new form of ethnic behavior and affiliation," but not necessarily "the emergence of a new form of acculturation and assimilation" (Gans, 1979, pp. 193, 198, 208). As suggested earlier, while much of extrinsic Jewish culture has disappeared among a significant proportion of the fourth generation, there are numerous manifestations of an intensification of intrinsic Jewish culture.

While much of the foregoing has been speculative because of the absence of empirical data on the subject, a recent study of upper-class Jews by Zweigenhaft and Domhoff has relevance for the discussion. On the basis of objective criteria and interviews, they found that longtime members of the corporate and social elite, the "Protestant Establishment," are much less likely to publicly identify as Jews and to be involved in Jewish activities than are more recent newcomers (Zweigenhaft and Domhoff, 1982). Their findings, they suggest, lend support to the argument that class identification becomes more important than ethnic-Jewish identification, as has been argued by Gans and others. Even Zweigenhaft and Domhoff do not suggest the disappearance of Jewish identification, however. They simply suggest that class identification becomes more important than Jewish identification, but that "people can retain an identification with Jewishness . . . while being members of the upper class" (Zweigenhaft and Domhoff, 1982, p. 110). It must also be emphasized that this was their finding and their conclusion with respect to that relatively small number of Jews in the upper class. For the vast majority of American Jews, who are in the middle class, there are far fewer pressures to maintain one's Jewishness in a low key. Finally, even the conclusion of Zweigenhaft and Domhoff can only be tentative without a more extensive longitudinal study, because possibly the differences in Jewish identification which they found between newcomers to the elite and long-timers may not be indicative of the impact of being in the elite;

they may be indicative of significant generational differences in intensity of Jewish identification. In other words, the more recent newcomers to the elite may have a stronger sense of Jewish identity than did the longtimers when they entered the elite, and the newcomers may retain their Jewish identification even as they are integrated into the elite.

Whether American Jewish ethnicity will persist even beyond the fifth and sixth generations is a question about which one can only speculate. In the social sciences as in the natural sciences, all predictions are qualified with the clause, "all other things being equal." Especially in the social sciences, things rarely are equal nor can we account for all of them. It would, therefore, be unsound to suggest a definitive response. Moreover, almost two thousand years ago, the Talmud stated that when the temple in Jerusalem was destroyed, prophecy was taken away from the prophets and given to fools.

References

Ackerman, Walter J. 1969. "Jewish Education—For What?" *American Jewish Year Book*. 70, pp. 3–36.

ADL. 1982. "Audit of Anti-Semitic Incidents." New York: Anti-Defamation League of B'nai B'rith.

Alder, Cyrus, and Aaron Margalith. 1943. *American Intercession on Behalf of Jews in the Diplomatic Correspondence of the United States 1840–1938*. Publications of the American Jewish Historical Society, 36.

Altizer, Thomas, and William Hamilton, eds. 1966. *Radical Theology and the Death of God*. Indianapolis: Bobbs-Merrill.

American Association for Jewish Education. 1979. "Jewish School Census 1978/79," Information Bulletin, No. 44.

Anthony, Dick, and Thomas Robbins. 1981. "Culture Crisis and Contemporary Religion." In *In Gods We Trust: New Patterns of Religious Pluralism in America*. Ed. Thomas Robbins and Dick Anthony. New Brunswick: Transaction Books, pp. 9–31.

Arendt, Hannah. 1963. *Eichmann in Jerusalem: A Report on the Banality of Evil*. New York: Viking Press.

Axelrod, Morris, Floyd J. Fowler, and Arnold Gurin, 1967. *A Community Survey for Long-Range Planning: A Study of the Jewish Population of Greater Boston*.

Balswick, Jack, 1966. "Are American Jewish Families Close Knit?: A Review of the Literature." *Jewish Social Studies*, 27, 3 (July), 159–69.

Barron, Milton C. 1946. *People Who Intermarry*. Syracuse: Syracuse University Press.

Bauer, Yehuda. 1974. *My Brother's Keeper: A History of the American Jewish Joint Distribution Committee 1929–1939*. Philadelphia: Jewish Publication Society of America.

Bauer, Yehuda. 1981. *American Jewry and the Holocaust: The American*

Jewish Joint Distribution Committee, 1939–45. Detroit: Wayne State University Press.

Bellah, Robert N. 1967. "Civil Religion in America." *Daedalus*, Winter, pp. 1–21.

Bellah, Robert N. 1976. "New Religious Consciousness and the Crisis in Modernity." In *The New Religious Consciousness.* Ed. Charles Y. Glock and Robert N. Bellah. Berkeley: University of California Press, pp. 333–52.

Benello, C. George, and Dimitrios Roussopoulos, 1971. Introduction to *The Case for Participatory Democracy: Some Prospects for a Radical Society.* Ed. C. George Benello and Dimitrios Roussopoulos. New York: Viking Press, pp. 3–9.

Berelson, Bernard. 1978. "Ethnicity and Fertility: What and to What?" In *Zero Population Growth—For Whom?* Ed. Milton Himmelfarb and Victor Baras. Westport: Greenwood Press, pp. 74–118.

Berger, Peter L. 1967. *The Sacred Canopy: Elements of a Sociological Theory of Religion.* Garden City: Doubleday.

Berger, Peter L. 1969. *A Rumor of Angels.* Garden City: Doubleday.

Berger, Peter L. 1977a. *Facing Up to Modernity.* New York: Basic Books.

Berger, Peter L. 1977b. "'A Great Revival' Coming for America's Churches." *U.S. News and World Report,* April 11, pp. 70–72.

Berger, Peter L., Brigitte Berger, and Hansfried Kellner. 1973. *The Homeless Mind: Modernization and Consciousness.* New York: Random House.

Berger, Peter L., and Richard John Neuhaus. 1977. *To Empower People: The Role of Mediating Structures in Public Policy.* Washington, D.C.: American Enterprise Institute for Public Policy Research.

Bergman, Elihu. 1977. "The American Jewish Population Erosion," *Midstream,* 23, 8 (Oct.), 9–19.

Bergman, Gerold S. 1976. "The Adaptable American Jewish Family: An Inconsistency in Theory." *Jewish Journal of Sociology,* 18, 1 (June), 5–16.

Berman, Saul J. 1973. "The Status of Women in Halakhic Judaism." *Tradition,* 14, 2 (Fall), 5–28.

Birmingham, Stephen. 1967. *Our Crowd: The Great Jewish Families of New York.* New York: Harper & Row.

Blau, Joseph L., and Salo Wittmayer Baron. 1963. *The Jews of the United States, 1790–1840: A Documentary History.* 3 vols. New York: Columbia University Press.

Blau, Zena Smith. 1967. "In Defense of the Jewish Mother." *Midstream,* 13, 2 (Feb.), 42–49.

Boroff, David. 1961. "Jewish Teen-Age Culture." *The Annals of the American Academy of Political and Social Science,* 338, Nov. 79-90.

Bremner, Robert H. 1960. *American Philanthropy.* Chicago: University of Chicago Press.

Briggs, Kenneth A. 1981. "Reform Jews to Seek Conversion of Non-Jews." *New York Times,* Dec. 9, p. A18.

Broun, Heywood, and George Britt. 1931. *Christians Only: A Study in Prejudice.* New York: Vanguard Press.

Bulka, Reuven P. 1979. "Women's Role—Some Ultimate Concerns." *Tradition,* 17, 4 (Spring), 27-40.

Cahnman, Werner J. 1952. "The Cultural Consciousness of Jewish Youth." *Jewish Social Studies,* 14, 3 (July), 195-208.

Cahnman, Werner J., ed. 1973. *Ferdinand Tönnies: A New Evaluation.* Leiden: E. J. Brill.

Cahnman, Werner J., and Rudolf Heberle, eds. 1971. *Ferdinand Toennies on Sociology: Pure Applied, and Empirical.* Chicago: University of Chicago Press.

Carlin, Jerome E., and Saul H. Mendlovitz. 1958. "The American Rabbi: A Religious Specialist Responds to Loss of Authority." In *The Jews: Social Patterns of an American Group.* Ed. Marshall Sklare. New York: Free Press, pp. 377-414.

Carmichael, Stokely, 1966. "What We Want." *New York Review of Books,* 7, 4 (Sept. 22), 5-8.

Carmichael, Stokely, and Charles V. Hamilton, 1967. *Black Power: The Politics of Liberation in America.* New York: Random House.

Carroll, Jackson W., Douglas W. Johnson, and Martin E. Marty. 1979. *Religion in America: 1950 to the Present.* San Francisco: Harper & Row.

Chenkin, Alvin. 1970. "Demography: Jewish Population in the United States." *American Jewish Year Book,* 71, pp. 344-53.

Chenkin, Alvin. 1972. "Demographic Highlights: Facts for Planning." *National Jewish Population Study.* New York: Council of Jewish Federations and Welfare Funds.

Chenkin, Alvin, and Maynard Miran. 1979. "Jewish Population in the United States, 1978." *American Jewish Year Book,* 79, pp. 177-89.

Chenkin, Alvin, and Maynard Miran. 1982. "Jewish Population in the United States, 1981." *American Jewish Year Book,* 82, pp. 165-77.

Cherlin, Andrew J., and Carin Celebuski. 1982. *Are Jewish Families Different?* New York: American Jewish Committee, National Jewish Family Center.

Clymer, Adam. 1978. "Voting Jews Remain Liberal, Poll Finds." *New York Times,* November 12, p. 27.

Cohen, Naomi W. 1972. *Not Free To Desist: A History of the American Jewish Committee 1906–1966*. Philadelphia: Jewish Publication Society of America.

Cohen, Naomi W. 1975. *American Jews and the Zionist Idea*. New York: Ktav Publishing House.

Cohen, Naomi W. 1977. "Pioneers of America Jewish Defense." *American Jewish Archives*, 29, 2 (Nov.) 116–50.

Cohen, Steven M. 1974. "The Impact of Jewish Education on Religious Identification and Practice." *Jewish Social Studies*, 36, 3–4, (July-Oct.), 316–26.

Cohen, Steven M. 1975. "On Our Minds." *Response*, 9, 3(Fall, 3–5.

Cohen, Steven M. 1980. "Trends in Jewish Philanthropy." *American Jewish Year Book*, 80, pp. 29–51.

Cohen, Steven M., and Paul Ritterband. 1981. "Why Contemporary American Jews Want Small Families: An Interreligious Comparison of College Graduates." In *Modern Jewish Fertility*. Ed. Paul Ritterband. Leiden: Brill, pp. 209–31.

Cohn, Werner. 1958. "The Politics of American Jews." In *The Jews: Social Patterns of an American Group*. Ed. Marshall Sklare. New York: Free Press, 1958, pp. 614–26.

Dashefsky, Arnold, and Howard Shapiro. 1974. *Ethnic Identification among American Jews: Socialization and Social Structure*. Lexington, Mass.: Lexington Books.

Davis, Moshe. 1963. *The Emergence of Conservative Judaism: The Historical School in the 19th Century*. Philadelphia: Jewish Publication Society of America.

Dawidowicz, Lucy, ed. 1967. *The Golden Tradition: Jewish Life and Thought in Eastern Europe*. New York: Holt, Rinehart and Winston.

Dawidowicz, Lucy. 1977. "Can Anti-Semitism Be Measured?" In *The Jewish Presence: Essays on Identity and History*. New York: Holt, Rinehart and Winston, pp. 193–215.

Dawidowicz, Lucy S., and Leon J. Goldstein. 1963. *Politics in a Pluralistic Democracy*. New York: American Jewish Committee.

Dinnerstein, Leonard. 1968. *The Leo Franks Case*. New York: Columbia University Press.

Dreier, Peter, and Jack Nusan Porter. 1975. "Jewish Radicalism in Transition." *Society*, 12, 2 (Jan./Feb.), 34–43.

Dye, Thomas R. 1976. *Who's Running America?* Englewood Cliffs: Prentice Hall.

Edelman, Joseph. 1977. "Soviet Jews in the United States: A Profile." *American Jewish Year Book*, 77, pp. 157–81.

Edelman, Joseph. 1982. "Soviet Jews in the United States: An Update." *American Jewish Year Book*, 82, pp. 155–64.

Elazar, Daniel J. 1973. "Women in American Jewish Life." *Congress Bi-Weekly*, 40, 13 (Nov. 23), 10–11.

Elazar, Daniel J. 1974. "Decision-Making in the American Jewish Community." In *The Jewish Community in America*. Ed. Marshall Sklare. New York: Behrman House, pp. 72–110.

Elazar, Daniel J. 1976. *Community and Polity: The Organizational Dynamics of American Jewry*. Philadelphia: Jewish Publication Society of America.

Elazar, Daniel J., and Rela Geffen Monson. 1981. "Women in the Synagogue Today." *Midstream*, 27, 4 (April), 25–30.

Elizur, Dov. 1980. "Israelis in the United States: Motives, Attitudes, and Intentions." *American Jewish Year Book*, 80, pp. 53–67.

Encyclopedia Judaica. 1971. Jerusalem: Keter Publishing House.

Engel, Sophie B., and Jane Rogul. 1979. "Career Mobility: Perceptions and Observations (A Survey of Women in Jewish Communal Service)." *Journal of Jewish Communal Service*, 56, 1 (Fall): 101–2.

Epstein, Melech. 1953. *Jewish Labor in U.S.A.: An Industrial, Political and Cultural History of the Jewish Labor Movement*. 2 vols. New York: Trade Union Sponsoring Committee.

Epstein, Melech, 1965. *Profiles of Eleven: Biographical Sketches of Eleven Men Who Guided the Destiny of an Immigrant Jewish Society*. Detroit: Wayne State University Press.

Fackenheim, Emil L. 1968. *Quest for Past and Future: Essays in Jewish Theology*. Boston: Beacon Press.

Fauman, S. Joseph. 1958. "Occupational Selection among Detroit Jews." In *The Jews: Social Patterns of an American Group*. Ed., Marshall Sklare. New York: Free Press, pp. 119–37.

Featherman Sandra, and William L. Rosenberg. 1979. *Jews, Blacks and Ethnics*. New York: American Jewish Committee.

Fein, Isaac. 1971. *The Making of an American Jewish Community: The History of Baltimore Jewry from 1773 to 1920*. Philadelphia: Jewish Publication Society of America.

Festinger, Leon. 1957. *Theory of Cognitive Dissonance*. New York: Harper & Row.

Feuer, Lewis S. 1969. *The Conflict of Generations: The Character and Significance of Student Movements*. New York: Basic Books.

Fisher, Alan M. 1979a. "Realignment of the Jewish Vote?" *Political Science Quarterly*, 94, 1 (Spring), 97–116.

Fisher, Alan M. 1979b. "Where Is the New Jewish Conservatism?" *Society*, 16, 4 (May/June), 5, 15–18.

Flacks, Richard. 1970. "Social and Cultural Meanings of Student Revolt: Some Informal Comparative Observations." *Social Problems*, 17, 3 (Winter), 340–57.

Fortune, editors of. 1936. *Jews in America*. New York: Random House.

Fowler, Floyd J., Jr. 1977. *1975 Community Survey: A Study of the Jewish Population of Greater Boston*. Boston: Combined Jewish Philanthropies of Greater Boston.

Frank, Shirley. 1977/78. "The Population Panic: Why Jewish Leaders Want Jewish Women To Be Fruitful and Multiply." *Lilith*, 1, 4 (Fall/Winter), 12–17.

Frazier, E. Franklin. 1957. *Black Bourgeoisie: The Rise of a New Middle Class*. New York: Free Press.

Friedman, Theodore. 1979. "Jewish Proselytism: A New Look." *Forum*, 34 (Winter), 31–38.

Fuchs, Lawrence H. 1956. *The Political Behavior of American Jews*. Glencoe, Ill.: The Free Press.

Gans, Herbert J. 1958. "The Origin and Growth of a Jewish Community in the Suburbs: A Study of the Jews of Park Forest." In *The Jews: Social Patterns of an American Group*. Ed., Marshall Sklare. New York: Free Press, pp. 205–48.

Gans, Herbert J. 1967. *The Levittowners: How People Live and Politic in Suburbs*. New York: Pantheon Books.

Gans, Herbert J. 1979. "Symbolic Ethnicity: The Future of Ethnic Groups and Culture in America." In *On the Making of Americans: Essays in Honor of David Riesman*. Ed. Herbert J. Gans, Nathan Glazer, Joseph R. Gusfield, Christopher Jencks. Philadelphia: University of Pennsylvania Press, pp. 193–220.

Gaon, Saadia. 1948 (circa 933). *The Book of Beliefs and Opinions*, trans. from the Arabic by Samuel Rosenblatt. New Haven: Yale University Press.

Gartner, Lloyd P. 1978. *History of the Jews of Cleveland*. Cleveland and New York: Western Reserve Historical Society and Jewish Theological Seminary of America.

Geertz, Clifford. 1976. *The Interpretation of Cultures*. New York: Basic Books.

Gitelman, Zvi. 1981. "'I Didn't Collect Baseball Cards': Soviet Immigrant Resettlement in the United States." Paper delivered at Tours College Conference on Immigration, New York City, Nov. 19. Forthcoming in *Soviet Jewish Affairs*.

Glanz, Rudolph, 1947/48. "The Immigration of German Jews up to 1880." *YIVO Annual of Jewish Social Science*, II–III.

Glazer, Nathan. 1969. "The Jewish Role in Student Activism." *Fortune*, Jan., 112 ff.

Glazer, Nathan. 1972. *American Judaism.* 2d ed. Chicago: University of Chicago Press.

Glazer, Nathan. 1979. "American Jews: Three Conflicts of Loyalties." In *The Third Century: America as a Post-Industrial Society.* Ed. Seymour Martin Lipset. Stanford: Hoover Institution Press, pp. 224–41.

Glazer, Nathan, and Daniel P. Moynihan. 1970. *Beyond the Melting Pot.* 2d ed. Cambridge: M.I.T. Press.

Glock, Charles Y. 1976. "Consciousness among Contemporary Youth: An Interpretation." In *The New Religious Consciousness.* Ed. Charles Y. Glock and Robert N. Bellah. Berkeley: University of California Press.

Glock, Charles Y. 1979. *Anti-Semitism in America.* New York: Free Press.

Glock, Charles Y., Gertrude J. Selznick, and Joe L. Spaeth, 1966. *The Apathetic Majority.* New York: Harper & Row.

Glock, Charles Y., and Rodney Stark. 1966. *Christian Beliefs and Anti-Semitism.* New York: Harper & Row.

Glock, Charles Y., Robert Wuthnow, Jane Allyn Piliavin, and Metta Spencer. 1975. *Adolescent Prejudice.* New York: Harper & Row.

Goldberg, David, and Harry Sharp. 1958. "Some Characteristics of Detroit Area Jewish and Non-Jewish Adults." In *The Jews: Social Patterns of an American Group.* Ed. Marshall Sklare. New York: Free Press, pp. 107–18.

Goldberg, Nathan. 1945. *The Classification of Jewish Immigrants and Its Implications.* New York: Yiddish Scientific Institute—YIVO.

Goldberg, Nathan. 1947. *Occupational Patterns of American Jewry.* New York: Jewish Teachers' Seminary and People's University Press.

Goldberg, Nathan. 1968. "The Jewish Attitude toward Divorce." In *Jews and Divorce.* Ed. Jacob Fried. New York: Ktav Publishing House, pp. 44–76.

Goldin, Milton. 1977. "The UJA: Losing Its Appeal?" *Interchange*, 2, 8 (April), 1 ff.

Goldscheider, Calvin. 1967. "Fertility of the Jews." *Demography*, 4, 1, 196–209.

Goldscheider, Calvin. 1978. "Demography and American Jewish Survival." In *Zero Population Growth—For Whom?* Ed. Milton Himmelfarb and Victor Baras. Westport: Greenwood Press, pp.119–47.

Goldscheider, Calvin, and Frances E. Kolbrin. 1980. "Ethnic Continuity and the Process of Self-Employment." *Ethnicity*, 7, 3 (Fall), 256–78.

Goldstein, Sidney. 1971. "American Jewry, 1970." *American Jewish Year Book*, 72, pp. 3–88.

Goldstein, Sidney. 1981a. "Jews in the United States: Perspectives from Demography." *American Jewish Year Book*, 81, pp. 3–59.

Goldstein, Sidney. 1981b. "Jewish Fertility in Contemporary America." In *Modern Jewish Fertility*, Ed. Paul Ritterband. Leiden: Brill, pp. 160–208.

Goldstein, Sidney, and Calvin Goldscheider. 1968. *Jewish Americans: Three Generations in a Jewish Community.* Englewood Cliffs: Prentice Hall.

Gordis, Robert. 1980. "The Ordination of Women." *Midstream*, 26, 7 (Aug./Sept.), 25–32.

Gordis, Robert, et al. 1981. "An Exchange: Women and the Rabbinate." *Midstream* 27, 4 (April), 60–64.

Gordon, Milton M. 1964. *Assimilation in American Life.* New York: Oxford University Press.

Gordon, Milton M. 1978. *Human Nature, Class, and Ethnicity.* New York: Oxford University Press.

Gorelick, Sherry. 1981. *City College and the Jewish Poor: Education in New York, 1880–1924.* New Brunswick: Rutgers University Press.

Goren, Arthur. 1970. *New York Jews and the Quest for Community: The Kehillah Experiment, 1908–1922.* New York: Columbia University Press.

Greeley, Andrew M. 1972a. *The Denominational Society: A Sociological Approach to Religion in America.* Glenview: Scott, Foresman.

Greeley, Andrew M. 1972b. *Unsecular Man.* New York: Schocken Books.

Greeley, Andrew M. 1974. *Ethnicity in the United States.* New York: John Wiley.

Greeley, Andrew M. 1977. *The American Catholic.* New York: Basic Books.

Greeley, Andrew M., William C. McCready, and Gary Theisen. 1980. *Ethnic Drinking Subcultures.* New York: Praeger Special Studies/ J. F. Bergin.

Greenberg, Blu. 1981. *On Woman and Judaism: A View from Tradition.* Philadelphia: Jewish Publication Society of America.

Greer, Colin. 1972. *The Great School Legend.* New York: Basic Books.

Grinstein, Hyman B. 1945. *The Rise of the Jewish Community of New York, 1654–1860.* Philadelphia: Jewish Publication Society of America.

Grinstein, Hyman B. 1959. "The Efforts of East European Jewry To Organize Its Own Community in the United States." *Publications of the American Jewish Historical Society,* 49, 2 (Dec.), 73–89.

Gurock, Jeffrey. 1979. *When Harlem Was Jewish, 1870–1930.* New York: Columbia University Press.

Gutman, Robert. 1966. "Demographic Trends and the Decline of Anti-Semitism." In Charles Herbert Stember, *Jews in the Mind of America.* New York: Basic Books, pp. 354–76.

Handlin, Oscar. 1951. "American Views of the Jew at the Opening of the Twentieth Century." *Publications of the American Jewish Historical Society,* 40, June, 323–44.

Handlin, Oscar. 1964. *A Continuing Task: The American Joint Distribution Committee 1914–1964.* New York: Random House.

Harrington, Michael. 1965. *The Accidental Century.* New York: Macmillan.

Heller, James G. 1965. *Isaac M. Wise: His Life, Work and Thought.* New York: Union of American Hebrew Congregations.

Helmreich, William G. 1982. *The World of the Yeshiva: An Intimate Portrait of Orthodox Jewry.* New York: Free Press.

Herberg, Will. 1960. *Protestant-Catholic-Jew: An Essay in American Religious Sociology.* Rev. ed. Garden City: Doubleday Anchor Books.

Herman, Simon N. 1977. *Jewish Identity: A Social-Psychological Perspective.* Beverly Hills: Sage Publications.

Hershkowitz, Leo, and Isidore S. Meyer, eds. 1968. *Letters of the Franks Family (1733–1748).* The Lee Max Friedman Collection of American Jewish Correspondence. Studies in American Jewish History, No. 5. Waltham: American Jewish Historical Society.

Hertzberg, Arthur. 1967. "Israel and American Jewry." *Commentary,* 44, 2 (Aug.), 69–73.

Hertzberg, Steven. 1978. *Strangers within the Gate City: The Jews of Atlanta 1845–1915.* Philadelphia: Jewish Publication Society of America.

Higham, John. 1975. *Send These to Me: Jews and Other Immigrants in Urban America.* New York: Atheneum.

Himmelfarb, Harold S. 1974. *The Impact of Religious Schooling: The Effects of Jewish Education upon Adult Religious Involvement.* Diss. Dept. of Sociology, University of Chicago.

Himmelfarb, Harold S. 1975. "Jewish Education for Naught: Educating the Culturally Deprived Jewish Child." *Analysis,* No. 51 (Sept.), Institute for Jewish Policy Planning and Research.

Himmelfarb, Harold S. 1979. "Patterns of Assimilation—Identification among American Jews." *Ethnicity,* 6, 3 (Sept.), 249–67.

Himmelfarb, Milton. 1973. *The Jews of Modernity.* New York: Basic Books.

Hoffman, Marcia Greenberg. 1980. "A Bi-Lingual Monthly Newspaper as an Acculturation Aid for Soviet Jewish Resettlement." *Journal of Jewish Communal Service,* 57, 1 (Fall), 87–90.

Horwitz, Allan V. 1982. *The Social Control of Mental Illness.* New York: Academic Press.

Howe, Irving. 1976. *World of Our Fathers.* New York: Harcourt, Brace, Jovanovich.

Isaac, Rael Jean. 1977. *Breira: Counsel for Judaism.* New York: Americans for a Safe Israel.

Jacob, Heinrich Eduard. 1949. *The World of Emma Lazarus.* New York: Schocken Books.

Jaffe, Frederick S. 1978. "Alarums, Excursions and Delusions of Grandeur: Implicit Assumptions of Group Efforts To Alter Differential Fertility Trends." In *Zero Population Growth—For Whom?* Ed. Milton Himmelfarb and Victor Baras. Westport: Greenwood Press, pp. 26–40.

Jaret, Charles 1978. "The Impact of Geographic Mobility on Jewish Community Participation: Disruptive or Supportive?" *Contemporary Jewry,* 4, 2 (Spring/Summer), 9–21.

Jick, Leon A. 1976. *The Americanization of the Synagogue, 1820–1870.* Hanover: University Press of New England and Brandeis University Press.

Joseph, Samuel. 1934. *The History of the Baron de Hirsch Fund.* Philadelphia: Jewish Publication Society of America.

Judah ben Samuel, "he-chasid" ("the Pious"). 1956 (circa 1217). *Sefer Hachasidim* (Hebrew). Jerusalem: Mosad HaRav Kook.

Kahane, Meir. Circa 1975. "Democracy in Jewish Life." An advertisement that ran periodically in *The Jewish Press* and other publications.

Kallen, Horace M. 1924. *Culture and Democracy in the United States.* New York: Boni and Liveright.

Kallen, Horace M. 1956. *Cultural Pluralism and the American Idea: An*

Essay in Social Philosophy. Philadelphia: University of Pennsylvania Press.

Kamerman, Sheila B. 1981. *Task Forces on the 80s: Family Policy.* New York: American Jewish Committee, Institute of Human Relations.

Kamerman, Sheila B. 1982. "Jews and Other People: An Agenda for Research on Families and Family Policy." In *Understanding American Jewry,* Ed. Marshall Sklare. New Brunswick: Transaction Books, pp. 146–62.

Kanof, Abram. 1949/50. "Uriah Phillips Levy: The Story of a Pugnacious Commodore." *Publications of the American Jewish Historical Society,* 39 (Sept./June), 1–66.

Kaplan, Mordecai M. 1934. *Judaism as a Civilization: Toward a Reconstruction of American-Jewish Life.* New York: Macmillan.

Karp, Abraham J. 1955. "New York Chooses a Rabbi." *Publications of the American Jewish Historical Society,* 44, 3 (March), 129–98.

Karpf, Maurice J. 1971 (1938). *Jewish Community Organization in the United States.* Repr. ed. New York: Arno Press & the New York Times.

Kass, Dora, and Seymour Martin Lipset. 1982. "Jewish Immigration to the United States, from 1976 to the Present: Israelis and Others." In *Understanding American Jewry.* Ed. Marshall Sklare. New Brunswick: Transaction Books, pp. 272–94.

Kennedy, Ruby Jo Reeves. 1944. "Single or Triple Melting-Pot? Intermarriage Trends in New Haven, 1870–1940." *American Journal of Sociology,* 49, 4 (Jan.), 331–39.

Kennedy, Ruby Jo Reeves. 1952. "Single or Triple Melting-Pot? Intermarriage Trends in New Haven, 1870–1950." *American Journal of Sociology,* 58, 1 (July), 56–9.

Kessner, Thomas. 1977. *The Golden Door: Italian and Jewish Immigrant Mobility in New York City 1880–1915.* New York: Oxford University Press.

Kilson, Martin. 1975. "Blacks and Neo-Ethnicity in America." In *Ethnicity: Theory and Experience.* Ed. Nathan Glazer and Daniel P. Moynihan. Cambridge: Harvard University Press, pp. 236–66.

Klaperman, Gilbert. 1969. *The Story of Yeshiva University: The First Jewish University in America.* New York: Macmillan.

Kobrin, Frances E., and Calvin Goldscheider. 1978. *The Ethnic Factor in Family Structure and Mobility.* Cambridge: Ballinger.

Koltun, Elizabeth, and Neil Schecter. 1977. "Whatever Happened to East Flatbush?" *Interchange,* 2, 7 (March), 1 ff.

Korn, Bertram Wallace. 1957. *The American Reaction to the Mortara Case: 1858–1859*. Cincinnati: American Jewish Archives.

Korn, Bertram W. 1961. *American Jews and the Civil War*. Philadelphia: Jewish Publication Society of America.

Kramer, Judith R., and Seymour Leventman, 1961. *Children of the Gilded Ghetto*. New Haven: Yale University Press.

Kranzler, Gershon. 1978. "The Changing Orthodox Jewish Family." *Jewish Life*, 3, Summer/Fall, 23–36.

Kutzik, Alfred J. 1977. "The Roles of the Jewish Community and Family in Jewish Identification." Mimeographed paper prepared for the American Jewish Committee, Jewish Communal Affairs Dept.

Kuznets, Simon. 1975. "Immigration of Russian Jews to the United States: Backgrounds and Structure." *Perspectives in American History*, IX, 35–124.

Landesman, Alter F. 1971. *Brownsville: The Birth, Development and Passing of a Jewish Community in New York*. 2d ed. New York: Block Publishing.

Lasch, Christopher. 1977. *Haven in a Heartless World*. New York: Basic Books.

Lazerwitz, Bernard. 1971. "Intermarriage and Conversion: A Guide for Future Research." *Jewish Journal of Sociology*. 13, 1 (June), 41–63.

Lazerwitz, Bernard. 1973. "Religious Identification and Its Ethnic Correlates: A Multivariate Model." *Social Forces*, 52, 2 (Winter), 204–20.

Lazerwitz, Bernard. 1979. "Past and Future Trends in the Size of American Jewish Denominations." *Journal of Reform Judaism*, 26, 3 (Summer), 77–82.

Lazerwitz, Bernard, and Michael Harrison. 1979. "American Jewish Denominations: A Social and Religious Profile." *American Sociological Review*, 44, 4 (Aug.), 656–66.

Ledeen, Michael. 1979. "Liberals, not the Jews, Have Changed." *Society*, 16, 4 (May/June), 5, 19.

Leff, Bertram A. 1974. "The Modern Orthodox Jew: Acculturation and Religious Identification." M.A. thesis. Adelphia University, Dept. of Sociology.

Leiby, James. 1978. *A History of Social Welfare and Social Work in the United States*. New York: Columbia University Press.

Lenski, Gerhard. 1963. *The Religious Factor*. Rev. ed. Garden City: Doubleday Anchor Books.

Lenski, Gerhard. 1966. *Power and Privilege: A Theory of Social Stratification.* New York: McGraw-Hill.

Lerner, Anne Lapidus. 1977. "'Who Hast Not Made Me a Man': The Movement for Equal Rights for Women in American Jewry." *American Jewish Year Book*, 77, pp. 3–38.

Leventman, Seymour. 1969. "From Shtetl to Suburb." In *The Ghetto and Beyond.* Ed. Peter I. Rose. New York: Random House, pp. 33–56.

Levine, Naomi, and Martin Hochbaum, eds. 1974. *Poor Jews: An American Awakening.* New Brunswick: Transaction Books.

Levy, Mark R., and Michael S. Kramer. 1973. *The Ethnic Factor: How American Minorities Decide Elections.* New York: Simon and Schuster, Touchstone Books.

Lewin, Kurt. 1948. *Resolving Social Conflicts.* New York: Harper & Row.

Liebman, Arthur. 1979. *Jews and the Left.* New York: John Wiley.

Liebman, Charles S. 1965. "Orthodoxy in American Jewish Life." *American Jewish Year Book*, 66, pp. 21–92.

Liebman, Charles S. 1970. "Reconstructionism in American Jewish Life," *American Jewish Year Book*, 71, pp. 3–99.

Liebman, Charles S. 1973. *The Ambivalent American Jew.* Philadelphia: Jewish Publication Society of America.

Liebman, Charles S. 1978. "Myth, Tradition and Values in Israeli Society." *Midstream*, 44, 1 (Jan.), 44–53.

Liebman, Charles S. 1979. "Leadership and Decision-making in a Jewish Federation: The New York Federation of Jewish Philanthropies." *American Jewish Year Book*, 79, pp. 3–76.

Liebman, Charles S. 1980. "The Future of Conservative Judaism in the United States." *Jerusalem Newsletter: Viewpoints*, No. 11, Center for Jewish Community Studies, March 31.

Liebman, Charles S., and Saul Shapiro. 1979. "A Survey of the Conservative Movement and Some of Its Religious Attitudes." Study released at the 1979 Biennial Convention of the United Synagogues of America, Nov. 11–15.

Lifson, David S. 1965. *The Yiddish Theater in America.* New York: Thomas Yoseloff.

Lindenthal, Jacob Jay. 1981. "*Abi Gezunt*: Health and the Eastern European Jewish Immigrant." *American Jewish History*, 70, 4 (June), 420–41.

Lipset, Seymour Martin. 1963. *Political Man: The Social Bases of Politics.* Garden City: Doubleday Anchor Books.

Lipset, Seymour Martin, and Earl Raab. 1970. *The Politics of Unreason:*

Right-Wing Extremism in America, 1790–1970. New York: Harper & Row.

Lipset, Seymour Martin, and Everett Carl Ladd, Jr. 1971. "Jewish Academics in the United States: Their Achievements, Culture and Politics." *American Jewish Year Book,* 72, pp. 89–128.

Lipset, Seymour Martin, and William Schneider. 1979. "Israel and the Jews in American Public Opinion." Unpublished.

Litt, Edgar. 1961. "Ethnic Status and Political Perspectives." *Midwest Journal of Political Science,* 5, 3 (Aug.), 276–83.

Loew, Judah ("Maharal mi-Prague"). 1969 (1593). *Tiferet Yisrael. Kol Sifrei Maharal mi-Prague"* ("The Complete Works of Maharal mi-Prague"), Vol. V. New York: Judaica Press.

Luckmann, Benita. 1970. "The Small Worlds of Modern Man." *Social Research* Vol. 37, 4 (Winter), 580–96.

Luckmann, Thomas. 1967. *The Invisible Religion: The Transformation of Symbols in Industrial Society.* New York: Macmillan.

Lurie, Harry L. 1961. *A Heritage Affirmed: The Jewish Federation Movement in America.* Philadelphia: Jewish Publication Society of America.

McWilliams, Carey. 1948. *A Mask for Privilege: Anti-Semitism in America.* Boston: Little, Brown.

Mandel, Irving Aaron, 1950. "Attitude of the American Jewish Community toward East-European Immigration." *American Jewish Archives,* 3, 1 (June), 11–36.

Marcus, Jacob Rader. 1970. *The Colonial American Jew, 1492–1783.* 3 vols. Detroit: Wayne State University Press.

Marty, Martin E. 1976. *A Nation of Behavers.* Chicago: University of Chicago Press.

Marx, Gary T. 1967. *Protest and Prejudice: A Study of Belief in the Black Community.* New York: Harper & Row.

Massarik, Fred. 1973. "Intermarriage: Facts for Planning." *National Jewish Population Study.* New York: Council of Jewish Federations and Welfare Funds.

Massarik, Fred. 1974. "Mobility: Facts for Planning." *National Jewish Population Study.* New York: Council of Jewish Federations and Welfare Funds.

Massarik, Fred. 1978. "Rethinking the Intermarriage Crisis." *Moment,* 3, 7 (June), 29–33.

Mayer, Egon. 1978. *Patterns of Intermarriage among American Jews.* New York: American Jewish Committee, Jewish Communal Affairs Dept. Mimeography ed.

Mayer, Egon, 1979a. *From Suburb to Shtetl: The Jews of Boro Park.* Philadelphia: Temple University Press.

Mayer, Egon, 1979b. "Intermarriage among American Jews: Consequences, Prospects and Policies." *Policy Studies '79,* February 15. New York: National Jewish Conference Center.

Mayer, Egon, 1979c. "A Cure for Intermarriage?" *Moment,* 4, 6 (June), 62–64.

Mayer, Egon, and Carl Sheingold. 1979. *Intermarriage and the Jewish Future: A National Study in Summary.* New York: American Jewish Committee, Institute of Human Relations.

Mayer, Egon, and Chaim I. Waxman. 1977. "Modern Jewish Orthodoxy in America: Toward the Year 2000." *Tradition,* 16, 3 (Spring), 98–112.

Mayer. Martin. 1969. *The Teachers Strike: New York, 1968.* New York: Harper & Row.

Michels, Robert. 1949. *Political Parties: A Sociological Study of the Oligarchical Tendencies of Modern Democracy.* Glencoe, Ill.: Free Press.

Miller, Alan W. 1969. *God of Daniel S.: In Search of the American Jew.* New York: Delta Books.

Mintz, Alan. 1976/77. "The People's Choice? A Demurral on Breira." *Response,* 32 (Winter), 5–10.

Mitchell, William E. 1978. *Mishpokhe: A Study of New York City Jewish Family Clubs.* The Hague: Mouton.

Moment magazine, editors of. 1979. "The Issue of Conversion." *Moment,* 4, 4 (March), 17–35.

Monson, Rela Geffen, 1977. *Bringing Women In: A Survey of the Evolving Role of Women in Jewish Organizational Life in Philadelphia.* Philadelphia: American Jewish Committee, Philadelphia Chapter.

Moore, Deborah Dash. 1981a. *At Home in America: Second Generation New York Jews.* New York: Columbia University Press.

Moore, Deborah Dash. 1981b. *Bnai Brith and the Challenge of Ethnic Leadership.* Albany: State University of New York Press.

Morgan, T. B. 1964. "The Vanishing American Jew." *Look,* May 5, pp. 42 ff.

Mosca, Gaetano. 1939. *The Ruling Class.* New York: McGraw-Hill.

Mostov, Stephen G. 1978. "A Sociological Portrait of German Jewish Immigrants in Boston: 1845–1861," *AJS Review,* 111, 121–52. Cambridge: Association for Jewish Studies.

Nahshon, Gad. 1976. "Israelis in America—Moral Lepers." *Midstream,* 22, 8 (Oct.), 46–48.

Nahshon, Gad. 1981. "The Thirteenth Tribe." *Midstream,* 27, 4 (April), 22–24.

Neusner, Jacob. 1972. *Contemporary Judaic Fellowship in Theory and in Practice*. New York: Ktav Publishing House.

New York Times. 1968. "A Bleak Outlook Seen for Religion." Feb. 25, p. 3.

New York Times. 1980. National Recruitment Survey. October 12, p. 15.

Newman, William, and Peter Halvorson, 1979. "American Jews: Patterns of Geographic Distribution and Change 1952-1971." *Journal for the Scientific Study of Religion*, 18, 2 (June), 183-93.

Nisbet, Robert. 1953. *The Quest for Community*. New York: Oxford University Press.

Novak, William. 1981. "From Somerville to Savannah . . . and Los Angeles . . . and Dayton . . . " *Moment*, 6, 2 (Jan.-Feb.), 17-21, 57-60.

Olsen, Mavin E., and Judith Corder Tully. 1972. "Socioeconomic-Ethnic Status Inconsistency and Preference for Political Change." *American Sociological Review*, 37, 5 (Oct.), 560-74.

Osofsky, Gilbert. 1960. "The Hebrew Emigrant Aid Society of the United States (1881-1883)." *Publications of the American Jewish Historical Society*, 44, 3 (March).

Park, Robert E. 1928. "Human Migration and the Marginal Man." *American Journal of Sociology*, 33, 6 (May), 881-92.

Parsons, Talcott. 1942. "The Sociology of Modern Anti-Semitism." In *Jews in a Gentile World: The Problem of Anti-Semitism*. Ed. Isacque Graeber and Steward Headerson Britt. New York: Macmillan pp. 101-22.

Parsons, Talcott, 1975. "Some Theoretical Considerations on the Nature and Trends of Change of Ethnicity." In *Ethnicity: Theory and Experience*, Ed. Nathan Glazer and Daniel P. Moynihan. Cambridge: Harvard University Press, pp. 53-83.

Patterson, Orlando. 1977. *Ethnic Chauvinism: The Reactionary Impulse*. New York: Stein and Day.

Phillips, Bruce. 1980. "Los Angeles Jewish Community Survey: Overview for Regional Planning." Los Angeles: Jewish Federation-Council of Greater Los Angeles.

Plaut, Gunther W., ed. 1965. *The Growth of Reform Judaism*. New York: Union of American Hebrew Congregations.

Pool, David de Sola. 1952. *Portraits Etched in Stone: Early Jewish Settlers, 1682-1831*. New York: Columbia University Press.

Porter, Jack Nusen, and Peter Dreier. 1973. *Jewish Radicalism*. New York: Grove Press.

Postal, Bernard. 1979. "Postal Card." *The Jewish Week*, March 11.

Poupko, Chana K., and Devora L. Wohlgelernter, 1976. "Women's Liberation—An Orthodox Response." *Tradition*, 15, 4 (Spring), 45–52.

Priesand, Sally. 1975. *Judaism and the New Woman*. New York: Behrman House.

Ramparts magazine, editors of. 1967. "Symposium: Chicago's Black Caucus." *Ramparts*, 6, 4: 99–114.

Raphael, Marc Lee, ed. 1979. *Understanding Jewish Philanthropy*. New York: Ktav Publishing House.

Rawidowicz, Simon. 1974. *Studies in Jewish Thought*. Philadelphia: Jewish Publication Society of America.

Rayback, Joseph G. 1966. *A History of American Labor*. Expanded and updated. New York: Free Press.

Reisman, Bernard. 1977. *The Chavurah: A Contemporary Jewish Experience*. New York: Union of American Hebrew Congregations.

Rezneck, Samuel. 1975. *Unrecognized Patriots: The Jews in the American Revolution*. Westport: Greenwood Press.

Reznikoff, Charles, and Uriah Z. Engelman. 1950. *The Jews of Charleston*. Philadelphia: Jewish Publication Society of America.

Rhodes, A. Lewis, and Charles B. Nam. 1970. "The Religious Context of Educational Expectations." *American Sociological Review*, 35, 2 (April), 253–67.

Riessman, Leonard. 1962. "The New Orleans Jewish Community." *Jewish Journal of Sociology*, 4, 1 (June), 113–17.

Riis, Jacob A. 1970 (1890). *How the Other Half Lives: Studies among the Tenements of New York*. Ed. Sam Bass Warner, Jr. Cambridge: The Belknap Press of Harvard University Press.

Ringer, Benjamin B. 1967. *The Edge of Friendliness: A Study in Jewish Gentile Relations*. New York: Basic Books.

Rischin, Moses. 1954. *An Inventory of American Jewish History*. Cambridge: Harvard University Press.

Rischin, Moses. 1970. *The Promised City: New York's Jews, 1870–1914*. New York: Harper Torchbooks.

Roof, Wade Clark. 1979. "Socioeconomic Differentials among White Socioreligious Groups in the United States." *Social Forces*, 58, 1 (Sept.), 280–89.

Rose, Peter I. 1977. *Strangers in their Midst: Small-Town Jews and Their Neighbors*. Merrick: Richwood.

Rose, Peter I. 1981. "Group Status in America." *Task Force on the 80s*.

New York: American Jewish Committee, Institute of Human Relations.

Rosen, Gladys. 1979. "The Impact of the Women's Movement on the Jewish Family." *Judaism*, 28, 2 (Spring), 160–68.

Rosenberg, Bernard, and Nathan D. Humphrey. 1955. "The Secondary Nature of Primary Groups." *Social Research*, 22, 1 (Spring), 25–38.

Rosenfeld, Geraldine. 1980a. "Attitudes of the American Public toward American Jews and Israel: December 1979." New York: American Jewish Committee, Information and Research Services.

Rosenfeld, Geraldine. 1980b. "Attitudes of the American Public toward American Jews and Israel: October 1–80, Gallup Poll." New York: American Jewish Committee, Information and Research Services.

Rosenthal, Erich. 1963. "Studies of Jewish Intermarriage in the United States." *American Jewish Year Book*, 64, pp. 3–53.

Rossel, Seymour. 1980. "'Can We Make Jewish Education Better?'" *Present Tense*, 7, 2 (Winter), 23–24.

Roth, Cecil. 1941. *A History of the Marranos*. Philadelphia: Jewish Publication Society of America.

Roth, Philip. 1969. *Portnoy's Complaint*. New York: Random House.

Rubinow, Isaac Max. 1959. "The Jewish Question in New York City (1902–1903)." Trans. Leo Shpall. *Publications of the American Jewish Historical Society*. 44, 2 (Dec.) 90–136.

Ruderman, Florence A. 1968. *Child Care and Working Mothers*. New York: Child Welfare League of America.

Ruppin, Arthur. 1973 (1934). *The Jews in the Modern World*. (Repr. of 1934 ed.). New York: Arno Press.

Russ, Shlomo M. 1981. *The Zionist Hooligans: The Jewish Defense League*. Graduate Faculty in Sociology, City University of New York Graduate Center. Ann Arbor: University Microfilms.

Sandberg, Neil C. 1974. *Ethnic Identity and Assimilation: The Polish-American Community*. New York: Praeger.

Sandberg, Neil C., and Gene N. Levine. 1981. "The Changing Character of the Los Angeles Jewish Community." Los Angeles: University of Judaism, Center for the Study of Contemporary Jewish Life.

Sarna, Jonathan D. 1981. "The Myth of No Return: Jewish Return Migration to Eastern Europe, 1881–1914." *American Jewish History*, 71, 2 (Dec.), 256–68.

Schappes, Morris U. 1971. *A Documentary History of the Jews in the United States 1654–1875.* 3d ed. New York: Schocken Books.

Schiff, Alvin Irwin. 1966. *The Jewish Day School in America.* New York: Jewish Education Committee Press.

Schmelz, U.O., and Sergio DellaPergola. 1982. "World Jewish Population." *American Jewish Year Book,* 82, pp. 277–90.

Schneider, William. 1978. "Anti-Semitism and Israel: A Report on American Public Opinion." New York: American Jewish Committee.

Schumpeter, Joseph A. 1962. *Capitalism, Socialism, and Democracy.* 3d ed. New York: Harper & Row Torchbooks.

Selzer, Michael, ed. 1972. *"Kike": A Documentary History of Anti-Semitism in America.* New York: World.

Selznick, Gertrude J., and Stephen Steinberg. 1969. *The Tenacity of Prejudice: Anti-Semitism in Contemporary America.* New York: Harper & Row.

Shapiro, Judah J. 1970. *The Friendly Society: A History of the Workmen's Circle.* New York: A Doron Book, Media Judaica.

Shapiro, Jonathan. 1971. *Leadership of the American Zionist Organization 1897–1930.* Urbana: University of Illinois Press.

Sherman, C. Bezalel. 1965. *The Jew within American Society.* Detroit: Wayne State University Press.

Sigal, John, David August, and Joseph Beltempo. 1981. "Impact of Jewish Education on Jewish Identification in a Group of Jewish Adolescents." *Jewish Social Studies,* 43, 3–4 (Summer-Fall), 229–36.

Silberstein, Laurence. 1974. "Religion, Ethnicity, and Jewish History: The Contribution of Yehezkel Kaufmann." *Journal of the American Academy of Religion,* 42, 3 (Sept.), 516–31.

Singer, David. 1967. "David Levinsky's Fall: A Note on the Liebman Thesis." *American Quarterly,* 19, Winter, 696–706.

Singer, David. 1979. "Living with Intermarriage." *Commentary,* 68, 1 (July), 48–53.

Sklare, Marshall. 1964. "Intermarriage and the Jewish Future." *Commentary,* 37, 4 (April), 46–52.

Sklare, Marshall. 1965. "Assimilation and the Sociologists." *Commentary,* 39, 5 (May), 63–67.

Sklare, Marshall. 1968. "Lakeville and Israel: The Six-Day War and Its Aftermath." *Midstream,* 14, 8 (Oct.), 3–21.

Sklare, Marshall. 1970. "Intermarriage and Jewish Survival." *Commentary,* 49, 3 (March), 51–58.

Sklare, Marshall. 1971. *America's Jews.* New York: Random House.

Sklare, Marshall. 1972. *Conservative Judaism.* Augmented ed. New York: Schocken Books.

Sklare, Marshall. 1974. "The Jew in American Sociological Thought," *Ethnicity,* 1, 1 (March), 151–73.

Sklare, Marshall 1976. "American Jewry—The Ever Dying People." *Midstream,* 22, 6 (June/July), 17–27.

Sklare, Marshall, and Joseph Greenblum. 1967. *Jewish Identity on the Suburban Frontier: A Study of Group Survival in the Open Society.* New York: Basic Books.

Sklare, Marshall, and Joseph Greenblum 1979. *Jewish Identity on the Suburban Frontier: A Study of Group Survival in the Open Society.* 2d ed. Chicago: University of Chicago Press.

Sklare, Marshall, and Marc Vosk. 1957. *The Riverton Study: How Jews Look at Themselves and Their Neighbors.* New York: American Jewish Committee.

Slater, Miriam K. 1969. "My Son the Doctor: Aspects of Mobility among American Jews." *American Sociological Review,* 34, 3 (June), 359–73.

Smolar, Boris. 1979. "Easy Marriages Bring Easy Splits: Jews in the 1 to 3 Divorce Scene." *New Brunswick Jewish Journal,* March 8.

Sofer, Eugene F. 1977. "Argentinian Jewry: What Do We Need To Know?" *Interchange,* 3, 1 (Sept.), 1 ff.

Soltes, Mordecai. 1969 (1925). *The Yiddish Press: An Americanizing Agency.* New York: Arno Press.

Somers, Robert H. 1965. "The Mainsprings of the Rebellion: A Survey of Berkeley Students in November 1964." In *The Berkeley Student Revolt: Facts and Interpretations.* Ed. Seymour M. Lipset and Sheldon S. Wolin. Garden City: Doubleday Anchor Books.

Sowell, Thomas. 1981. *Ethnic America: A History.* New York: Basic Books.

Span, Paula. 1979. "Half-Jews: Sooner or Later the Children Grow Up." *Present Tense,* 6, 4 (Summer), 49–52.

Spiegel, Irving. 1973. "Conservative Jews Vote for Women in Minyan." *New York Times,* September 11, pp. 1 ff.

Spiegel, Irving. 1974. "Rabbi Deplores Small Families." *New York Times,* January 24, p. 40.

Stark, Rodney, Bruce Foster, Charles Y. Glock, and Harold Quinley. 1971. *Wayward Shepherds: Prejudice and the Protestant Clergy.* New York: Harper & Row.

Stein, Herman D. 1956. "Jewish Social Work in the United States (1654–1954)." *American Jewish Year Book*, 57, pp. 3–98.

Steinberg, Stephen. 1974. *The Academic Melting Pot: Catholics and Jews in American Higher Education.* New York: McGraw-Hill.

Stember, Charles Herbert. 1961. *Education and Attitude Change: The Effect of Schooling on Prejudice against Minority Groups.* New York: Institute of Human Relations Press.

Stember, Charles Herbert, et al. 1966. *Jews in the Mind of America.* New York: Basic Books.

Stern, Malcolm H. 1967. "Jewish Marriage and Intermarriage in the Federal Period (1776–1840)." *American Jewish Archives*, 1g, 2 (Nov.), 142–43.

Stern-Taubler, Selma. 1955. "Problems of American Jewish and German Jewish Historiography." In *Jews from Germany in the United States,* Ed. Eric E. Hirshler. New York: Farrar, Strauss and Cudahy, pp. 3–17.

Stroock, Sol. M. 1903. "Switzerland and the American Jews," *Publications of the American Jewish Historical Society,* 11.

Sussman, Marvin B. 1978. "The Family Today: Is It an Endangered Species?" *Children Today*, 7, 2 (March/April), 32–37, 45.

Swichkow, Louis J., and Lloyd P. Gartner. 1963. *The History of the Jews of Milwaukee.* Philadelphia: Jewish Publication Society of America.

Szajkowski, Zosa. 1951. "The Attitude of American Jews to Eastern European Jewish Immigrants." *Publications of the American Jewish Historical Society*, 40, March, 221–80.

Tarshish, Allan, 1959. "The Board of Delegates of American Israelites (1859–1878)." *Publications of the American Jewish Historical Society.* 44, 1 (Sept.), 16–32.

Taylor, Philip. 1971. *The Distant Magnet: European Emigration to the U.S.A.* New York: Harper & Row.

Tcherikower, Elias, ed. 1961. *The Early Jewish Labor Movement in the United States.* New York: YIVO Institute for Jewish Research.

Thernstrom, Stephen. 1973. *The Other Bostonians: Poverty and Progress in the American Metropolis, 1880–1970.* Cambridge: Harvard University Press.

Tocqueville, Alexis de. 1969 (1850). *Democracy in America.* New York: Doubleday.

Tönnies, Ferdinand. 1957 (1887). *Community and Society (Gemeinschaft und Gesellschaft).* Trans. and ed. Charles P. Loomis. New York: Harper Torchbooks.

und Gesellschaft). Trans. and ed. Charles P. Loomis. New York: Harper Torchbooks.

Trainin, Isaac N. 1981. "The Acculturation of Iranian Jews in America." Paper delivered at Touro College Conference on Immigration, New York City, Nov. 19, 1981.

Tsukashima, Ronald Tadao. 1978. "Selective Black Hostility toward Jewish and Non-Jewish Whites." *Contemporary Jewry*, 4, 2 (Spring/Summer), 51–59.

United States Bureau of the Census. 1958. "Religion by Civilian Population of the United States." *Current Population Reports*, Ser. P-20, No. 79, Feb.

Urofsky, Melvin I. 1975. *American Zionism from Herzl to the Holocaust.* Garden City: Anchor Press/Doubleday.

Vitz, Paul C. 1977. *Psychology as Religion: The Cult of Self-Worship.* Grand Rapids: Wm. B. Eerdmans.

Warner, W. Lloyd, and Leo Srole. 1945. *The Social Systems of American Ethnic Groups.* Yankee City Series, Vol. III. New Haven: Yale University Press.

Wasserman, Harry. 1979. "The Havurah Experience." *Journal of Psychology and Judaism*, 3, 3 (Spring), 168–83.

Waxman, Chaim I. 1976. "The Centrality of Israel in American Jewish Life: A Sociological Analysis." *Judaism*, 25, 2 (Spring), 175–87.

Waxman, Chaim I. 1977a. *The Stigma of Poverty: A Critique of Poverty Theories and Policies.* New York: Pergamon Press. 2d ed., 1983.

Waxman, Chaim I. 1977b. "Perspectives on the Family and Jewish Identity in America." New York: American Jewish Committee, Jewish Communal Affairs Department, Mimeographed.

Waxman, Chaim I. 1977/78. "Psalms of a Sober Man: The Sociology of Marshall Sklare." *Contemporary Jewry*, 4, 1 (Fall/Winter), 3–11.

Waxman, Chaim I. 1979a. "Bringing the Poor Back In: Jewish Poverty in Education for Jewish Communal Service," *Forum* 35 (Spring/Summer), 133–43.

Waxman, Chaim I. 1979b. *Sustaining the Jewish Family: A Task Force Report on Jewish Family Policy.* New York: American Jewish Committee, Jewish Communal Affairs Department.

Waxman, Chaim I. 1980. *Single-Parent Families: Challenge to the Jewish Community.* New York: American Jewish Committees, National Jewish Family Center.

Waxman, Chaim I. 1982. "The Sabbath as Dialectic: The Meaning and Role." *Judaism*, 31, 1 (Winter), 37–44.

Waxman, Chaim I., and William B. Helmreich. 1977. "Religion and Communal Elements of Ethnicity: American Jewish College Students and Israel," *Ethnicity*, 4, 2 (June), 122–32.

Weinberger, Paul E. 1974. "Religious Tradition and Social Services." In *Perspectives on Social Welfare: An Introductory Anthology*, Ed. Paul E. Weinberger. Second edition. New York: Macmillan, pp. 402–11.

Weinryb, Bernard D. 1958. "Jewish Immigration and Accommodation to America." In *The Jews: Social Patterns of an American Group*. Ed. Marshall Sklare. New York: Free Press, pp. 4–22.

Weinstein, Bernard. 1929. *The Jewish Unions in America* (Yiddish). New York: United Hebrew Trades.

Westerman, Jacqueline. 1967. "Note on Balswick's Article—A Response." *Jewish Social Studies*, 29, 4 (Oct.), 241–44.

Winch, Robert F., Scott Greer, and Rae Lesser Blumberg. 1967. "Ethnicity and Familism in an Upper Middle-Class Suburb." *American Sociological Review*, 32, 2 (April), 265–72.

Winter, Nathan H. 1966. *Jewish Education in a Pluralist Society: Samson Benderly and Jewish Education in the United States.* New York: New York University Press.

Wirth, Louis. 1928. *The Ghetto*. Chicago: University of Chicago Press.

Wirth, Louis. 1938. "Urbanism as a Way of Life." *American Journal of Sociology*. 44, 1 (July), 3–24.

Wirth, Louis. 1964. "Some Jewish Types of Personality." In *Louis Wirth on Cities and Social Life*, Ed. Albert J. Reiss, Jr. Chicago: University of Chicago Press, pp. 99–105.

Wischnitzer, Mark. 1948. *To Dwell in Safety: The Story of Jewish Migration since 1880*. Philadelphia: Jewish Publication Society of America.

Wischnitzer, Mark. 1956. *Visas of Freedom: The History of HIAS*. New York and Cleveland: World.

Wise, Isaac Mayer. 1973 (1901). *Reminiscences*. Trans. from the German and ed. David Philipson. New York: Arno Press.

Wolf, Edwin 2nd and Maxwell Whiteman. 1975. *The History of the Jews of Philadelphia: From Colonial Times to the Age of Jackson*. Philadelphia: Jewish Publication Society of America.

Woocher, Jonathan S. 1978. *"Civil Judaism" in the United States*. Jerusalem and Philadelphia: Center for Jewish Community Studies.

Woocher, Jonathan S. 1979. *"Civil Judaism": The Religion of Jewish Communities*. New York: National Jewish Conference Center.

Woocher, Jonathan S. 1981. "The 'Civil Judaism' of Communal Leaders." *American Jewish Year Book*, 81, pp. 149–69.

Wuthnow, Robert. 1982. "Anti-Semitism and Stereotyping." In *In the*

Eye of the Beholder: Contemporary Issues in Stereotyping. Ed. Arthur G. Miller. New York: Praeger, pp. 137–87.

Yankelovich, Skelly and White, Inc. 1981. *Anti-Semitism in the United States*, Vol. II: The Detailed Findings. New York: American Jewish Committee.

York, Alan S. 1981. "American Jewish Leaders from the Periphery." *Jewish Journal of Sociology*, 23, 1 (June), 25–36.

Zborowski, Mark, and Elizabeth Herzog. 1952. *Life Is with People: The Culture of the Shtetl*. New York: Schocken Books.

Zweigenhaft, Richard L., and G. William Domhoff. 1982. *Jews in the Protestant Establishment*. New York: Praeger.

Index